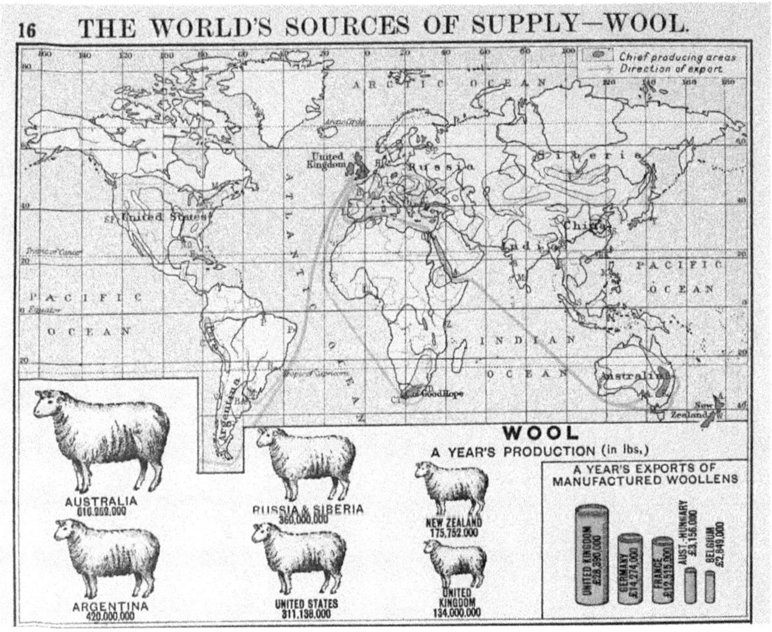

"The World's Sources of Supply - Wool," Philips Chamber of Commerce Atlas, A Graphic Survey of the Worlds Trade. 1912 (Alamy).

Fleeced

Fleeced

Unraveling the History of Wool and War

Trish FitzSimons and Madelyn Shaw

ROWMAN & LITTLEFIELD
Lanham • Boulder • New York • London

Cover design concept by Matt Pfeffer. Sheep icon courtesy of Sandra McEwen.
Graphics by Cheryl Hill.

Published by Rowman & Littlefield
Bloomsbury Publishing Inc, 1385 Broadway, New York, NY 10018, USA
Bloomsbury Publishing Plc, 50 Bedford Square, London, WC1B 3DP, UK
Bloomsbury Publishing Ireland, 29 Earlsfort Terrace, Dublin 2, D02 AY28, Ireland
www.rowman.com

British Library Cataloguing in Publication Information Available

Library of Congress Cataloging-in-Publication Data Available

Library of Congress Control Number: 2025932164.

ISBN: 979-8-8818-0380-3 (cloth)
ISBN: 979-8-8818-0381-0 (electronic)

For product safety related questions contact productsafety@bloomsbury.com.

♾™ The paper used in this publication meets the minimum requirements of American National Standard for Information Sciences—Permanence of Paper for Printed Library Materials, ANSI/NISO Z39.48-1992.

For Edith Hobbs, Merrie FitzSimons, Désirée Koslin, and Angela K. Shaw. Each in their own way encouraged this book into being.

Contents

Preface

This book is what happens when an American textile curator and an Australian documentary filmmaker get together to talk about wool for an hour. Ten years, innumerable research trips, a pandemic, and two moves to independent employment later, our collaboration has led us from Jason's Golden Fleece to the Great Pacific Garbage patch, with myriad stops in between.

One of the questions that has informed this book, "Why Wool?," is something each of us had asked ourselves well before we knew each other. At least six generations of the men in Trish FitzSimons' mother's family were wool buyers, wool brokers, and wool staplers, working predominantly among Yorkshire in the UK, Australia, and the United States. Wool had financed a comfortable life for one line of her family tree, but she wondered who all that wool had been for, and why the demand, and with it the family company, had fallen away. Madelyn Shaw's family tree includes men and women across Germany, Scotland, and the United States who wove, knitted, sewed, and tailored textiles and clothing, including but not only with wool, and whose ability to provide for their families depended on those skills. While working on an exhibition and book on the American Civil War, she kept tripping over the outsize role access to wool played in that conflict—and wondering why nobody seemed to dwell on it much. So, wool claimed headspace in our lives—one personal, one professional—in a desultory way until those two lives happened to intersect.

The two of us met in 2014, when Trish, visiting the United States on an unrelated research project, saw that Civil War exhibition. She also happened to be reading letters written by her wool-buyer grandfather, Frederick Booth, to his family in Australia when, from 1905–1907, he was working in England and the United States, learning about the wool business. Trish looked Madelyn up, the two had lunch, and after that initial hour of discussion turned into four, they emerged with the kernel of an idea: for at least a century, from the Crimean War to the Korean War, wool was a vital strategic military commodity, like steel or gunpowder. Access to wool during wartime in that century of cold climate warfare by massed—and massive—armies was a kind of "behind the curtain" facet of the story of both Australia's wool selling industry and the United States's wool-buying and textile production industries.

Madelyn is a curator specializing in textiles and dress. Her occupation wields the power of objects to engage people in questioning and understanding complex and nuanced histories. Trish is a documentary filmmaker, steeped in oral history and the capacity of an individual's story to encapsulate bigger histories. For both of us, learning and teaching are visual exercises as much as intellectual ones. We value "feet on the ground" visits to key sites, along with photographs, archival film, advertising and other ephemeral artifacts, as well as the evidence found in government archives and business records, letters, and diaries as pieces of the puzzle of historical understanding. Across Australia, New Zealand, the United States, the UK, and parts of Europe, we visited, separately and together, dozens of museums, historical societies, libraries, government archives, working farms, working and abandoned mills, and the sites of strikes, massacres, and discoveries. Our research partnership has thrived on the joy of understanding that knowledge is cumulative: sharing the stored-up bits and pieces of interesting information we've picked up individually from different sources has led us to many exciting AHA! moments.

We've learned a lot.

More than we had thought about when we started.

About a lot more things than we had realized were related.

This book is the outcome of a shared quest to understand wool as a strategic resource and how the military dimension of that trade was a catalyst for the close to complete transformation of the textiles that we wear from natural fibers to synthetics. This project started out just being about wool—we called it *Fabric of War: A Hidden History of the Global*

Wool Trade. Because, if you survey a line-up of sample uniforms from every combatant nation in the first year or so of each cold climate war between about 1850 and 1950, they are all very likely to have as part of the mix, wool from Australian and/or New Zealand sheep. Would the same hold true for uniforms from later in those same wars? Not without a lot of back door smuggling and financial chicanery. Britain used its privileged access to its Empire's supply of apparel wools to its own advantage, and secondarily for its allies. Britain's enemies were out of luck: the world was divided by war into the wool haves and the wool have-nots: a very significant discrepancy.

Along the way, for reasons linked to this division, we discovered that we could neither understand nor explain the rise and fall of the military uses of wool without also understanding its eventual competitors—synthetic fibers—and that indeed we were also writing the history of how they came into being. Thus did our title change.

We have come to realize that the meanings of the terms natural, synthetic, and semi-synthetic fibers, relatively common knowledge 50 years ago, are no longer so widely understood. In a nutshell, natural fibers are those that are recoverable from plants or animals by mechanical processes. Common plant fibers are cotton, linen (from flax), jute, and hemp. Animal fibers include silk, extruded as a long fiber called a filament by silkworms and also by certain spiders; and the hair or fur or wool grown by a variety of animals, such as Angora and cashmere goats, camels, llamas, vicunas, alpacas, and sheep. Sheep's wool is the most common, and in this book that's what we mean by wool. (Not all sheep are woolly—some breeds are hairy, but the complexities of wool will be revealed in all their glory as you read on.) Natural fibers must be processed into usable thread first by twisting them together—called spinning. Wool can also be felted.

In contrast, synthetic fibers were developed by humans from chemicals derived from fossil fuels. Synthetic fibers are extruded—the process is much like a silkworm, but on a scale of thousands of individual fibers at a time. The most common synthetic fibers—polyester, nylon, acrylic, and their variants—are all synthetic polymers. In other words, plastics, a key part of a global economy based on carbon. In between the two categories, and thus known as a semi-synthetic, is rayon, derived from naturally occurring cellulose, primarily wood pulp but also other sources, including bamboo. The cellulose pulp is reduced chemically to form a liquid that is then extruded, again similar to the workings of the silkworm. Unsurprisingly, rayon was originally called artificial silk. All of these different fibers can be mixed in various combinations to make threads and textiles, and their history too is related to the way that resources get allocated and withheld during war and the build-up to war.

We were young adults before the fully synthetic "test-tube" fibers—nylon, acrylic, polyester—took over much of the textiles market from the most popular natural fibers—cotton, wool, linen, and silk. In adulthood we both had careers that involved adherence to certain dress codes, and while rayon and polyester crept in, we still chose to wear mostly natural fibers, widely available even in moderate-priced clothing. This was possible into the early 2000s, but the use of natural fibers on their own has steadily decreased since then, even in the holdout market of menswear. Natural fibers now must be sought out and are typically significantly more expensive. So, in many parts of the world young people have little or no understanding, nor even experience, of the natural fibers that have been so important to human history. We think it's past time to change that.

The wool industry has been transnational for centuries, becoming even more so once the factory mechanization of creating woolen textiles met the newly productive southern hemisphere sheep markets in the first half of the nineteenth century. But it has tended to be understood partially, from the perspective of whichever nation is telling the story. In Australia this means that "wool industry" refers to sheep pastoralism—the primary production of woolen fiber. There are occasional nods to the global wool market based there, but little focus on who used all that wool—or why. In the United States, which had both substantial sheep pastoralism and a woolen textile manufacturing capacity rivaled only by the UK, wool's story has essentially faded from view, overshadowed in American history by another textile fiber, cotton.

We found that many different kinds and degrees of warfare arose in relation to sheep and wool—not all confined to battlefields. Land wars between indigenous inhabitants and the colonist-invaders who wanted their land to raise sheep occurred in many parts of the world. The western United States saw range wars erupt between cattlemen and sheepmen who wanted to run their animals on the same open ranges, which couldn't support both. Additional complications, sometimes involving physical violence, arose in decades of strife between labor and capital, while the business and economic warfare of industrial espionage, the metaphorically cut-throat business of buying and brokering wool, and the constantly changing tariff laws sparked discord not only between companies, but among countries, and even between manufacturers and primary producers within countries. Behind those fluffy fleecy mounds of wool fiber lies much that is not warm and fuzzy.

A transnational approach aids in understanding both wool and the synthetics that have largely replaced it. Our research has been wide ranging, necessary in a global story. New directions were sparked by conferences we've participated in, questions we've been asked, objects we've analyzed. But what we cover here is also idiosyncratic: how the topic looks from the perspective of two women, one residing in the Northeastern US and the other in Eastern Australia. While we've braided this history together from many different strands and national perspectives, we are aware that our account is by no means definitive, and that many players we mention in passing or not at all also have significant skin in the wool game. But we believe our framework can be applied across nations and help to understand the world we live in now: the world of fast fashion made of cheap synthetic fibers, junked after a few wearings, and the alarming, related problem of microplastic pollution, now understood as connected to textiles as well as more obvious plastics such as bags and bottles.

We've headed each chapter with an object that we hope will surprise and intrigue you, and also introduce you to why and how we see objects/artifacts as so central to our understanding of the topic. More objects will crop up along the way; links to various repositories are noted. You will also meet an incredibly broad range of interesting people whose lives were either briefly touched by or deeply entwined with wool. All in all, you'll see how wool, which in 1938, according to the Royal Statistical

Society, was the fourth most valuable international trade commodity, fueled textile industries in 46 countries, frames and molded the lives and economies and cultures of so many, in even unlikely places.[1] And equally, how and why synthetic textiles have largely supplanted wool, becoming in the process one of the most ubiquitous pollutants in the world today.

Chapter 1

Wool

A Fabric of War

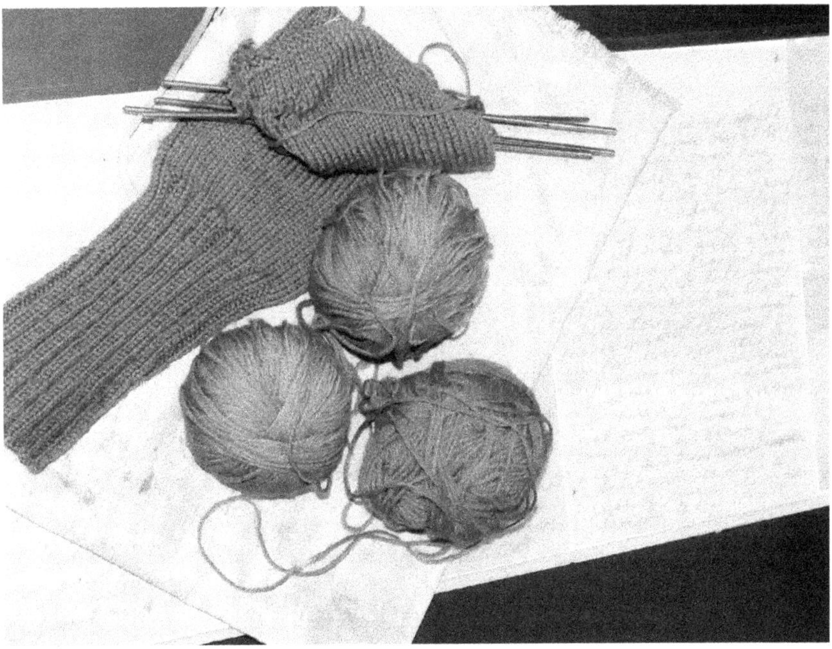

A pair of unfinished knitted woolen socks, still on the knitting needles, and an accompanying letter from John Angus McDonald to his mother, Fanny McDonald, dated October 14, 1917 (courtesy of the Zara Clark Museum, National Trust Queensland, Australia).

> While wool socks and blankets do not win wars, they do contribute immensely to the health and efficiency essential to any military action. . . . wool remains the one proven fabric for insulation and resiliency under conditions of extreme cold, heat, or humidity.[1]
>
> Donald M. Blinken, 1948

Wool was important enough to entice 23-year-old Harvard University Economics graduate Donald Blinken to write a book about its place in the post-World War II world economy. Blinken had served in the recent war, and no doubt had first-hand experience of wool's utility. Perhaps not the same experiences that those in places suffering from a lack of wool had, however, or he may have added to his statement above the words "on their own" to his comment about socks and blankets. Until the late 1950s wool had high value as a strategic resource, sometimes requiring whole government entities, such as Australia's Central Wool Committee, the UK's Wool Textile Executive, and the US'sWar Production Board Wool Branch, to deal with its wartime logistics. Wool was a fabric of war for a whole host of reasons.

John McDonald's unfinished socks represent both the practical and emotional side of wool's place in war. Hand-knitted socks were a common request by servicemen writing home to mothers, wives, sisters, sweethearts—across many wars, and many countries. While army-issue machine-knitted socks were expected to last about a month amidst the rigors of war, thicker, denser woolen socks from skilled knitters were warmer, more comfortable, and more durable. They were also an important reminder of a service person's connection to home. From Belgium, in October 1917, the 20-year-old John, called Jim by his family, wrote to his mother in outback Queensland, Australia: "The weather over here at present is very wet and the winter is coming on us again. You might knit me some socks and send me a pair of warm gloves."[2]

Jim's mother Fanny had been knitting socks for him even before he asked. She received his letter in December 1917—a month after she had learned of his death on October 22nd, one of many thousands who fell at the Third Battle of Ypres (Passchendaele).[3] Fanny never finished the socks. She died in 1924. While we know little about the McDonalds' lives and relationship, we absolutely understand that knitting socks for her son was a way for Fanny to express her love and do all practically possible to keep him warm and connected to home in the debilitating conditions of the Western Front's trenches. For Jim, the socks would meet at least one everyday need while reinforcing his ties to home.

Wool, the soft, pliable fiber shorn annually from living sheep, is precisely the fiber that a soldier from a tropical climate—indeed, any climate—needed to survive a wartime winter. Historically, wool's physical characteristics have given the textiles made from it a special, and especially multivalent, place in wartime. It is literally warm and fuzzy. Wool cloth holds warmth even when wet. Although wet wool has its own odor, it resists picking up human body odor, and it's naturally flame resistant. Wool is tough, withstanding even a frontline soldier's hard use and constant wear. It takes dyes easily, which is useful for differentiating between armies or among ranks or specialties. And, importantly, it is a renewable natural resource. Quartermasters who outfitted armies preferred it for these reasons, and also because good quality wool textiles can be repaired and re-issued until they are ready for the rag bin, when they can be recycled back into fiber either to be turned into compost or to start the manufacturing process all over again. While in wartime this can be a cost-cutting measure for nations that have access to new wool supplies, it can mean life or death in those that don't. As the head of the Textiles Branch of the US government's War Production Board during World War II wrote, "wool is considered a strategic fiber not only for the military front but for the health and morale of the home front."[4]

* * *

The story of wool during wartime really begins with who has the wool and who wants it—and when. This has been understood in the wool business for centuries, and its risks and rewards can be seen in the life of the old Queensland politician, newspaper proprietor, and businessman, Thomas Blacket Stephens. Stephens, born and raised in the Lancashire, England, wool stapling (brokering) community, emigrated to Australia in 1849. He established himself in Sydney as a wool buyer and broker and opened a wool scouring (cleansing) business to process wool for export. A few years later he moved to Brisbane, Queensland, and started a new scour there.

When the news that the Crimean War had begun in October 1853 arrived, some months later, in Australia, this enterprising young man and his business partner James Atkinson bought up a goodly percentage of the Queensland wool clip and commenced sending it to England for sale. Even with the fastest mode of transport then available, clipper sailing ships, Australia to Britain took a minimum of 11 weeks. After that the fiber had to be cleaned, spun into yarn, woven into cloth, turned into uniforms, and shipped out again to make its way onto the backs of soldiers suffering in the frigid Crimean winter.

News took as long to travel to Australia as wool did to reach London. In the first quarter of 1856 Stephens and Atkinson sent about 170 bales of wool per month to Britain, and during the next quarter an average of 400 bales per month. Unfortunately for them, the war had ended in February 1856. Three months' worth of their wool was either en route to or unsold in London, or still sitting on the docks in Sydney. Amidst the ensuing glut of wool and declining prices they dissolved their partnership. James Atkinson went bankrupt, but T. B. Stephens traded his way out of his debts and expanded his Brisbane wool scouring, tanning, and fellmongery (sheepskin) businesses. Perhaps Stephens' hard-won knowledge of the value of accurate and timely information factored in his purchase of a local newspaper in 1861. He died in 1877, a very wealthy man.[5]

We like to think that American author Mark Twain heard this story during his 1895 visit to Australia, and that it inspired his charming little fable, in *Following the Equator* (1897), that British imperialist politician and businessman Cecil Rhodes got his start by cornering the wool market in Sydney, Australia, in 1870. Down and out on a Sydney harbor beach, he helped a fisherman land and gut a shark and found a fragment of a newspaper in the shark's stomach that told, days before the news could arrive by ship, of the outbreak of the Franco-Prussian war in Europe. Rhodes then asked a local wool broker to lend him the money to buy the whole of the Australian wool clip, "Because France has declared war against Germany, and wool has gone up fourteen percent in London and is still rising."[6] Twain's point was that the shark was faster than the ship. We took to heart the fact that fortunes in wartime were made not only by armaments makers but by wool brokers and textile manufacturers as well. Or, without accurate and timely information on hand, could equally be lost.

* * *

Wool's many uses within the military explain why access to wool supplies was so important in wartime and became more so as the size of armies increased from the mid-nineteenth century, culminating in the gigantic armies of World War I (1914–1918) and World War II (1939–1945). For one thing, military personnel were often furnished pretty much from the skin out, and head to toe, in garments made at least partly of wool. Undershirts, drawers, and shirts were either wholly wool or half cotton, half wool. Uniform tunics or jackets, knitted waistcoats or cardigans, trousers or breeches, socks, puttees, overcoats, and caps were usually all wool. Since protection from the elements was a big part of uniform functionality, and the wear and tear of military life greater than for most civilians, military textiles were usually four to ten ounces heavier per yard than those meant for civilians—a significant difference that increased the quantity of wool needed per soldier.

Many books have been written about the evolution of military dress. This is not one of them. But since woolen uniforms are one of the reasons for woolen textile production, a nod to the topic is in order.[7] Outfitting military personnel with uniforms, of course, is essential to war-making, and important to both the cloth manufacturers and the garment trades. Military demand for wool and the clothing made from it in wartime can be seen as the Janus face of peacetime demand and civilian fashion.

For centuries military officers, usually from the upper levels of the social hierarchy, purchased their own uniforms, made to order, matching a model, made from the finer, more expensive, elegantly finished grades of woolen cloth. In the UK, by 1800 the best London tailors, serving the most exclusive clientele, began to cluster in an area which became known as Savile Row. Several of the earliest of these bespoke tailoring establishments, notably Meyer & Mortimer, Adeney & Boutroy, Davies & Son, and James Poole, owed their initial success partly to the uniform commissions they fulfilled during the Napoleonic Wars.[8] Although Savile Row became the heart of British elite men's outfitting, military and civilian, military tailoring was widespread across Britain. American actor Clark Gable, serving in the US Army Air Force in Britain during World War II, had one of his uniforms tailored by a Yorkshire firm, E. Abington & Sons.[9]

Enlisted personnel, however, wore standard garments, also produced to a model. These were originally known as "slops," similar to the ready-made clothing of merchant seamen and whalers. These garments were the purview of small tailoring workshops and larger concerns called Merchant Tailors, often relying on both in-house and outwork labor.

As armies became larger in the 1800s, government departments evolved to outfit enlisted personnel in more "uniform" uniforms, often establishing army-run manufacturing facilities or depots, which used hard-wearing worsted fabrics, such as kersey, serge, covert cloth, or cavalry twill. The US Army set up its first "Clothing Establishment" during the War of 1812. While capable of outfitting that army and the subsequent peacetime army, in later wars it had to be expanded and supplemented by outworkers and contractors. Large armies created a need for standard sizing to enable cutting out hundreds of garment pieces at a time, and mass producing of same, either in workshops or with outworkers, and eventually in factories. The clothing needs of the Union army in the American Civil War encouraged the eventual adoption of sewing machines by the US Army Quartermaster Depot and its contractors. Hand-stitching a man's shirt took a seamstress some 14 hours. Machine-stitching the same shirt averaged an hour and a quarter.[10] Ready-made civilian menswear developed rapidly as a result, becoming accepted and commonplace by the 1870s.

Uniforms were just a part of the wartime wool surge. Garrison flags, naval ensigns, signal flags, artillery marking flags, and flags for purposes you've never imagined, such as a pennant that marked the New Zealand Field Pay Office at Gallipoli, were all made of wool. And flags could be pretty sizable: the Pay Office pennant measures nearly four and a half meters by six meters—it was meant to be seen from a distance (one does wonder in an uninformed way whether it also made a good artillery target).[11] Then, of course, there were blankets. Millions and millions of them. Trish's father, serving in the Middle East during World War II, was issued four blankets: three to fold underneath for insulation from the ground, one to sleep under. Front line World War I soldiers rarely had as luxurious a bed.

There were other uses, less familiar but equally important, and sometimes in response to new dangers, such as the woolen gas mask or "hypo helmet" of World War I.[12] Woven wool covers for canteens helped keep the contents cool, while saddle and horse blankets were vital to the well-being of transport and cavalry animals. And wool didn't have to be woven or knitted to have value and find use. Coats, vests, and overalls made from sheepskin and shearling (a skin from a sheep shorn once) warmed British soldiers in the Crimean War, ANZACS on the Western Front during World War I, British merchant seamen during World War II, and flying crews from many nations in both. Wool felt of varying thicknesses made gaskets and washers for machinery and insulated everything from cold weather boots to aircraft and tanks.

* * *

All of these products were vulnerable to the "wastage and the hazards of war."[13] The hazards contributing to wastage were innumerable and inescapable. Front-line troops or those on the move rarely had adequate bathing and laundry facilities; soldiers wore their clothing long and hard, and depending on conditions could be wet through, caked with mud or dust, or worse. Soldiers' clothes, and bodies, were scraped and torn by close encounters with stony ground, barbed wire, crumbling buildings, and jagged tree limbs. When army supply lines couldn't keep up with advancing troops, soldiers might supplement their uniforms with whatever they could pick up along their route. US Civil War soldier William Bluffton Miller compared how he and his comrades in Union General William T. Sherman's army looked in early 1864, when they began their March to the Sea in Tennessee, and when they finished that campaign a year later in North Carolina: "our Boys wore the 'Blue' entirely and was in a splendid condition. . . . [But] we enter here with ranks depleted and hardly two men dressed alike."[14] Even if they had extra clothes, front line troops might have little opportunity to change them. In his World War I diary, Jack Martin, an English sapper, described removing his woolen socks, which had been "soaked through time after time with rain and mud and perspiration . . . I had to cut them and tear them . . . the soles were as hard as boards."[15]

In frontline conditions items simply wore out. They were also taken as souvenirs, lost or abandoned during battles, cast aside from the wounded, or buried with the dead. Men on the march were particularly prone to shedding extra weight when heat or distance tired them out. Another Civil War soldier, William Wiley of Illinois, disparaged the behavior of an "eastern" regiment ahead of his own: "The day being rather warm they soon began to lighten up by throwing away their extra blankets, shirts, etc. and the roadside was lined with them for miles."[16] A soldier's blanket might also serve as a makeshift shroud in the hurried burials that often occurred amid battle.

Also part of the equation was the tiny but inescapable misery of lice. Union soldiers in the Civil War even had a song about them, "The Graybacks so Tenderly Clinging." The lyrics made it clear that even generals suffered: "And never partial were those bugs, no mortal would they spare, No dignity could keep them off, they just bit everywhere. . . ."[17] At the end of World War I an estimated 90 percent of American soldiers were infested with this pest, a calculation arising from the necessity of separating the men from their insect companions before they shipped back home. A textile industry article in March 1918 discussed what the British had learned about lice during their three-plus years of war, zeroing in on the knitted undershirt as the worst offender for "the myriads of vermin that find lodgment in it. . . . It is a saying at the front that they do not wash their shirts or the insects thereon would swim away with them. . . ."[18] Shirts subjected to the rough laundering and boiling necessary to kill lice and their eggs might shrink enough to become unwearable.

Hence, the need for constant replacements, and for the anxieties that arose about where all that wool, and all that cloth, was going to come from, and how to ensure that, in its myriad final forms, it made it to those who desperately needed it. Entering World War II, the US Army estimated needing 26 sheep to outfit one soldier, one time—up from 20 sheep in World War I.

* * *

Army quartermasters were not, however, the only consumers of wool in wartime. For many women, the end of a (paid or volunteer) workday was not the end of their war work. Like Fanny McDonald, they went home to knit and sew "comforts" for their "boys" in uniform, and their girls too, providing the support and warmth of socks, gloves and mittens, caps and scarves. American artist Winslow Homer's "Christmas Boxes in Camp, 1861," the front cover of *Harper's Weekly* magazine in January 1862, depicts a dozen or so US (Union) soldiers scuffling over the contents of a crate of presents. Books and bottles lie discarded, while the men try on the hand-knitted socks, undoubtedly of wool, that will contribute most to their comfort.[19]

Knitting patterns approved for military use were distributed through yarn manufacturers, Women's Institutes, newspapers and magazines, and government agencies. Some knitters joined large, nationally or even internationally active societies, such as the Red Cross, or the Sanitary Commission during the American Civil War. Others participated through local church groups, neighborhood work parties, at work or at school, or at home on their own for family members and friends. All contributed from a sense of patriotism, a need to feel useful, and a hope that their actions might mitigate, in some small way, the misery of war, while reassuring those in harm's way that they had not been forgotten at home. Meanwhile civilians regularly faced restrictions on their own consumption of wool, and learned to make do and mend, to conserve, to explore alternatives.

Wool and woolen crafts have also been important to prisoners of war, to internees, and to those rebuilding their lives, bodies, and psyches after war. Wounded and demobilized veterans were taught new skills to help them find work after the war: French *mutilés de guerre* (veterans with severe injuries) learned to shear sheep; New Zealand amputees were taught wool grading and classing in hospitals in England; Australian soldiers were given wool classing lessons on board ship in 1919 on their long journey home from France.[20] Occupational therapy for wounded soldiers often included learning to weave or embroider to regain fine motor skills.

These skills were not necessarily new to the servicemen and women, who routinely repaired their own clothing or stitched on new insignia. At least as far back as the Crimean War soldiers have cut and sewed scraps and pieces from their own and their comrades' woolen uniforms into bed covers, table covers, and other mementos, the pattern built up from hand-stitching together tiny diamonds of different colors. One American soldier, Jewett Washington Curtis, made three of these pieced woolen "mosaics," now held by three different US museums.[21] He sewed dates into the pieces, made during two periods of hospitalization in the 1880s and 1890s, although family history says that he also sewed during a tour of duty in Alaska, where winters were both long and dark. Other soldiers created their quilts in hospitals or convalescent homes, or in lonely huts in frontier outposts. These intricate masterpieces certainly helped occupy and perhaps helped heal both mind and body—the makers metaphorically stitching themselves back together.

Prisoners and internees whose resources were limited also stitched and knitted—and sometimes even wove—useful items for themselves and other inmates. Lionel Granville Burnett, an Australian POW in Burma in 1942, constructed a pullover using the good bits from a knitted scarf, puttees, a blanket, and a pair of long johns: a classic example of "Make Do and Mend."[22] Items beyond reuse could be unraveled, the resulting odd lengths of yarn spun or knotted together to knit new items, such as Jim Simpson's knitted blanket, housed in a tiny museum in Australia's Snowy Mountains. Simpson, a gunner and navigator with the Royal Australian Airforce, was shot down on his very first bombing sortie over Germany in 1943. Sent to Stalag IVB camp in Germany, he was warned by American POWs that his military-issue woolen jumper would be confiscated for German soldiers on the Russian front. He determinedly retired into a toilet, unraveled the jumper, and hid the yarn on his person, denying his captors this precious wartime resource. His mother had taught him how to knit as a child, and he pressed the wire handles of Italian military-issue "Dixie pans" into service as knitting needles. Simpson's skill was in high demand in camp, and during his long incarceration he taught many of his comrades to knit their own socks.[23] After 13 months of purloining and bartering for fragments of wool, he had enough to knit himself a blanket. A masterpiece of improvisational design, its central motif is a map of Australia, drawn from memory. Simpson recalled that the wool scraps were often lice-infested and had to be boiled to free them of vermin. Wool is tough as well as warm, as everyone affected by that war had cause to know.

In the same war but thousands of miles away, Japanese-Americans were interned by the US government in rough camps, scattered from California to Arkansas, hastily erected to house them after the United States entered World War II. Sewing and knitting were essential to furnishing their living cubicles and clothing themselves and their children. Alice Imamoto Takemoto was only 15 when her family was removed from their California home. After stops in the county jail system and the Santa Anita racetrack camp, the girls and their mother were interned in Arkansas, while their father was sent elsewhere. Alice's mother, Yoshiko Imamoto, knitted a good deal, sometimes incorporating fur from the family's dog into the yard she spun. She also taught her daughter to knit in the Arkansas camp.[24]

* * *

The mental and physical work that went into making objects like these—in homes, hospitals, camps, and prisons—could help keep boredom at bay and bring some satisfaction, and even creativity and color, into an otherwise very restricted existence. The physical warmth they gave is not the only thing about them that might have been life-saving, nor is the wearer or user the only one who may have benefitted. The survival of these items, carefully kept by the makers, or by the families of those who did not return, or by the soldiers themselves and the militaries that employed them, suggests another reason for the enduring power of wool as a fabric of war: it lasts. Worldwide, museum collections hold quantities of what might be termed the relics of war, tangible *aides memoires* that speak to the visceral experiences of those that served and those that waited at home. We have viewed hundreds of objects in person and hundreds more in online collection databases from museums around the world. While the stories of individuals and specific relics are moving and important, if we look deeper we can find too the legacies of the multitudes of people whose labor and skill and intellect ensured that the needed wool was available and usable, as one of the strategic necessities of war.

Certain kinds of objects speak clearly to this duality. Among the hundreds of uniforms held by the US Army Quartermasters Museum is a Union army infantry officer's overcoat, made of dark blue wool broadcloth, tightly woven and heavily fulled (a treatment that deliberately washed and shrank woolen cloth to increase durability, so that coat hems, for example, were rarely turned up because they simply wouldn't fray). The coat is one of literally millions produced by workers in northern mills and factories during the war, and shows the even, hand-stitched seaming and tight buttonholes one would expect of professional tailors and seamstresses (including one set of Madelyn's great-great grandparents, German immigrants to New York City in 1860, who tailored Union uniforms). Yet it also displays the handiwork of its wearer: hastily stitched repairs of rips and tears, and a very uneven turned-up hem. The coat's scars embody its wearer's close encounters with rough surroundings during his service, which the sturdy wool coat saw him through.[25]

Uniforms were also reincarnated. The Civil War collections at the Atlanta History Center in Georgia contain a little boy's dark blue wool suit, the jacket emblazoned with a silk ribbon reading "My Father was a Soldier."[26] Soldiers in that war often sent their dress uniforms home when starting on a campaign, knowing they would not be needed in the field. The pure wool cloth was too good to waste, especially if you were a war widow trying to raise small children on an inadequate government pension. The military was also adept at reusing, recycling, and remaking woolen uniforms. The British army in France, which greatly depended on the support of the non-combatant Indian Labour Corps (ILC), issued them, and other non-combatant support personnel of color, who were often conscripts, with recycled uniforms, including "military coats unfit for combatant use."[27]

Bits and fragments of uniforms, such as two items held by the Australian War Memorial, can be equally eloquent. Shoulder straps that identified German regiments in World War I, cut from the uniforms of prisoners and the dead for gathering intelligence on units met in combat, were carefully mounted on a series of framed display boards, originally for Australian General John Monash, eventually as victory trophies for fundraising. Viewing the boards as samples of uniforms arranged in rows, however, emphasizes how fiber and dye shortages, visible in the variations in both the color and the quality of the fabrics, affected the German military. A fragment of an Australian officer's tunic collar, retrieved in 1919 from the position known as the "Bloody Angle" in Gallipoli, Turkey, was traced using the badges remaining on it to one of seven officers of the 16th Infantry Battalion, which had arrived only a week before the battle they died in, on 2nd May 1915.[28]

Relics like these speak both of individuals and of the shattering of generations, across national borders and wartime occupations. The malleable wools retain something of the physical imprint of those that used or wore them. They certainly hold the metaphorical imprint of those who stood behind their creation. Their survival, in whatever condition they might have been found or returned or brought home, whether carefully stored in a trunk in an attic or picked up among the detritus of a field hospital, connects us to their legacies of hard work and hard fighting, courage and heartbreak, suffering and resilience.

* * *

Just as the uses of wool in wartime are varied and complex, it is also true that wool and sheep are *not* simple. Viewing wool in the aggregate as simply fluffy masses of white fiber shorn from sheep and spun, woven, knitted, crocheted, or felted into several useful and possibly decorative items ignores a phenomenal amount of complexity. Indeed, first century Roman writer Columella moaned that while all animals required different management, that in sheep husbandry, "The Tarentine [sheep] breed demands a different method from the coarse-wooled; a still different treatment is required by the goat kind, and of these the hornless and thin-haired are cared for in one way, the horned and shaggy-haired, as in Cilicia, in another way."[29] This was echoed, more succinctly, in 1961 by Ken Ponting, a British historian with a long family history in the wool trade, who wrote that "wool varies more than any other raw material."[30]

The fact that sheep provide meat and wool, milk and hides, all valuable commodities, is part of this complexity, because for many centuries, not only was the wool valued in wartime, the sheep were, too. A history of wool's place in war must then also be a history of sheep *husbandry*, the breeding of sheep to develop particular characteristics, over time creating new breeds and variations within breeds. Recent genetic studies of sheep populations suggest that while sheep and goats were the first animals domesticated by humans, with evidence from southwestern Asia dating back as far as 10,000 BCE, they have been moved around, crossed and recrossed, resulting in a quite remarkable amount of genetic diversity.[31] Some breeds, known collectively as crossbreds, are bred to produce satisfactory meat and wool, whereas others, usually incorporating the genetic material of the Spanish merino, are bred for the finest possible woolen fiber.

The merino sheep is not wholly native to Spain. The founding stock likely resulted from myriad crosses. During the Roman Empire settlers took Italian Tarentine sheep to Spain, crossing them with another breed from Africa. Centuries later this strain was intermixed with sheep brought by the Moors from North Africa during their rule of most of modern-day Spain and Portugal, then known as Al Andalus (711–1492). By the fifteenth century the Spanish merino was both renowned and coveted for its fine fleece. For a few centuries merinos collectively were controlled by the Spanish monarch, who occasionally presented a small flock to a fellow ruler, spreading merino genes in the eighteenth century into France, where the breed became known as the Rambouillet, and Germany, where it became the Saxony.

Spain's involvement in the Napoleonic Wars destroyed that nation's elaborate systems of control over merino genes. Invading soldiers ate the unlucky sheep, generals and diplomats carted them off to found their own flocks, and fleeing Spanish flock-owners sold them to finance their escape from the devastation of war. Pirates were even said to target ships carrying cargoes of merino sheep, knowing their high resale value. Over time the merino became a bearer of and synonym for fine wool around the world. Adapting it to thrive in the new climates and ecologies to which it was transplanted, though, required decades of sheep husbandry.

Nineteenth-century Britain dominated both industrialized woolen textile manufacturing and the shipping needed to carry the wool back to those factories. It is no coincidence that the diaspora of merino sheep and the breeding efforts that allowed them to flourish in difficult terrain occurred during that century largely in British colonial territories or in regions influenced by British capital and the British textile industry. Australia, New Zealand, and the United States were the most significant early players in this field.

* * *

Britain's first domestic sheep appeared in the Neolithic era, around 3,000 BCE, increasing in number as inhabitants cleared forests for agriculture and timber. Britain's Roman colonizers brought additional sheep, and promptly established textile production centers, including an important one at Winchester, to supply the occupying army. The Norman Conquest of 1066, however, really set the stage for England's close economic relationship with wool. William the Conqueror's followers established monasteries with large tracts of land to maintain them, suited to the rhythms and needs of sheep herding. Medieval Britain had the space in many of its counties for sheep to roam and eventually wool was grown across much of England, not only by the church but also by aristocrats, by peasants with their own flocks, and by villagers who shared ownership of flocks, using town and manor common land. Over the following centuries, regions, counties, and even individual farms across Britain would develop sheep breeds whose wools would be sought after around the world, and form the foundation of other nations' flocks.

In the nineteenth and twentieth centuries, most European and many Asian, North African, and North and South American nations produced at least some wool, if only for domestic purposes. By 1900, the powerhouses were the United States, Argentina and Uruguay, and collectively, the British Empire. The Empire controlled the wool production of the British Isles, Australia, New Zealand, Canada, India, the Union of South Africa, and smaller sources such as the Falkland Islands—about a third of the world's wool. The two largest producers of fine merino wools were Australia, very much in first place, and South Africa, a distant second. The rest of the world either split production between merino and crossbred, focused on crossbred, or produced the so-called carpet wools.

The ragtag mixture of sheep that came to Australia along with the first convicts were there primarily for meat. With the early decades of the colonizing of the Australian continent roughly coinciding with the Napoleonic Wars and their supply chain interruptions, a focus on fine wool production quickly took precedence. The Australian colonies needed a source of export income and Britain wanted a reliable supply of raw wool for textile manufacturing. Some sheep breeders focused on the wool fiber's fineness, others on maximizing the length of the staple, and some far-sighted folks melded the two. In 1827 a breeder (and parson) named Samuel Marsden won an award at the Sydney Agricultural Show for sheep that showed "extraordinary length of staple, with extreme smallness [ie fineness] of fibre."[32]

Longer fibers made machine-processing of woolen textiles in factories much easier, but this was not the only characteristic necessary to create the Australian merino. As sheep pastoralism moved inland on the driest continent on earth, with its regular fierce droughts, producing physically strong animals that could survive a tough climate was equally important. From the late 1850s until the mid-1870s breeders such as the Peppin family methodically bred animals in dry inland Australia that were both hardy and productive, carrying a much greater quantity of wool than previous strains. Fine merino wool dominated the Australian market until crossbred wools staged a comeback in the early twentieth century. New Zealand built on Australian sheep husbandry, but with a greater focus on crossbreds valued for both meat and wool.[33]

The United States essentially inherited two strains of sheep from Colonial times. Spanish explorers brought their country's common sheep—meat and coarse wool providers—to their settlements in Central America. These *churro* sheep moved northward into what became the American southwest, becoming the foundation of the Navajo Indian flocks. English and Dutch settlers brought small numbers of sheep with them, again for meat and coarse wool, but since Britain preferred to keep the American colonies dependent on its woolen textiles, and Spain restricted the export of merino sheep, little breed improvement was attempted until after the Revolutionary War. Both George Washington and Thomas Jefferson then experimented with sheep breeding, eventually participating in the merino diaspora of the Napoleonic Wars, which reached the United States from about 1801. Widespread "merino mania" arose only after access to British cloth ceased in 1808 with the US trade embargo against British goods. In 1809 even "hard-headed entrepreneurs" Paul Cuffe and Isaac Cory from New Bedford, Massachusetts, dispatched a ship to Spain, bringing back 87 merino sheep—some for sale, some for local breeding purposes.[34] The War of 1812 also kept British cloth off the American market, inspiring new Societies for the Promotion of Agriculture, whose interests dovetailed with the push for national self-sufficiency. The minute the war was over, however, Britain began recovering its US market by dumping fabrics at very low prices, smothering both the nascent American woolen textile industry and the need for fine-wooled sheep.[35]

Variations on this theme occurred throughout the nineteenth century. English breeds were imported for "mutton and wool" crosses, and Saxony and Rambouillet merino variants for their fine wool and their adaptability to harsher climates. Changing consumer preferences, periodic economic problems, and tariff laws that variably favored growers or manufacturers created boom and bust cycles for wool growing. Merino flocks often ended up in the slaughterhouse or tallow vats. Nevertheless, American farmers did not totally give up on "grading-up" their sheep, particularly as the nation expanded westward from the 1840s. The state of Vermont became internationally known for its merino sheep: a dozen or so breeders developed animals with a high yield of longer staple, medium-fine wool, on a slightly larger body adapted to the local environment. In its extreme form it was bred for numerous folds and wrinkles in its skin, which increased wool yield. In the 1880s this type of Vermont merino was exported in quantity to Australia, where its folds entered the genes of the Australian merino. The much warmer climate engendered a practice known as mulesing, which removes folds of skin around the sheep's anus to prevent flystrike: maggots infesting the damp cracks. The United States's far western flocks balanced merino genes, suited to the rough range conditions and producing fine wool, with

English and (in the twentieth century) Australian long-wooled breeds contributing heavier fleeces and better meat. Not only was the manufacturing of woolen cloth multi-national, the continual tinkering with the genetic material of sheep also involved breeders around the globe, as they searched for a "golden fleece" that would meet the needs of the textile manufacturers—and both their military and civilian customers.[36]

* * *

Why did the physical characteristics of a sheep's wool *matter* so much? As discussed above, wool fiber varies markedly across different breeds of sheep, in relation to length, thickness, and uniformity of fiber. Other fiber qualities, such as wavy or curly, crimped or straight, also determine what they are suited for. These characteristics must be considered, and balanced, in creating the yarns that are woven or knitted into finished cloth.

Some breeds, aptly called "long-wooled," give wool fibers of eight to twenty centimeters (three to eight inches) long. Fibers from short-wooled breeds are around eight centimeters. The term for fiber length is staple. Short staple wools are carded, meaning they are run through a series of rollers studded with metal teeth, which remove really short fibers but leave the rest loosely arranged, crisscrossing, and ready for spinning into soft or lightly twisted yarns. Long staple wools are combed, which also removes the short and imperfect fibers, but then aligns the fibers more or less in parallel. This, and the length of the fibers, allows them to be more tightly spun, in what are called hard yarns. This distinction led to two distinct woolen textile sectors: woolens (from short staple) and worsteds (from long staple). Across the centuries, they have traded places at the top of the profit heap, as fashion favored first one and then the other, and both may incorporate other fibers. All wools have scales that allow the fibers to latch onto one another when heat, moisture, and friction are applied. The processes of fulling and felting common to woolen (as opposed to worsted) fabrics take advantage of this, making the cloth more resistant to abrasion and moisture.

Even with sheep of the same breed, wool differs according to where the sheep are raised and what they feed on, as well as temperature and rainfall variations from year to year. Wool also varies in length and fineness according to where it grows on the sheep. In order of desirability: first, the back, from the neck to within several inches of the tail; second, the sides; third, the neck and nearer to the tail; last, the belly. The fleece around the base of the tail is usually discarded because it is covered with dried dung, known as dags. This type of wool has contributed the term "daggy" to the Australian vernacular, from the 1930s a synonym for "unconventional, unkempt . . . unfashionable, graceless" but in recent decades often used affectionately.[37]

Wool quality, and therefore price in the market, also depends on factors such as whether the sheep were washed before shearing, or the wool was sold in its raw state ("greasy" or "in the grease") as it came from the sheep, or had been washed (scoured) after shearing; or whether the fleece had been "skirted" to remove the ragged bits, and "classed" (sorted by quality) before packing for the salesroom. Australia and New Zealand had the best systems for processing the fleeces before they came to market. American wools, on the other hand, particularly the range wools, for decades were reputedly dirty and ill-packed, with a shrinkage rate during scouring of as much as 60 percent, making them unappealing to the international market.

Australian wool in the 1910s had a price list with 848 separate classifications based on quality.[38] For the most part those variations were fitted into a much smaller set of standards. Wool Standards boxes, containing samples of raw wool of verified diameter, put together by and available to interested parties through the US Department of Agriculture, ensured that wool grades were clear to both sellers and buyers. The US Army Quartermaster's Museum holds two, dated 1926 and 1946. The 1926 box has 12 graded samples, the 1946 box contains 16. Today's standards still number 16, ranging from the finest merinos down through various crossbreds, ending with carpet or braid wools.[39]

Since wool varies much more than cotton (or any synthetic fiber, which is one reason why synthetics triumphed), historically wool markets and auctions depended on buyers being able both to view and to touch the actual wool prior to purchase. Photographs of wool stores (warehouses) show open sample bales from the various sellers in what seems like chaotic clutter but must have been an orderly chaos for the sales to proceed. The profits of the woolgrowers, the buyers and brokers who got the wool to market, the yarn and textile manufacturers—and all the middlemen in between—depended on selling the right wool to the right buyer for the right job. At the heart of the process was the wool buyer, skilled in determining, largely by sight and touch, the qualities of raw wool. Only in the 1970s was this skill made partly redundant by scientific measurement.

Although sheep were a part of pastoral life in many countries and regions, not all sheep produce wool that humans want to wear. The finer and softer wools were more lucrative and sought after than the coarser, but often more lustrous, carpet wools (which made excellent floor coverings), although carpet wools were sometimes spun with better quality wools to make them go farther, especially in manufacturing cheap cloth and military blankets. In the Europe of around 1800, wool comprised more than three-quarters of the total amount of textile fibers consumed.[40]

It lost that supremacy to cotton within a few decades. Cheap cotton from the American slave states began feeding England's Lancashire spinning and weaving mills, whose powered machinery and factory organization of labor are generally recognized as at the forefront of the Industrial Revolution. By the 1840s, however, carding and combing machinery, looms, and other equipment had been developed specifically for woolen fibers. Advances in sheep husbandry had brought fineness to long wools and greater length to short wools. With wool fibers long and strong enough to be processed on the new machines, they joined cotton in being manufactured primarily in factories, on water- and steam-powered, and in time fully automated machinery that would be tended, rather than operated, by a weaver.

Wool's status as a reliable source of export income depended on webs of international connections, not only geographically, but through the ties of commerce, chemistry, genetics, industrial espionage, technology, and even, perhaps especially, families. The industry's complexities however, mean that overall, wool has varied in price more than most other commodities. Pulses of demand for wool associated with warfare were just one of the factors in these constant price fluctuations. Drought or flood didn't just affect the quality of a sheep's wool—in many cases, the animals didn't survive the catastrophic event—perhaps starving or drowning, but equally possibly being sent to slaughter for meat or tallow in order that a farmer might retrieve some income from the stock. So, fewer sheep, less wool, but higher prices for the better grades. Had a nation decided to try manufacturing its own woolen textiles rather than buying from another country? More competition for the available wool, higher prices. Did a stock market crash? Economic dislocation meant less competition and lower prices. The wool business has never been for the fainthearted.

* * *

It does, however, seem to arouse a certain devotion among its practitioners. Our intergenerational connections to wool and woolen textiles are by no means unusual, and this book uses many family histories to illustrate the larger global story. In peacetime or war, the work of raising sheep for wool and getting it to market requires—at a minimum—farmers and entrepreneurs, shepherds or fencers and fences to keep the sheep together, shearers, sorters, packers, wool buyers and brokers, ship owners and transport workers. Producing cloth and clothing, blankets, and all the other myriad uses wool had in daily life, required mill owners and their bankers, and tens and hundreds of thousands of sorters, spinners, weavers, loom fixers, dyers, cutters, fitters, stitchers, and finishers in woolen mills and garment factories. We cannot tell all their stories, but several names will recur across these chapters.

Kathy "Tup" Bateman is a proud Gamilaraay/Kamiliaroi woman, probably the first Aboriginal woman in Queensland to have registered as a wool classer and a wool classing trainer. Her maternal family includes at least seven generations of shearers, wool classers, roustabouts, and shearer's cooks, their labor central to the success of the Australian wool industry. The Mackay/Baldry/Jacobs family have raised sheep on land near Canberra for over six generations, and managed sheep stations in other parts of South-Eastern Australia, experiencing every aspect of pastoral life, from the tough early frontier, to drought and flood, wool booms and busts, to a new focus on producing wool via regenerative agriculture. After World War I, Agnes Mackay married into the interconnected—and intercontinental—Lohmann/Waldthausen/Noltenius families from northern Germany, who for several generations bought, sold, and shipped wool to, from, and among Europe, Australia, the United States, South Africa, and South America. Wool buyer Frederick Booth, Trish's grandfather, was another Australian with international connections, including the Hainsworths in Britain, and the American wool families of Marland, Hobbs, and Stevens, who in turn intersect with the German-American Julius Forstmann.

France, too, is represented, but this story has a twist—E.I. du Pont emigrated to the United States from France in 1800. His first order of business was to open a gunpowder mill in Wilmington, Delaware. His second was to establish a small flock of sheep sired by a merino ram, Don Pedro. Importing additional merino sheep, du Pont sold the offspring to neighboring farmers, improving the quality of the fleece in the local area. In 1811 he opened his own woolen mill. The du Pont family (alternate spellings over time include duPont and DuPont) would not remain in the wool business for long, but their success in the gunpowder field would lead them back to textiles, and back into this story, after World War I.

Given how historically widespread the growing and manufacturing of wool was, why has the memory of its prominence in so many national stories diminished? In the American colonies and during the first decades of the United States, sheep and wool symbolized freedom from the economic restrictions imposed by Britain's mercantilist philosophy, which viewed colonies first as providers of the raw materials Britain desired to feed its industrial base, and second as consumers of British-made goods. Starting from small flocks and community fulling (cloth finishing) mills, the American woolen textile industry grew into one of the world's largest, both for grazing sheep and for producing woolen textiles. This was aided by slave owners who wanted cheap woolen cloth and blankets, by the federal government which imposed protective tariffs, and by regular influxes of foreign capital and skilled immigrants.

In the UK, wool growing was a primary industry for hundreds of years, gradually supplanted by textile production, which by 1800 would be at the heart of the industrial revolution. Bradford became the center of Britain's wool manufacturing industry, but it had competitors across Europe, such as Milan in Italy and Roubaix in France. As wool textile production expanded, the question of where all the wool would come from became more urgent. For Britain, its empire was the obvious answer, rooted in the mercantilism that the emerging United States had rejected.

Australia for many decades was said to have "ridden on the sheep's back." This certainly acknowledges wool's place at the heart of the national economy for 150 years. Prior to the development of refrigerated shipping, wool—which would not decay on the months-long journey to its markets—was vital to developing an economy that would allow Australia to grow beyond a series of convict settlements. It was equally important to the nation's "squatter" myth, whereby an odd assortment of largely young men ignored government restrictions and settled themselves outside the boundaries of the established colonies, opening up the Australian interior and becoming a wealthy "squattocracy" from their wool earnings.

Few Americans today know anything about how entwined wool and sheep were in the nation's economic growth and immigration patterns, although the craft market for knitting and weaving remains popular. Britain retains the remnants of both its sheep and wool industries, but as in the United States, many mill buildings have either found new uses or been demolished. In Australia wool has been pushed to the edges, replaced by the more profitable extractive industries. We have some ideas about why and how this has happened but would like to share an anecdote that spells out the current state of affairs—at least in Australia, and anecdotally, we hear, in many other countries as well.

Yass is a quintessential wool town an hour from Australia's capital, Canberra. The explorer and later pastoralist Hamilton Hume lived on its edge, having "discovered" the Yass Plains with the scouting party he led in 1821. It developed into a town with a reputation for stud sheep producing the finest wool. As you drive into town today, a few plastic sheep sculptures greet you. The Merino Nightclub and the Ewe and Me restaurant compete for the tourist dollar. In 2022 the local gift shop's front window featured a fleecy sheep doorstop. According to the manufacturer's tag, the sheep was made in China, of 100 percent polyester. It was cold the day we drove in and Trish decided she needed a woolen beanie and pullover. We went into two "op" or "thrift" shops in the town. Both were full of caps and sweaters, some hand-knitted but all from synthetic yarns. A craft shop in town apparently sells handmade woolen goods but we didn't find it that day.

So why—apart from the myriad sheep and wool festival markets—is it so hard to find wool now? What on earth happened? How is it that synthetic polyester fiber is currently far and away the most common clothing textile—*and* the biggest source of microplastic pollution? Why is the marketing of certain fibers, such as bamboo rayon, clearly greenwashing? Did the surge of demand for wool in the wars of the nineteenth and twentieth centuries play a part in the disappearance of wool? Before we are ready to answer these questions we need to first understand how wool came to establish its position as such a precious textile fiber.

CHAPTER 2

Golden Fleece/White Wealth

SHIPS & WOOL
The Age-old Quest of the Golden Fleece
In the weird and fantastic craft that plied the Mediterranean in the dawn of history; in the schooners and brigantines that sailed the seven seas in mediaeval times; in speedy clippers and power driven merchantmen of later times—wool, in some form or other, was invariably an important part of the most valuable cargoes.
Isaac
Naylor
& SONS LTD

Ad for Isaac Naylor, Import/Export. Bradford, UK, 1953. (Courtesy of The National Library of Australia).

Chapter 2

> In the weird and fantastic craft that plied the Mediterranean in the dawn of history; in the schooners and brigantines that sailed the seven seas in mediaeval times; in speedy clippers and power-driven merchantmen of later times—wool, in some form or other, was invariably an important part of the most valuable cargoes.
>
> Ad for Isaac Naylor, Export and Import Business,
> *Wool Record,* Bradford, UK, 1953

Wool, and transporting wool, equals money in the eyes of Isaac Naylor and Sons, a Bradford, England, import-export business. One of the "most valuable cargoes," wool was not only worth traveling long distances for, but also a cargo for which complex transport was necessary. Across thousands of years, it was carried from growers to markets in a myriad of ships: the fabled Argo of Greek mythology, powered by sail and oar; the fast-sailing square-rigged clippers that brought wool from Australia to Britain in the nineteenth century; and the coal and oil powered steamships that cut the transport time from months to weeks.

What is this "Age Old Quest of the Golden Fleece?" How is it that wool became associated with wealth? And how does that association relate to the historical role of wool in wartime?

As the advertisement suggests, the relationship of wool to wealth can be traced back in history both far and wide. Sheep were domesticated more than 10,000 years ago in what is known as the Fertile Crescent of Mesopotamia, for milk, meat, and wool. For centuries in most of Europe and parts of Asia, wool, a renewable resource, was the most commonly available textile fiber. It was also portable, unbreakable, non-perishable, and desirable—a perfect cargo. In the ancient Greek myth of Jason and his band of Argonauts, who pursue a quest to seize the Golden Fleece (the pelt of a winged Ram sacrificed to the gods), Jason steals the fleece and brings it back to Athens, presenting it to the king. Vase paintings depicting the story use the Golden Fleece as a symbol of the monarch's power, authority, and wealth. Several origin stories exist for the idea of a Golden Fleece. The one we like best relates it to Georgians, to the east of Greece, using sheepskins to filter the water of creeks and rivulets that contained flecks of gold, the wool becoming infused with gold and quite literally the source of wealth.

The symbol of the Golden Fleece would be widely taken up, including in "The Order of the Golden Fleece," a fifteenth century chivalric order instituted by the ruler of Flanders. But perhaps nowhere more so than in England. In the British city of York, the sign for the Golden Fleece Inn, a pub dating to the sixteenth century, is a listless golden sheep, constrained by the rope around its middle. The history of the city of York and its surrounding county of Yorkshire is, like the sheep, tightly bound up with the British wool trade. The region was renowned in medieval Europe for raising quality sheep and selling their wool, and famous for woolen cloth-making as far back as the eleventh century. England would also become the key source of wool for the cloth-making industries in Flanders (an area of Europe now divided among The Netherlands, Belgium, and France), and a little later in the Medieval period, in the Italian peninsula, centered in Florence in Tuscany. Indeed, the relationships among Flanders, Italy, France, Spain, England, and Ireland across medieval and early modern history—as their borders and conflicts and place in the woolen textile supply chain shifted—are crucial to understanding the intersection of wool, war, and money in the nineteenth and twentieth centuries.

The "Golden Fleece" of mythic memory would morph over time into "White Wealth" that helped support Britain and its Empire. This was overtly recognized, although seemingly without understanding the possible double meaning, in a 1933 Pathé newsreel about the wool market and Australia. The narration boasted that "Sydney Royal Exchange is the largest wool selling center in the world . . . in the City the great wool stores are crammed with bale after bale of White Wealth."[1] This transformation was aided by Cistercian monks, Florentine bankers, Flanders merchants, Australasian farmers, British industrialists, and countless inventors of new technologies. Although other nations invested in sheep, their wool, and the products made from it, by the late nineteenth century Britain was the center of the world's wool trade. The people and businesses whose stories follow will lead us through centuries of the associations between land and wool, between wool and wealth, and show what ready access to wool in the medieval and early modern eras meant for the wealth of those nations fortunate enough to have it. They illustrate the wool trade's global connections, and the ways in which wool supply chains have—for centuries—been fraught with financial and political intrigue and social upheaval. The effects of twentieth-century Britain's power over the world's wool would be felt around the globe, especially in wartime. To understand why, we must look farther back.

* * *

The era of Britain's Golden Fleece begins in the early twelfth century, when an order of Cistercian monks began to specialize in growing fine wool for the Flanders cloth industry in the North Yorkshire countryside. Flanders had grown its own wool until population pressures reduced the land available for pasturage. This is a familiar refrain in the history of sheep herding: sheep need space and movement to grow their best wool, so as people move in, sheep must move on.[2]

The Flanders wool trade depended on the Merchants of the Staple, a guild that at least as far back as 1319 controlled the export of the precious fleeces from Britain. Members had exclusive rights to buy and sell English wool in certain cities in Flanders and in Calais (which although geographically French was held by England from 1337 to 1548). Guild members, who represented all of England rather than any particular city, collected taxes that supported the British monarchy.

In 1353 the raw wool England exported, or perhaps more accurately the revenue it produced for the English crown, was described in the Parliament of Edward III as "The sovereign merchandise and the jewel of England."[3] Since that time the holder of the office of Lord Chancellor has been seated in the British Parliament's House of Lords on a red "wool sack," an oversized cushion of woolen cloth tightly stuffed with raw wool, as a symbol of the status and power of this commodity. England's wish to ensure that its wool trade with Flanders would continue without French interference was one factor in the Hundred Years War between those two nations. The peaks and troughs of this conflict, however, did affect the trade. The surviving letters of Thomas Betson (died 1486), a Merchant of the Staple, describe the drama and dullness of wool trading.[4] He bargained for wool and sheepskins in the Cotswolds; waited in an agony of uncertainty for wool shipments to arrive in Calais unharmed by Scottish raiders; competed for buyers at the seasonal market fairs held in cities across Flanders and France; and courted buyers from Italy, Scotland, and Spain.

Wool, money, and war-making were also closely connected in other regions of Europe. Florence became a center of finance and of wool cloth production during the papacy of Gregory IX, beginning in 1227. Saddled with debt from his participation in Crusades and other military actions, Gregory enlisted a series of trading families from Florence, who combined moneylending with wool-trading, to collect taxes from Europe and England on behalf of the papacy and the Church. They used these sinecures to enlarge and enhance their commercial reach and roles: for example, buying wool from England's monastic suppliers in quantities that supported the foundation of a substantial cloth production industry in Florence.[5]

The "Golden Fleeces" coming from England to the Italian peninsula created great wealth in Florence. In time even British monarchs would take loans from Italian financiers to allow them to wage wars and undertake other grand affairs of state. By the beginning of the fifteenth century the Medici family had become the leading Florentine family at the intersection of wool and finance, both fabulously wealthy and extremely powerful. A Medici Pope (Clement VII) rejected the request of Henry VIII of England to divorce and remarry, which led to Henry and England breaking away entirely from the Catholic Church and absorbing the resources of England's Catholic monasteries into the English monarchy.

* * *

For several centuries, Britain was not only a raw-wool-producing nation but also, and ultimately pre-eminently, a textile producing one. During Medieval times, the high export taxes on raw wool encouraged the development of artisanal wool textile production in England, particularly the tightly fulled, hard-wearing woolens known as broadcloth. An Act of Parliament in 1337, in the reign of Edward III, made it a felony to export raw wool from England unless the king decided otherwise. As it happens, the king often did decide otherwise, as the crown depended on the revenue from the wool exports it licensed. The act, however, remained in place to encourage English cloth manufacturers to have first pick of English wool.[6]

It also encouraged foreign cloth-workers to come to England, an invitation taken up by weavers exiled from Flanders after the periodic labor disputes in the wool workshops there. They brought vital skills with them, including those required to produce lighter fabrics called worsteds, named for the village of Worstead in Norfolk, the site of their first production in England.[7] Influxes of skilled textile workers from the continent would continue in successive centuries, whenever religious persecution led Protestant craftspeople to flee across the Channel. British monarchs tended to support these immigrants, including offering tax relief for several years after arrival, but the guilds that controlled labor in the towns and cities to which they moved, not so much.[8]

In all the excitement of expanding production, it's important to remember that before the invention in the eighteenth century of machines that allowed one spinner to control several spindles and produce copious quantities of yarn in a day, it took about four spinners working on individual spinning wheels to produce enough yarn per day to keep a single weaver working. This was a pretty serious bottleneck in the cloth production process. A new occupation, the clothier, arose to handle this and all the other intersecting processes and craftspeople necessary to create woolen textiles. Clothier Thomas Paycocke, who lived in Coggeshall, in Essex, in the sixteenth century, employed spinners, weavers, finishers, and dyers—each of whom worked in their own households—and when the cloth was ready for market, collected it and found buyers. Clothiers assumed the risks of production and reaped the rewards of the sales. By Paycocke's time they were assembling the various wool workers they employed under one roof. These were still workshops using hand tools and equipment, not factories with powered machines, but they allowed more control over the flow of the work between the various production processes. This control concentrated capital in the hands of the clothiers, who became an economic force. Thomas Paycocke was a master of this profession, and at his death in 1518, a wealthy man.[9]

England's shift from a raw wool to a textile producing nation had many stages, and as with most things woolen, complications and conflict. The rise of English woolen cloth-making created friction between the Merchant Staplers and another guild known as the Merchant Adventurers. The Adventurers, whose Royal Charter dated to 1505, sold woolen cloth on the Continent, and levied duties. By selling English cloth they not only undercut the Flanders textile industry but reduced the quantities of English raw wool purchased by Flanders merchants. Cloth export duties were never as big a source of revenue to the Crown as raw wool had been, and increased demand by domestic cloth makers kept more English raw wool in England.[10]

Disputes over wool were not limited to the various English merchant guilds. In the late 1400s through the 1500s, high wool prices and a growing population sparked clashes between farmers who had been using land to raise a variety of crops and small numbers of livestock with those wanting to use the land for grazing large numbers of sheep. Complaints began to be heard that sheep were taking over the island. The Enclosure Movement, which had started in the 1450s and went on intermittently for centuries, was led by big landowners, including monasteries. Enclosures commandeered common land to create larger tracts for private use. Land that had been used in a complex system of rotating each field between different agricultural crops and a range of livestock, including sheep, with the animals mainly fed on stubble and other byproducts of growing crops, became dedicated pasture for larger, and therefore more profitable flocks.[11] Over time a rather unfortunate side effect of feeding the sheep better in enclosed lands and breeding for meat quality emerged: their wool became longer but less fine—and therefore less valuable.[12]

As the English wool spinning and cloth weaving sector developed, there was simply not enough native raw wool available to feed both it and the important continental buyers in weaving centers such as Flanders and Florence. In 1660, England banned the export of raw wool altogether, and two years later made the death penalty the highest punishment for this crime, though we've found no records of capital punishment being meted out, and a few decades later it went off the statute books. The

Scottish Parliament, a separate institution until 1707 even though the monarch was shared with England from 1603, also acted in the seventeenth century to protect and encourage its own wool industries, passing laws against exporting wool, or wearing wool cloth not of native manufacture.[13] Wool yielded serious money, and was worth controlling.

* * *

Britain's efforts to encourage cloth production would lead to a new set of trading relationships, money flows, and supply chains for wool, with a new dependence upon imports of Spanish wool, particularly as prices for English woolen textiles gradually climbed. Until the 1840s, when industrialization of woolen textile production took hold across Europe, Britain was for the most part the primary importer of wool; other nations met their needs with their own flocks.

Exports of British wool textiles declined during the English Civil War—war generally interrupts agricultural and pastoral pursuits. After the austerity of Cromwell's Commonwealth, however, the Restoration of Charles II in 1660 saw the production of both wool and woolen cloth begin again to flourish across the islands. At the end of the century, the poet John Dryden described sheep pastoralism as "growing gold." By 1700 wool represented nearly 70 percent of all British exports.[14]

This rise coincided with more legislation regarding the trade in both raw wool and wool cloth, and enormous increases in the crime of "owling"—smuggling raw wool or sheep out of Britain. The Wool Act of 1699 prohibited Britain's North American colonies from selling any domestically produced wool or woolen cloth across colonial boundaries, or even very far from where it was made within a colony, and certainly not across the ocean either to Europe or the Caribbean. Not only was transport by ship denied, but even loading wool onto a carriage or a horse was made illegal. Ireland, by the same law, was forbidden to export raw wool except to England and Wales, its burgeoning wool textile production similarly constrained. The Act also established a kind of coast guard of ships tasked with interdicting wool smugglers.[15]

Eventually this created tensions between the British woolen textile sector, which wanted domestic wool to remain in Britain, and the landowners growing sheep for wool, who wanted the higher prices offered on the Continent. The British Crown and Exchequer were also determined not to miss out on income from wool sales, needing the revenue to fund England's many wars during the 1700s, which ranged over continental Europe, North America, and India.

Sheep and wool and the restrictions on their export were central to Scottish philosopher Adam Smith's 1776 work, *An Inquiry into the Nature and Causes of the Wealth of Nations.* He argued that "our woolen manufacturers have been more successful than any other class of workmen, in persuading the legislature that the prosperity of the nation depended upon the success and extension of their particular business."[16] Parliament only removed the restrictions on exports of British wool in 1824, perhaps because by the start of the nineteenth century, with the production of cotton fabric having been mechanized earlier than wool, cotton textiles (42 percent) had taken over from wool (16 percent) as Britain's prime export commodity.[17]

The financing of and supply chains for wool shifted many times in Europe between the twelfth and eighteenth centuries. No European nation ever had a constant full range of "sheep-to-suit" capacity within its borders to a degree that would provide for both domestic needs and an export commodity. Throughout this period war disrupted wool and cloth production and transport and encouraged revenue measures that in turn led to a shadow economy of smuggling. But the outfitting of huge militaries was not in and of itself in these centuries a cause of huge demand for wool. It would take the Napoleonic Wars (about 1799–1815), which involved—repeatedly—most of Europe, to really stimulate the acquisition of wealth derived from outfitting ever larger military contingents in wool.

* * *

That series of wars, following the American and French Revolutions, saw many nations begin to establish substantial national militaries, as opposed to the small armies of professional or feudally bound soldiers that had preceded them. This in turn was linked to an escalation, at first gradual and then exponential, of the scale of war across the nineteenth and into the twentieth centuries. Producing cloth for the military became a significant sector of the European economy, with a corresponding increase in demand for wool.

The value of wool in relation to military needs, however, depended on being able to process huge quantities of wool into cloth and make clothing in bulk to outfit armies that grew ever larger. These two manufacturing sectors became cornerstones of the Industrial Revolution, starting in Britain. As mechanization, which required capital, crept into the woolen textile industry, decades later than it did for cotton textiles but adopting and adapting similar technologies, wool textile production moved from the home and small workshop in places like Coggeshall and Norwich to the factory. Factories with water-powered equipment needed land and rivers, both in short supply in the old wool towns. The West Riding of the county of York, around Bradford and Leeds, had plenty of waterways to power the machines and became the center of the factory system of wool textile production.

Perhaps most importantly in the long term, the region also had an abundance of landless laborers, many of whom drifted to the towns because of the enclosure movement. From the factory owner's perspective, workers in these new towns and cities were free of the guilds and apprentice/journeyman/master forms of labor organization common in the old established cities. Laborers appreciated that the cost of living in the newer towns was much cheaper than in the wealthy city of York. As the Industrial Revolution unfolded for wool, the cities of Yorkshire's West Riding grew quickly, along with the industry that supported it. In 1800 Bradford's population was estimated at about 6,000. By 1850 it numbered more than 100,000. An industrial city, it grew around the physical locations and requirements of its mills and their workers.

Why is the shift to factory production and mechanization important to the historical relationship of wool and war? Well, for an extreme example, A Vikingskibsmuseet (Viking Ship Museum, in Roskilde, Denmark) project reported on the person-hours necessary to make a single, ten-meter square woolen sail for an eleventh-century Viking longship, using the hand processes of the time. First, preparing 50 kilos of wool, shorn from 150 sheep, for spinning would take 1,666 hours.

Add in 400 days to spin the necessary 200,000 meters of yarn for 100 meters of cloth. Thirty days to set up the warp-weighted loom then in use, and another 200 days to weave it by hand. All in all, a single sail required about 800 person-days, or five workers for about a year.[18] By the eighteenth century, spinning wheels, and then spinning frames, flying shuttles, and carding machines had sped up the creation of woolen thread, but until some degree of automation was introduced to the weaving looms, the bottleneck at the end was still one weaver to one loom.

Compare this to the vast consumption of wool during World War II. In peacetime, a mid-twentieth century civilian consumed an average of one kilo (2.2 pounds) of scoured (clean) wool per year. Heading into World War II, the US Army estimated that each combat soldier required gear consuming 100 pounds of scoured wool, with an annual resupply of 40 pounds. One hundred pounds scoured could be almost double that in raw wool and represent the fleeces of 26 sheep. During 1942, the first full year of US involvement in that war, 125,000 workers—mechanized, automated, and organized into factories—produced 227 million linear yards of woven wool textiles for consumption by the American military.[19] This total does not even include the statistics for the knitting mills, which produced woolen underwear, socks, caps, and pullovers by the millions.

While armies march metaphorically on their stomachs, food is not their only requirement. The reality is that they literally march on their feet, and their ability to do so is affected by the quality of the textiles that clothe them. If the production of woolen textiles had not moved to mechanized factories in the mid-nineteenth century, would warfare at the ever-increasing scale that pertained from the Crimean War through the Korean War even have been possible? The ability to fight a war efficiently and effectively, particularly one engaging hundreds of thousands, if not millions of combatants, and especially in cold climates, depends on military personnel outfitted with uniforms and blankets that keep them warm, insulated, and when you get right down to it, *alive.*

* * *

Which means that an infrastructure that can manufacture the yarns and cloth necessary for those blankets and uniforms, underwear and socks, must exist. Business in wartime was (and is) immensely risky. As with most strategic wartime commodities, wool rose and fell in price for any number of reasons; the pulses of demand caused by war are important but *not* the only determinant. Interruptions of the flow of wool by organized blockades of trading ports and by surface and later submarine and aerial warfare, and virtual monopolies, such as Britain's commandeering of its Dominion's wool in the twentieth century's two World Wars were just some of the hazards to be navigated. Yet individual companies managed to flourish despite the risks.

Britain's Hainsworth family has produced military textiles in Pudsey, Yorkshire, for seven generations, since the Napoleonic Wars. Over 250 years or so the family has owned three different woolen mills in and around Leeds and Bradford and intermarried with several other "wool families" such as the Gaunts and the Knoxes. A.W. Hainsworth & Sons, Ltd., in addition to producing a wide range of fabrics for civilian markets, remains an important supplier of scarlet red woolen cloth to Britain's military for ceremonial uniforms—a focus of attention at royal funerals and coronations. It now comprises a single factory complex in Pudsey that undertakes every stage of manufacture from raw wool to finished fabric. It is the last such business in and around Bradford. From the beginning, military textiles have been their biggest, albeit not their only, product line. They first exhibited Army cloths at the London Exhibition in 1840 and took on contracts for the Army the next year. By the 1880s, the British War Office was their main client. In 2016 Tom Hainsworth, the firm's managing director, summed up that aspect of the business simply: "In wars, if you're making a [woolen] military product, it's financially very good."[20]

The first Hainsworth in the area known to be involved with textiles was a mid-seventeenth-century clothier, in trouble for drying fulled wool on a lord's private land. The first known direct ancestor to the current firm was Abimelech Hainsworth, a clothier who from around 1783 was buying woolen cloth from local weavers and selling it in Leeds. Abimelech is said to have encouraged Samuel Marsden to continue his Australian sheep breeding experiments during Marsden's visit to England in 1807. He was also the first family member to run a textile mill, buying his first woolen mill in 1811, in Farsley. The previous owners had gone out of business due to the French navy's blockade of Britain, the explicit intention of same being to stop the island's exports during the Napoleonic Wars. Hainsworth would prove luckier: his woolen cloth, according to company history, was worn by British soldiers at the final battle of those wars, at Waterloo.

It would not be the firm's only, nor even its most important connection to war and the military. In 1854, smack in the middle of the Crimean War, family member Israel Roberts noted in his diary that that year's profits were the "greatest ever." In 1859, Reuben Hainsworth wrote in *his* diary, "Trade in a most deplorable condition. A very deal out of work and some families I do believe perishing." At about the same time another of the Hainsworth family's woolen mills was toasting the Army and the Navy, presumably on the strength of orders related to the Indian Mutiny of 1857–1858. Just a few years later, during a blockade associated with the American Civil War, which prevented both Confederate state cotton from getting to Britain and British goods—including much sought after woolen uniform cloth—from entering the Confederacy, again Reuben noted, "the whole village at a standstill and has been for about a month."[21] The family managed to consolidate its business with good years in the 1870s, amidst the Franco-Prussian and Russian-Turkish wars.

The Hainsworth family mills illustrate the complexities of the mechanization of the woolen industry. There are so many different stages in creating finished textiles from raw greasy woolen fiber that developing the technology to completely mechanize the process took about 80 years. In 1830 the word "factory" in the family's documents meant not mechanization, but a building where multiple workers could be supervised. Establishing oversight and central organization was an important step toward introducing the technology to mechanize the production of woolen fabric. Steam-powered spinning mules (machines allowing a single spinner to control many spindles) arrived in the 1840s, powered carding and fulling equipment in the 1850s. Most weaving was still, however, home based. This system supported production levels that would outfit an army then still numbering "only" in the tens of thousands. In 1869 powered looms were installed in the Farsley mill, and in 1884 modern equipment was installed in a second mill, completing the mechanization of the textile manufacturing process. This, and similar stories in dozens of other wool textile businesses around the UK, Europe, and the United States, would enable the outfitting of an army in the millions by 1914.

* * *

The late eighteenth-century woolen mills of England generated one of the most important American woolen dynasties, appropriately enough in New England. The Marland, Stevens, and Hobbs families, who share roots in English wool, are intertwined both through businesses and marriages, and are forever linked in the nineteenth-century creation and twentieth-century demise of the woolen industry of North Andover, Massachusetts. Abraham Marland, woolen mill worker from Lancashire, England, emigrated to Massachusetts in 1801, at the age of 29. Although Samuel Slater, an acquaintance in Pawtucket, Rhode Island (who became known as the founder of America's cotton manufacturing industry), supposedly counseled him to take up farming instead of textiles, Marland's cotton mill experience was highly desirable in New England's tentative steps toward a textile industry.

At the time it seemed that the United States had everything necessary to challenge Britain as a producer both of raw wool and the products made from it. The country had started on its bumpy road to becoming a wool-growing, as well as wool-manufacturing, nation in the seventeenth and eighteenth centuries. Relatively small flocks of sheep were brought by European colonizers to the Eastern seaboard of North America, and northward from Mexico to California. Britain continually fretted that if its American colonists raised too many sheep and wove anything other than the coarsest, most utilitarian cloth, British woolgrowers and industry would suffer. Britain's mercantilist economic philosophy greatly irritated the resourceful, and literally, resource-full, colonists. So, the British Parliament enacted legislation forbidding Americans from selling woolen cloth to other colonies and restricting imports from Britain of machinery and the emigration of workers with technical know-how. These laws were both perpetually re-enacted and routinely, if clandestinely, ignored. In the eighteenth-century workshop production of woolen cloth for local sale was well established in cities and towns from Philadelphia north through Massachusetts. After the American Revolution, with the United States established as a growing nation, economic and social disruption in Britain led many British textile workers, like Marland, to emigrate to the United States in search of greater opportunity and stability.[22]

Just two years after his arrival, Marland had earned enough cash and experience to buy a small cotton-spinning mill of his own in Lynfield, Massachusetts. Lured by the siren call of the Shawsheen River with its abundant waterpower, Marland moved in 1807 to Andover, Massachusetts, first opening a second cotton-spinning mill and quickly adding wool carding to the mix. These were the standard factory operations of the time. Wool spinning and most weaving were still done either in a small workshop or by a single weaver. In fact, a family history maintains that Marland began his weaving business "on a handloom with a spring shuttle," an improvement that "people flocked to see."[23] At a time when a family's cloth requirements could cost a third of its annual income, improvements that increased efficiency and productivity and lessened costs were welcome.

Marland might have felt some divided loyalties during the War of 1812; the US part of the Napoleonic Wars, which from a US perspective concerned both its territorial boundaries in North America and freedom of the seas: specifically, Britain's penchant for stopping American ships and forcing (impressing) American sailors into its Navy. He had then been in the United States only 11 years. Nevertheless, he started a putting-out system, giving local weavers yarn from his mill, and turning the cloth they wove for him into blankets which he sold to the US Army. His business prospered during the war, and survived the period immediately after, when British textile manufacturers made a concerted effort to quash the upstart American textile industry by dumping their goods at prices low enough to outcompete US-made goods, even with the then current tariff rate on imported woolen fabrics of 25 percent of their value.

Congress enacted much higher protective tariffs, 40 percent and up, against competition from Britain and other European nations in 1828, and the US industry grew steadily. New England, in particular Andover and Lawrence, Massachusetts, became the first American center of large-scale factory production of woolen textiles, after waterpower arrived with a canal system and dams on the Merrimack River in 1845. The state of Rhode Island and the region around Philadelphia, Pennsylvania, drew in part on their histories of producing coarse woolen or mixed wool and cotton cloth marketed to slave-holding states to establish their places in the woolen industry.

Marland's son and heir, John, expanded the business he inherited from his father in 1849, adding new, more fashionable worsted goods to the blankets and flannels his father had produced. His Ballard Vale Mills received a gold medal for these in 1844 for "the attainment of such great perfection, in articles never before made in this Country." The occasion was the Fourth Exhibition of Domestic Manufactures held by the Massachusetts Charitable Mechanic Association, in Boston.[24] The newfangled products proved less profitable than the flannels, and in 1853 that branch of the business was sold. John Marland died in 1865; his company passed out of family hands but remained in business until 1930. His sister Mary, however, provided the next generation of wool men: her daughter, also Mary, would marry William Hobbs. Their son Franklin W. Hobbs would become the treasurer and in 1912 President of the Arlington Woolen Mills, and later President of the National Association of Wool Manufacturers.

* * *

John Marland had lived to see the American Civil War (1861–1865) give a giant boost to the woolen industry. The number of woolen mills in the United States grew from 1,260 in 1859 to 2,891 in 1869, spurred by the need for blankets, uniform cloth, overcoats, undershirts and drawers, mixed wool and cotton flannel shirts, and let us not forget, the voracious need of an army for woolen socks.[25] Records from the Cocheco Woolen Mill (Rochester, New Hampshire) and the Stevens Woolen Mill (North Andover, Massachusetts), which each had army contracts, show that during the war they purchased large quantities of domestic raw wool from Michigan, Wisconsin, Ohio, Pennsylvania, California, Oregon, and Washington, as well as from overseas sources in use before the war, including Argentina and the Levant, and tentatively, from new sources, buying small quantities from New Zealand and the Sandwich Islands (Hawaii).[26]

The profits made from selling woolen cloth to the US government during the Civil War enriched the owners of the woolen companies, and provided capital for new machinery, mills, and production systems. By the end of the nineteenth century, these investments would make the American textile industry the largest in the world. Like the Marland family had found half a century earlier, it was not the fancy goods that filled their coffers, but the standards (confusingly, for our purposes, called "staples"), which for woolens meant the flannels, broadcloths, kerseys, and blankets that served the everyday needs of millions of office workers, laborers, and of course, soldiers and sailors. Andover became an important center of the concentration on staple cloths, and home to several of the mills that would be amalgamated to form the American Woolen Co., an immense conglomerate built by William Wood from the late nineteenth into the early twentieth centuries.

Tariff protection, which woolgrowers and woolen manufacturers each sought for themselves and opposed for the other, encouraged this growth, fueled by the demand from a rapidly increasing population. High import duties on many European-made textiles made it cheaper for firms that had the capital to simply open a subsidiary mill in the United States, often staffed by family members and skilled workers brought over from the home country. This made the later-nineteenth-century American wool business especially multi-national. Julius Forstmann, founder of the important New Jersey woolen manufacturing firm Forstmann & Huffmann, was a fourth-generation wool man born in Germany, but whose uncle, along with a Huffmann of the same generation, opened a business in the United States in the 1850s, selling their family's products to the American market.[27] The McKinley Tariff of 1890 impelled Julius to emigrate to the United States at the age of 23, first to work in the Botany Mills (also in New Jersey, and German-owned, by the Stöhr family, which owned mills in Leipzig). In 1904, Forstmann opened an US offshoot of his German family's company. By the time he renamed his company the Forstmann Woolen Co. in 1931, it was a leader in quality and innovation in the American woolen industry.

The ins and outs, ups and downs, and endless reversals of the tariff laws that helped shape the US woolen industry are impossible to lay out clearly in anything less than an encyclopedia. Testimony at tariff hearings encompassed many points of view: woodgrowers who wanted to maintain the value of their wool through tariffs on raw wool imports; free traders who said tariffs of any kind simply raised the prices on goods for the many in favor of the few who raised sheep or made cloth; manufacturers of cloth who wanted their products protected from foreign competition; and manufacturers of clothing and other finished goods who wanted low tariffs on cloth imports to reduce their cost of production.[28] (You can't please everybody.)

Whether despite or because of the tariff laws, the size of the American wool textile business and the challenges of domestic wool growing created opportunities for those who understood wool as a global commodity. Just as England had grown its own wool but also depended on imports from Spain, the US woolen textile industry purchased both domestic and imported wool, and after the Civil War steadily expanded the scope of its imports. Whatever the tariff rates on wool imports were, manufacturers needed foreign wool.

The Boston wool brokerage and buying firm established in about 1880 by Sidney Clementson was one of the first to sell Australian wool to American manufacturers. A T. Clementson (a partner or employee) boasted to an Australian newspaper in November 1896 that he was on his fifteenth buying trip for that purpose.[29] James Booth, who had emigrated to Australia from England in 1867, worked for Sidney Clementson, making the rounds of Australian sheep stations buying wool to suit US requirements. His son Frederick joined the firm at the age of 14, in 1894, but left to serve as a private in the Victorian Light Horse Regiment during the Boer War of 1899–1902. Restless upon his return to Australia, and keen to learn more about the family trade, he headed to England in 1904. For a year he tried to find a suitable position in Bradford, but mostly gained experience in unpaid roles.

At a low ebb in his fortunes, relatives advised him to head to the United States, where the wool business was thriving. Frederick found great opportunity there, working in 1905–1906 for the A. J. Cameron and Co. worsted spinning mill in Philadelphia, which also had offices in Boston. His letters home to his parents make it very clear why American-grown wool was not highly prized by US textile manufacturers. On a buying trip in Missouri, Nebraska, and Colorado in July 1905, he wrote, "So I have seen just where this wool is grown. It is entirely different to Australian wool, not nearly as good and very dirty." In September he described buying "Territory" or "range" wools, from the States west of the Mississippi River: "These wools are very hard to value being full of sand and shrinkage anywhere from 55% to 75%."[30] By 1907 Frederick had a generous contract from yet another firm, Jeremiah Williams, in Boston, to buy Australian wool for their clients, a role he undertook from Australia for several decades. In the 1910s, he took on another client, the Arlington Woolen Mills, with his key business contacts being Franklin and Marland Hobbs, descendants of Abraham Marland.

In 1913, Dartmouth College gave Franklin W. Hobbs the honorary degree of Master of Science in recognition of his contributions to the textile industries in the United States. Hobbs had graduated from the Massachusetts Institute of Technology and had been in the forefront of technical education and technological development in the textile field. In reporting on his honor from Dartmouth, the Bulletin of the National Association of Wool Manufacturers commented: "As an illustration of the growth of the woolen industry it may be remarked that the Arlington Mills, of which Mr. Hobbs is the head, could now comb in five hours the quantity of wool which it took his great grandfather one year to manufacture."[31]

* * *

Britain's failure to retain its American colonies as providers of the wool it needed to sustain its textile industry had a far-ranging ripple effect. One of these was the last iteration of its enclosure movement: the land clearances of the Scottish Highlands and the western islands of the Inner and Outer Hebrides that replaced crofters with sheep. The Clearances had begun in the middle of the eighteenth century, but by the early nineteenth century were regarded as an answer to Britain's need for wool and mutton as its various wars with, on, and around the continent of Europe dragged on, damaging trade and driving the nation inward on its own resources. Donald MacLeod, who lived through the Sutherland clearances in the early nineteenth century, wrote in 1840 of the connection between the Napoleonic Wars (1803–1815) and the Clearances:

> *The late war and its consequences laid the foundation of the evil complained of. Great Britain with her immense naval and military establishments, being in a measure shut out from foreign supplies, and in a state of hostility or non-intercourse with all Europe and North America, almost all the necessities of life had to be drawn from our own soil. . . . Hence also, all the speculations to get rid of human inhabitants of the Highlands and replace them with cattle and sheep for the English market.*[32]

By the early 1800s, Britain was out of land that could be pressed into service for sheep. When Spain's involvement in the Napoleonic Wars disrupted Britain's access to the fine merino wool that had been vital to its textile export industry for several centuries, Britain saw, not for the first time, the dangers of being dependent upon wool from nations not under British control.[33] To allow for continued growth of Britain's woolen mills, the economic elites and the government encouraged the growth of sheep pastoralism throughout the Empire.

In the times of swirling change following the Napoleonic Wars, a Royal Charter would again be the vehicle chosen to secure the nation's fortune. One final representation of the Golden Fleece says a lot about the longevity of the relationship of Crown, Money, and Empire in relation to wool. The Australian Agricultural Company, at its inception in 1824 neither Australian nor agricultural, had on its seal a "hung sheep" image of the kind associated with the mythical Golden Fleece. During a phase of the Clearances in the 1840s and 1850s, titled Scottish landowners often facilitated surplus crofters emigrating to other parts of Britain's empire. Exporting British expertise—and personnel—in sheep pastoralism would drive developments in nineteenth-century Australia, New Zealand, South Africa, and in other, less well-known places.[34]

* * *

These developments would depend on technologies that emerged alongside the advances in textile manufacturing. Even before the Industrial Revolution, Britain's wealth was closely aligned with its wool industry. By the mid-nineteenth century, Britain had changed from a nation known for producing raw wool to a nation renowned for producing woolen fabric. Its failure in one colonial enterprise had precipitated the growth of an important competitor, as the United States emerged as a consumer of raw wool beyond what it could produce, and a manufacturer of woolen textiles almost entirely focused on its own domestic market, largely excluding Britain from a growing source of potential profit. Meanwhile Britain came to depend on its far-flung empire for raw wool production. It is no accident that the advertisement at the start of the chapter focused on shipping. Transport across these extended supply lines was both crucial and a weak link in times of war.

Steam-powered shipping developed in stages from the late 1700s. By the 1850s paddle steamers on inland rivers were an important means of moving wool to Australian coastal ports. Not until the opening in 1869 of the Suez Canal, however, would steamships decisively shape the wool industry. The canal, designed for steamers, radically cut the time and distance for transport between Europe and Asia and the Pacific. Ocean-going steamships capable of carrying bulk wool as a long-distance cargo came into play in the 1870s, although, as hinted at by the wool clipper in the Naylor advertisement, sailing ships put up a fight. A "clipper" is a sailing ship of various kinds and shapes built for speed rather than to maximize storage. The famed clipper *Cutty Sark* was built in Scotland the same year as the Suez opened, originally for Britain's tea trade with China. The tea trade quickly turned to steam transport, and the clippers, including the *Cutty Sark*, switched to wool cargoes instead.

In 1891, Sydney Harbour still had 77 sailing ships loading wool for London, each carrying up to 10,000 bales. By then, however, more than half of Australia's wool was traveling by steamship, and within a decade steam was king. Time was a huge factor: steamships made it possible for the wool from sheep shorn in a southern hemisphere spring to get to London in good time for the wool sales traditionally held in November, giving growers a quicker return on their investment. Ultimately, though, steamships helped move the largest wool sales from the northern to the southern hemisphere, carrying not just cargoes of raw wool to Europe, but many of the world's wool buyers to increasingly important southern hemisphere auctions.[35]

Even before the industrial era, and overwhelmingly important thereafter, technological advances and governments controlling imports and exports were integral to the wool trade. War was a key thread of this tangled skein of history. Wool caused wars, funded wars, and its trade was regularly disrupted by wars. Its industrialization coincided with a sharp rise in the scale of wars. Where the wool would come from to support this growth, and what such a collaboration meant for the continent of Australia and its Indigenous peoples, as well as others around the globe, is where we'll take you next.

Chapter 3

Agents of Empire

Wool bag for carrying pituri, handle made from an old ration blanket. Queensland, Australia. Collected 1949, age unknown (courtesy of the University of Queensland Anthropology Museum. Acc. No. 1742).

Chapter 3

> The white settler revolution . . . transformed the hunting grounds of Australia's Indigenous peoples into a vast sheepwalk for the production of raw wool for the textile mills of England.[1]
>
> Lyndall Ryan, 2015

This pithy summary of the textile industry's role in the radical changes to Australian land and land use wrought by British nineteenth-century colonization emerged from historian Lyndall Ryan's analysis of Aboriginal societies in the states now known as Tasmania and Victoria. The catastrophic population loss that opened the land for sheep resulted from the conflict-ridden intersection of the settler occupiers and the Aboriginal peoples of Australia. Settler violence was ecological as well as human to human.

Starting this project, we knew Australia's history included frontier warfare connected to sheep and wool, although not its extent, and that during the American Civil War, the Union's textile manufacturers went far afield for wool to clothe the burgeoning ranks of soldiers, including to Hawaii (then known as the Sandwich Islands) and New Zealand. Seeing a French documentary film[2] about how Rapa Nui (Easter Island) had been taken over in the late 1800s as a sheep station led us to research how Indigenous peoples of Australasia, the Americas, Southern Africa, and the Pacific faced the imposition of large-scale sheep grazing.

Trial and error marked invaders' efforts to establish sheep and wool. Which climates and geographies suited sheep? Where would the capital and labor come from? How would the wool get to distant markets and manufacturing centers and be best prepared for sale. Most importantly, where would all the *land* come from? The lands of Indigenous peoples became the main answer to this question, creating a different kind of war, not only in Australia. Wherever sheep were introduced, their grazing damaged the land, with native grasses largely replaced by imported fodder species and water sources despoiled by stock.

Britain was not the only nation to face these questions in the nineteenth century, though it was central, not only within its empire but through its capital in places such as Patagonia in South America.[3] The vast expansion of woolen textiles spelled trouble for Indigenous peoples around the world. Conversely, First Nations peoples often became important parts of the wool industry's workforce, alongside new immigrants of color, in a complex web of survival, adaptation, and exploitation.

The invasion of the Australian continent forced First Nations' exposure to new animals, materials, and technologies. Sometimes these were selectively incorporated into Aboriginal cultures. At the head of this chapter is a bag woven using traditional methods, most likely by Aboriginal women, to transport pituri (a psycho-active drug related to nicotine), derived from a native plant found in the sandhills of Australian deserts. Pituri was highly prized by Aboriginal people for ceremonies; traded along ancient routes stretching from the Kimberley in North-Western Australia down to South Australia and east to Queensland's central coast.[4] Pre-invasion, bags for carrying pituri were woven with human hair. This bag's maker incorporated some hair, but mainly used wool yarns, adding a section cut from a gray woolen blanket to form its top cover.

A yearly ration of blankets was commonly included in the *quid pro quo* for the largely unpaid labor Aboriginal people provided for pastoralists. Where much of the year is blazingly hot, wool may have been as valuable for the qualities that would make a strong bag as it was for its warmth. While the strip of blanket in this bag was used as is, blankets were also sometimes unraveled, the yarn re-used for weaving and embellishment. Adapting European materials to traditional uses is one way in which Aboriginal culture, and many other Indigenous peoples, demonstrated resilience and ingenuity in the face of invasion of their lands and the mass introduction of an animal at odds with their environment.

As the nation that came to have the largest apparel-wool export industry, Australia is our key example to understand the impact of large-scale sheep pastoralism on Indigenous peoples and their ecologies. This is a vast history, and we can only summarize key trends and explore indicative examples, while surveying several other nations for context and to see patterns. There is more to this story from nations only mentioned here. Wool markets followed sheep to the southern hemisphere, creating hyper-extended supply lines, manageable in peacetime but vulnerable in war. Wool is *not* a friction-free fiber.

The far-flung British colony of Australia was initially designed as a literal dumping ground for convicts, replacing the colonies lost in the American War of Independence. Australia's emergence as an unrivaled global center for fine wool production seemed unlikely. But as it had done (less successfully) in North America, Britain imposed its mercantilist system: its southern hemisphere colonies would supply raw materials but not compete with the mother country's growing manufacturing sector. The British did not acknowledge the semi-nomadic Aboriginal peoples' deep connection to specific land as ownership, nor did they ever negotiate a treaty with Indigenous Australians. All land was deemed Crown land, justified by the concept of *terra nullius,* or empty land. The chaos that followed was closely linked to the British woolen textile industry's interests.

Britain's search for Australian primary products to feed its industries started early. On August 29, 1802, Lord Hobart, Secretary of State for War and the Colonies, wrote to Phillip Gidley King—then Governor of New South Wales (NSW), asserting:

> *The exertions that have been made by certain of the settlers to improve the quality of wool are highly creditable to the individuals and cannot be too much encouraged with a view to the future exportation of the finest quality of that article for the market of this country rather than for the employment of it in the manufactures of the colony, which should be confined to the coarser kind of cloth.*[5]

Lord Hobart's statement indirectly references John Macarthur: an important, if controversial, figure in the Australian wool industry's development. Macarthur, the son of a Plymouth draper (textile merchant), came to Australia as a lieutenant in the British Army in 1790, shortly after the colony's founding. Within three years he had been promoted and granted 100 acres of land on the outskirts of present-day Sydney. The ambitious Macarthur took advantage of his new position, commissioning his brother back in England to produce "regimental slops" (ready-made military uniforms) for his fellow soldiers in Australia.[6]

John was a divisive character. Governor King sent him back to England in 1801 for court martial after repeated conflicts with other officers and a series of governors, including King himself. But the year before, King had sent samples of eight different Australian-grown wools back to England, including some of Macarthur's. Britain, suffering trade interruptions from the war with France, was hungry for wool. London wool buyer George Laycock dismissed one sample as hairy, barely wool at all, but another, of mixed merino genetics, he proclaimed to be "nearly as good as the King's Spanish wool at Oatlands," remarking that such samples, if replicated, would be "a great acquisition to our manufactory in England."[7]

Accompanied by two of his children and more samples of his family's wool, Macarthur spent a year traveling to England. Upon arrival he wriggled out of the court martial and wrote effusively of Australia to Lord Hobart: "The climate of NSW is peculiarly adapted to the increase of fine-wooled sheep," with "unlimited extent of luxuriant pastures" where "millions of these valuable animals may be raised in a few years," requiring only "the hire of a few shepherds."[8] Amidst the exigencies of the Napoleonic wars, these assertions, while questionable, had their effect. Spending two years in Britain before returning to Australia, Macarthur secured more sheep, more land, and more powerful contacts.

* * *

Britain's interests in securing a reliable raw wool supply influenced discussions of Australia's future. In 1819, Judge John Bigge, former Chief Justice of the British Caribbean colony of Trinidad, toured NSW and Van Diemen's Land (Tasmania) as Britain's special commissioner investigating those colonies' governance and economic future. He published his findings in the early 1820s, nominating wool as "the great staple article of [the colony's] future exports."[9] In an era of sail power and before refrigeration, wool was an ideal export commodity, withstanding months of transport, first to Australian ports and then to the UK, without deterioration.

Bigge envisaged that both assigned convicts and those who had completed their sentences would provide the "few shepherds" Macarthur recommended. He also, however, promoted attracting "men of real capital" to Australia. One result was the Australian Agricultural Company (AA Co), created by Royal Charter of November 1, 1824. A privately owned joint stock company, it was authorized to choose a million acres of the Australian continent. Its first selection on the NSW mid-central coast proving ill-suited to raising sheep for wool, the company swapped half of it for some of the finest pastoral land of NSW's inland Liverpool plains. The land they kept included major coal deposits, adding coal mining to the AA Co's goals. The underlying legislation referred to the "Waste Lands of NSW," ignoring Aboriginal sovereignty.[10]

Despite its title and sprinkling of Australian shareholders (including John Oxley, explorer and Surveyor General of NSW), the company was fundamentally British. Its hundreds of British shareholders included 19 Members of Parliament, the Ebsworths—a London family that sold the Macarthur family's first wool—and Judge Bigge. The extended Macarthur family, in Australia and the UK, were heavily involved, including John and Elizabeth Macarthur's son John, who had accompanied his father to Britain as a child and remained there. The AA Co was not primarily agricultural, although wartime trade interruptions in grapes and olives placed growing them among its subsidiary goals. Its primary aim was "producing fine wool as an export commodity to Great Britain" at a time when the industrial revolution in woolen textiles was accelerating. It would also provide gainful employment for freed convicts to be trained by "competent, free persons with experience gained in the Continental woolen industry," sent by the company to NSW.[11]

In 1825, the same year that the colony of Van Diemen's Land separated from NSW, another Royal Charter ceded 350,000 acres of that island's northwest to 22 persons associated with the British woolen industry: wool importers, exporters and buyers, bankers, and a military outfitter. They formed the Van Diemen's Land Company (VDL), also with the primary purpose of providing British textile manufacturers with a steady supply of wool. The AA Co, flexing the muscle of its slightly earlier incorporation, insisted that the VDL's land grant be outside the colony of NSW, and on land that had not previously carried sheep. The chosen land was wet, windy, and cold, and would (eventually) fail abjectly as a commercial wool enterprise.[12]

The initial efforts, both troubled and troubling, of these two vast British companies to secure supplies of wool from far-off colonies positioned Australia to become the world's largest producer of fine wool, with sheep numbers increasing from around 156,000 in 1820 to 100 million in 1890.[13]

* * *

But the two Royal Charter land grants were the exception, not the rule of land tenure for Australia's sheep pastoralism. Devising a system of land ownership for the rest of the continent had several stages. From 1818 until 1831, those with at least 500 pounds were granted land in proportion to their capital, within the defined boundaries of the colony of NSW. Tasmania's colonial administration followed a similar model, routinely assigning convicts as labor and assuming sheep as the primary industry. The defining reality of land tenure for sheep pastoralism in Australia, however, was the "squatter."

In its original 1820s Australian usage, the word described "one, especially an ex-convict, who occupies Crown Land without legal title." Squatters acting privately and illegally left governments conveniently free of responsibility. But from the mid-1830s, squatter meant "one who occupies a tract of Crown Land in order to graze livestock, having title by either license or lease."[14] Eventually the term denoted those with substantial land, a lot of livestock (especially sheep), and an entrepreneurial attitude, whether they had bought, leased, licensed, or simply occupied the land.

Despite squatters' portrayal as individual entrepreneurs, British and colonial governments were pivotal to the continent's occupation, though official statements and actions were complex and often contradictory. For several years from the mid-1820s the NSW government tried to contain settlers within the colony's mandated boundaries, partly to retain the vast Crown Lands of Australia for Britain, and partly to protect the Aboriginal inhabitants.[15] But squatters and their flocks continuously exceeded those boundaries, in NSW and elsewhere. In the 1830s, Tasmanian sheep pastoralists crossed the Bass Strait to find pasture on the mainland (now Victoria). Explorers such as John Oxley and Major Thomas Mitchell journeyed in their roles as government surveyors, searching for—and mapping—land suitable for sheep and cattle, opening Australia's interior for settler invasion.[16]

The squatting land rushes of the 1830s and 1840s coincided with a high point of humanitarian sentiment in Britain, after reports of the horrors of the Tasmanian frontier had filtered through, and following a series of bans on various aspects of the slave trade.[17] In 1834 the House of Commons unanimously asserted the king's "duty of acting upon the principles of justice and humanity" in relationships with Australia's "native inhabitants," and charged colonial governors to further "the protection of their rights, promote the spread of civilization amongst them and lead them to peaceful and voluntary reception of the Christian religion."[18] This document, although duly distributed to all colonial governors, conflicted with the realpolitik of the emerging Australian economy. NSW Governor Bourke informed London in 1835 that constraints "expedient elsewhere" could not apply because

> *the wool of NSW forms at present, and is likely long to continue, its chief wealth. It is only by free range over the wide expanse of native herbiage that the Colony affords that this staple article can be upheld at its present rate of increase in quantity . . . or quality.*[19]

On the horns of this dilemma, land policy in Australia vacillated for 20 years. At first colonial governments tried to oversee the treatment of First Peoples by offering squatters licenses to graze stock, rather than lease or free-hold title to specific land. In 1837, the British government affirmed that Aboriginal people had an "incontrovertible right to their own soil," a precept appearing in documents until at least 1850 but rarely honored. After squatter advocacy, Parliament in 1846 approved the granting of pastoral leases by colonial governments. Land commissioners were appointed to determine the boundaries of different squatters' runs, which were often contentious. Though the commissioners' remit included the welfare of Aboriginal people, who supposedly retained the right to use land leased by pastoralists, once fencing was introduced during the 1860s their land rights effectively disappeared, "a ghost in the fine print of pastoral leases."[20] Colonial governments set up reserves for Aboriginal people, supposedly giving them the "use and benefit" of that land, but reserves often became staging posts for forced removal of Aboriginal people from the land.[21] These tenuous early rights, however, would aid recognition of native title for Australia's First Peoples in the 1990s.

Historian Eric Rolls describes squatting around central NSW as having "rules more complicated than chess. And it was a rough game that extended outside the law of the land and often outside any moral laws."[22] Dreams of an easy fortune were sometimes realized, but more often evaporated. Losers and even winners moved on to new opportunities, though some squatters remained on land that their descendants have lived on ever since. Macarthur's promise of an "unlimited extent of luxuriant pastures" ignored that these pastures belonged to another people, whose culture and economy depended on quite different uses of the land.

The upshot was an undeclared war whose goal was to establish sheep pastoralism in Australia at a scale that supported Britain's manufacturing aspirations. Until around 1980 the language of invasion, occupation, and war in relation to Australian settlement was rarely used. Aboriginal people were believed to have thinly populated the continent prior to colonization, and to have been hyper-susceptible to the settlers' diseases—surely deadly, but in no way accounting for the radical population decline after colonization.[23]

* * *

For more than a hundred years, a violent frontier accompanied the establishment of broad-scale sheep pastoralism in Australia, moving north and west from the cities of Sydney, Hobart, Melbourne, and Perth. At a meeting in 1842, Aboriginal people in the Western Districts of Victoria told the man appointed by the Victorian government as their "Protector":

> *Some White men . . . very good, but plenty very bad, these shoot too much black fellow and take away their Lubra and picaninny and that by and by Black fellow all gone. They were poor men now.*[24]

The violence of those occupying the continent with their flocks was often matched by fierce resistance from Aboriginal people, including lethal force, although not to the extent used against them.[25] Aboriginal warriors lit blazes close to shepherd's huts to scare them, burned crops being counted on as food by the settlers, and destroyed fences to hinder stock management. The oral traditions of the Gunditjmara people of Western Victoria describe sheep as particular targets of Aboriginal retribution: "they would kill and maim them, breaking their hind legs, skinning them and taking their kidney fat, as they would an enemy."[26] Sheep could be immediate food for Aboriginal people whose hunting and gathering had been interrupted, but were sometimes captured and contained *en masse*, suggesting intent to establish some form of Indigenous pastoralism.[27] One landowner in northwestern Australia in 1888 claimed he had lost two thousand sheep to Aboriginal attacks and was thinking of abandoning his pastoral operation.[28]

Tasmania was relatively densely populated when invaded, and its governors also flagrantly disregarded Aboriginal peoples' land or human rights. In February 1828 at Cape Grim, at the edge of Van Diemen's Land company territory, a horrific massacre took place. After VDL employees kidnapped Aboriginal women, Aboriginal people killed a reputed 118 sheep in reprisal. VDL employees retaliated by murdering at least 28 Aboriginal people. This crime was never properly investigated: the Chief Agent of the VDL was also the responsible magistrate. The colonial governor eventually instituted an enquiry but ultimately took no action for justice.[29] Frontier wars destroyed nine of Tasmania's northwest region's Aboriginal clans, but the pervasive myth that Aboriginal people of Tasmania had suffered complete genocide is resisted powerfully by the contemporary Palawa people of wider Lutruwita/Tasmania.[30]

Common threads emerge from the innumerable different local and regional histories. With the non-Aboriginal population on the frontier overwhelmingly male well into the 1900s, conflict often began, as at Cape Grim, with Aboriginal women being abducted and assaulted. Despite the (intermittent and largely ineffectual) efforts of Britain and some colonial governments *not* to condone violence, it was regularly tacitly sanctioned by, and often organized by, governments as a tool of colonization. Colonial systems of criminal justice rarely protected Aboriginal people despite official "Protectors" being appointed from the 1830s.

Native Police Forces appeared in Australian colonies from around the same time: an ancient tool of empires to enlist "the conquered to fight on their side."[31] These para-military organizations, led by non-Aboriginal people, murderously pitted Indigenous people from distant areas against locals who challenged squatters' land tenure.

Frontier conflict also features in stories handed down in non-Aboriginal families. Mary Durack, descended from Irish Australian cattle and sheep pastoralists in Queensland's Channel Country and the Kimberley of Western Australia, recounted family lore:

> *What wonder that the white mens' herds became scapegoats for the bewildered rage of the tribespeople. Tongues and tails were hacked from living animals, horses hamstrung, maimed and left to die . . . many settlers now openly declared that Western Queensland could only be habitable for whites when the last of the blacks had been killed out—"by bullet or by bait."*[32]

Many early sheep stations had at least one building where settlers could shelter from attack while aiming guns at Aboriginal warriors. After the rare and cautionary judicial execution of the murderers of Aboriginal people in the Myall Creek massacres of 1838 in Northwestern New South Wales, poisoned flour became a more common tool of settler reprisal, though armed killing/massacres dubbed "dispersals" continued too in a cone of silence.[33]

No simple binary divides those who resisted the colonists and those who worked for them. The fiercest resistors, such as Western Australia's Bunuba warriors of the 1880s and 1890s, were often those whose labor pastoralists most prized. Once the initial stage of frontier war was over and a district became "settled," armed resistance became impossibly dangerous. Just as the pituri bag shows traditional Aboriginal culture integrating wool fiber, so some Aboriginal families adapted to the new realities; developing skills critical to sheep pastoralists and becoming highly respected in settler society. Kathy "Tup" Bateman's family is one such. Tup, a retired wool classer, is researching her family history, with new facts and interpretations emerging.

Tup's third great-grandmother Jinnie Griffin (tribal name Ibidah) was born around 1822 in central western NSW. Records exist of massacres and "dispersals" for her Gamilaraay/Kamilaroi people as the settler economy of cattle, crops, and sheep was established.[34] In 1840, Jinnie married "ticket-of-leave" convict Eugene Griffin, with whom she worked on a sheep station near Coonabarabran, central NSW. She returned after his death to a more traditional life with an Aboriginal man known as King Cuttabush. A local policeman, Sergeant J. P. Ewing, as an old man, told his son stories he had heard as a child from Jinnie about conflict between different Aboriginal clans.[35]

Jinnie's daughter Mary Jane Griffin (b. 1844) married a shearer, George Cain. Mary Jane worked as a shepherd and, like many Aboriginal women, she also looked after the squatters' children. Her obituary asserted that "many of today's most powerful scions of the House of Merino were nursed or fondled by her . . . and entertain feelings of belligerent and fierce affection."[36] In the 1890s, Mary Jane Cain successfully petitioned the NSW government to allocate the 600-acre Burra bee dee Mission near Coonabarabran, to her extended family (many of them shearers), and to other local Aboriginal families.[37] In total, eight generations of Tup's family have worked in the Australian wool industry, latterly as shearers and wool classers running their own company.

* * *

The widespread displacement of Aboriginal peoples by sheep required more than the meager savings of former convicts. Although numerous convicts became squatters after completing their sentences, it was typically non-convicts who successfully established large sheep runs. The word "squattocracy," first recorded in Australia in 1843, connotes the collective land, wealth, and formal and informal political power of squatters. Whether or not the land was bought, capital and cash flow were essential to establish a sheep station, both for infrastructure and to purchase, transport, and breed appropriate sheep. It took a huge investment of time and money to create sheep hybrids that could survive the globe's driest continent and grow the kind of wool the industrialized textile industry needed.[38]

Fortunes were lost as well as made in squatting, with the difference often the depth of capital available to survive the vagaries of wool growing. Until regular wool auctions were established in Australia, wool had to be exported to Britain for sale, requiring connections to London wool merchants and waiting up to two years for the return of profits to Australia. Pastoralist John Robertson, of Wando Vale station in Victoria's Western Districts, asserted in 1853 that in his district "the so-called fast men" who squatted with little capital and an expectation of quick profits ended up going broke. Robertson, with capital amassed from several years work for a Tasmanian pastoralist, could survive waiting for payment and periodic fierce droughts.[39]

Some squatters were absentee landlords, funding land acquisition in their names and providing other necessary resources but hiring others to turn the holding into a profitable pastoral venture. One such relationship, displaying the tangled threads of British Empire, was between James Matheson (b. 1796) and Alexander Mackay (b.1815), hailing from nearby villages in the Scottish Highlands. Matheson's mother was a MacKay; possibly the two were related. Together with his business partner William Jardine, Matheson made a vast fortune in the 1830s and 1840s, trading tea, silk, and opium between China and the UK, benefitting from Britain's Opium Wars with China. While residing in China, he invested in Australia in tea, sugar, and wheat. During the Depression of 1841–1842, he bought several sheep stations through an agent, spending the huge sum of £11,000, hoping that the properties could both make a profit and provide a home and employment for some of those displaced by the Highland Clearances.[40] At the end of the Opium Wars, Matheson returned to Scotland. In 1844 he purchased the Isle of Lewis (then suffering from a potato famine) off the west coast, and eventually became the second largest landowner in Britain—and Governor of the Bank of England.[41]

Meanwhile, Alexander Mackay, who had worked for Matheson in China, came to Australia in 1840, at the age of 25. First working as a "jackeroo" or trainee manager on a sheep station on the South Coast of NSW, he managed two stations before re-entering Matheson's employ in 1842, as primary manager for Wallendbeen Station, about 90 miles northwest of present-day Canberra. He also oversaw his younger brother Donald's management of another Matheson-owned station.[42] Adaptability was essential to establishing and managing a successful sheep station. During the drought and depression of 1851, Alexander regularly slaughtered and boiled down many of Wallendbeen Station's sheep, filling their carcasses with the rendered fat (tallow) so there would be *some* return on Matheson's capital when wool prices fell on the global market.[43]

In 1856, Mackay married Annie Mackenzie, a relative of James Matheson and of James Matheson Mackenzie, who was then managing Wallendbeen under Mackay's supervision.[44] In the early 1860s, the NSW government instituted land reforms designed to break up the huge squatters' holdings amidst public disquiet about how much Australian land was tied up in relatively few hands. To encourage small agricultural pursuits alongside the huge pastoral enterprises, smaller farmers, called selectors, were able to buy or to lease land. If they lived on the land for three years and improved it (as defined by the government), selectors got up to 640 acres. For £1/acre they got freehold title; otherwise, they paid a small annual lease fee. Many squatters, including Mackay on Matheson's behalf, encouraged "dummy selectors" (often employees) to select choice sections of land with good soil and water in their own names, with the understanding that they would later then sell it back to the big pastoralists. The American Civil War of 1861–1865, which drove wool to premium prices, benefitted squatters by giving them more capital to purchase land under this system.[45]

Alexander Mackay, who by 1867 held the leasehold of Wallendbeen Station in his own name, was likely so advantaged. He had been making independent decisions and buying other properties for several years before that. Over the next two decades he repurchased lands from dummy selectors.[46] Five generations of Mackay's descendants have run and cared for the land since.

Other Empire commodities and activities provided the substantial capital essential to supporting the export wool industry in Australia, including the compensation paid by British taxpayers to slave-owners after slave emancipation in 1834.[47] The Malcolm family of Poltalloch in western Scotland, for example, invested capital derived from Caribbean slave enterprises in Australian sheep farms.[48] Ben Boyd, son of Scottish slave ship owners, arrived in Australia in 1842. His business enterprises included a wool scour in Neutral Bay; a bank, a whaling and cargo transport enterprise in southern NSW; and several sheep stations in NSW and Victoria.[49]

A reliable source of labor was also critical, especially in the early decades when sheep stations were unfenced and needed many shepherds. Once the transportation of convicts to Eastern Australia, and their forced labor, ended in 1839, pastoralists were desperate. Forms of labor that resembled slavery resulted. Indentured laborers from other nations, including Germany, India, and China, were provided passage to Australia; its cost worked out over several years against minimal, and often notional, wages. Ben Boyd, in 1847, supplemented the ex-convicts working on his sizable sheep stations by forcibly removing a group of South Sea Islanders from their homes, ostensibly under indenture. The NSW Parliament amended the Masters and Servants Act to frustrate Boyd's scheme, determined not to allow slavery in disguise. Boyd left Australia in 1849 in financial ruin and died soon after.[50]

Even if labor could be found, without effective roads, sea transport, or railways, workers could not easily be *got* to inland sheep stations. Indentured laborers often never arrived or soon absconded. The gold rushes of the early 1850s in Eastern Australia exacerbated labor shortages. Mary Jane Cain's obituary reported her childhood memory that in 1850s Bathurst, NSW, "many of the bigger squatters had supplanted their black labour with Chinese." With the Chinese laborers heading for the goldfields without notice, sheep were left to the predations of dingoes and "the squatters had to go practically cap in hand to the blacks they had dispensed with" who then saved the day.[51] Mary Jane's 1920 memoir located this story near Ballarat, Victoria, but with the same import: squatters aimed for a non-Aboriginal workforce, but utterly depended on under- or un-paid Aboriginal labor.[52] Ultimately, ongoing troubles in Scotland and Ireland in the 1850s associated with the Highland Clearances and potato famines brought many impoverished migrants to Australia, which along with the end of the gold rushes eased extreme labor shortages.

In Australian national mythology squatters grew rich through hard work and business acumen. The "Golden Fleece" fable fused with the legend of the Australian squatter to form a romantic image of peace and plenty, as in Australian impressionist painter Tom Roberts' works *The Golden Fleece* (1894) and *Shearing the Rams* (1890).[53] The myth persisted: in 1926 Arthur Streeton painted *Land of the Golden Fleece*, an idyllic rural Australian landscape bathed in golden light, a flock of sheep in the foreground.[54] Although ubiquitous (a print of *The Golden Fleece* decorated the office of wool-buyer Frederick Booth), the myth ignored vicious battles over land and sheep, the fierce industrial battles between pastoralists and shearers, and the two groups that transported wool—Afghani, Pakistani, and Punjabi cameleers and Anglo teamsters using wagons and horses.[55]

By 1851, the wool of two of six wool-producing Australian colonies provided fully half the wool needed by the northern British mills.[56] A decade later the world's largest sheep pastoral economy was well established in Southeastern Australia, the frontier moving to the north and west of the continent. This process was frantic, expensive, violent, intricately connected to governors and government, and to wool manufacturers a hemisphere away. Australia was the largest but not the only nation, or British colony, to develop large-scale sheep pastoralism as the Industrial Revolution in textiles unfolded.

* * *

The economy of the two substantial islands of New Zealand/Aotearoa, across the Tasman Sea from Australia, also developed around sheep and wool, but with substantial differences. The Māori had arrived in the islands from East Polynesia in a wave of fourteenth century canoe migrations, bringing with them their village-based economy, with communal vegetable gardens supplemented by gathering seafood, fishing, and hunting. Initial European contact was largely through whaling, sealing, and missionary outposts from the early nineteenth century.

The New Zealand Company and the closely affiliated Wakefield scheme, New Zealand's equivalents of Australia's Royal Charters, envisaged the islands as a source of flax, timber, and seal fur and oil, but sheep and wool proved easier to establish. Samuel Marsden, a parson influential in breeding the Australian merino, sent sheep and cattle to some New Zealand missions from 1814. The 1840 Treaty of Waitangi recognized that New Zealand's land belonged to the Māori and that negotiation and compensation were needed to secure its use, paving the way for their wool industry. In the early 1840s, the first commercial scale sheep runs appeared on the Wairarapa plateau above Wellington on the North Island. Many Australian sheep pastoralists relocated to New Zealand during those years, fleeing severe drought and associated economic depression.[57]

The Waitangi Treaty did not mean that sovereignty over New Zealand land was easily or fairly ceded. Between 1845 and 1872 Māori and the occupiers fought a series of long land wars, but since early sheep pastoralism was centered on the sparsely inhabited South Island, those wars were not primarily about sheep. Historian John MacGibbon asserts that whilst some Māori were "dispossessed, willingly or unwillingly . . . local Māori also made money leasing land to early runholders in the Wairarapa."[58] Māori were among the earliest shearers in New Zealand, becoming dominant in the shearing workforce. Sheep pastoralism surged during the 1850s; by 1860 wool represented 90 percent of New Zealand's export income. Sheep numbers increased fivefold by 1870.[59] After the development of refrigerated transport in the 1880s, New Zealand's pastoralists mostly balanced wool with meat as sources of export income from their mainly crossbred sheep.

Many Māori embraced the wool introduced by the colonizers. Mark Sykes, formerly senior curator of an exquisite collection of Māori cloaks or Taonga in the New Zealand/Aotearoa Te Papa Tongarewa National Museum, explained that many of these ceremonial objects included wool alongside traditional materials, even those worn in battle against the invading colonists:

> *The new wools and the new materials that the Europeans were bringing out here, they came with prestige. We as a people were innovative enough to take on all this new fiber that had suddenly come with all these amazing colours. One of my sister-in-laws got a cloak reputed*

> *[to include] the red fiber . . . from the British soldier's uniform which they unwound and reincorporated.*[60]

Missionary Thomas Grace, at Lake Taupo in the middle of the North Island from 1850, noted that wool was often preferred by local Māori to their traditional textiles and that "our Māori are most anxious to learn to weave."[61] Portraits of Māori men and women from the late nineteenth and early twentieth centuries demonstrate their ready adoption of wool clothing.[62] Wool and other textiles were also traded for land or welcomed as recompense for Māori labor. The Greenwood brothers from Yorkshire leased a large amount of land for their commercial sheep station after 1843 for "an annual rent of seven blankets and some printed calico."[63] By 1859 Rev. Grace and his district's paramount Māori chief had collaborated to buy some sheep for local weaving rather than for export. This joint enterprise became a model for subsequent sheep pastoral enterprises run by Māori. Māori society's village economy helped mitigate the scale of devastation wrought by the settler invasion.

* * *

The American sheep story is also one of continual encroachment on Indigenous peoples and ecologies, but across a continent spanning a huge range of climates, environments, cultures, and histories. It began with the eighteenth-century movement of colonists northward from Mexico to California, and westward from the Atlantic coast. East of the Mississippi, flocks tended to be small and rarely a sole or even major source of income for the farmer. West of that river was a different story. The Spanish brought sizable flocks, often with Indigenous shepherds from Mexico, into what would become the Southwest United States, inciting fierce resistance from local tribes. In the 1840s, Manifest Destiny ideology, claiming a kind of moral right for US expansion from the Atlantic to the Pacific oceans, and reinforced by the discovery of gold in California and in the 1860s in the Pacific Northwest, resulted in a tidal wave of settler/invaders migrating westward.[64]

Many Indian nations negotiated treaties for their own lands but faced forced removal and/or perpetually diminishing reservations as incoming settlers pushed them aside.[65] In Oregon and Idaho, for example, the Nez

Perce saw their lands, seen as prime grazing territory by the incomers, reduced from an original 7.5 million acres to fewer than one million in a (disputed) 1863 treaty. In 1890 the reservation was cut again, to about 150,000 acres, just before the 1891 Forest Reserves Act claimed federal control of many acres for the leasing of various rights, including grazing. In 1906 the remaining reservation Nez Perce, who had by custom used those lands for seasonal hunting and grazing, were required to apply for permits to do so.[66] We have found no comprehensive history of Indigenous perspectives regarding sheep pastoralism. Settler perspectives usually have little regard for the loss of lives, land, livelihood, and culture faced by the dispossessed.

The textile arts of Native American nations, including those who adopted sheep and wool into their cultures, are well documented. In the Southwest, the Navajo, Hopi, and Pueblo peoples, who made the Spanish/Mexican *churro* sheep their own, developed weaving techniques, products, and trade routes that spanned Indigenous and settler markets. Other Indigenous groups across the continent chose, or were forced, to adopt manufactured wool cloth, yarns, and blankets into or in place of their traditional garments and artworks.[67]

Indigenous access to their lands across the west, from Utah and New Mexico north to Oregon, Idaho, Montana, and Wyoming, were further complicated by the emergence of a different frontier war in the late 1800s. Range wars saw sheepmen and cattlemen fight bitterly over access to public grazing lands, cattlemen contending that sheep ate the grass down too much for cattle to share the pastures. Sheep and shepherds (many of them immigrants) both suffered episodic violence; sheep were maimed or slaughtered, shepherds injured or killed. By the 1920s, over-grazing by both sheep and cattle had damaged the western ranges to the point that fewer and fewer sheep could be profitably run there, and the populations of native animals hunted by the Indigenous peoples also decreased.[68]

US woolgrowers faced other challenges. Selling lambs for meat was more profitable than selling raw wool. Farms and factories competed for labor, particularly scarce in the west where distances were vast, predators (wolves, bears, coyotes) abundant, and shepherds led hard and lonely lives. Western Territory wools, as they were known, were less desirable than those from Australia and New Zealand, where growers carefully prepared their shorn fleeces for market. Sustained primarily through high protective tariff rates on imported raw wool, the industry rarely produced even half the wool the nation's textile industry consumed and never developed export markets.[69]

* * *

By the mid-nineteenth century even relatively small islands were attracting the attention of sheep entrepreneurs. Before the 1850s, the few sheep in the Hawaiian Islands descended from those dropped off as food sources by explorers such as James Cook and George Vancouver, or by the whalers who used the islands for refitting and recreation. But the Great Mahele (literally, the divide or portion) of 1848, instituted a version of Hawaiian land title that was supposed to result in one-third of the land for the king, one-third for chiefly families, and one-third for commoners. In practice most land ended up owned by foreigners, including cattle and sheep ranchers. Several relatively short-lived sheep ranching ventures existed in the archipelago. The Parker Ranch on the Big Island of Hawaii, for example, subsumed several smaller holdings and ran sheep until the 1920s.[70]

On the Hawaiian Island of Ni'ihau, the island's commoners wanted to buy their island in 1848 but could not raise sufficient capital. They were offered and accepted a lease from the king, but soon fell into arrears. In 1864, King Kamehameha V sold the whole island to the Sinclair family, headed by widowed matriarch Elizabeth, for $10,000. She and her family, emigrants from Scotland via New Zealand and Canada, arrived at the island in their own ship, complete with stud merino sheep and cattle. They promptly cleared the land for their flock by moving about half of the 650 Indigenous inhabitants, and the native dog population, off the island. By 1885 the island held about 40,000 sheep, and was maintained as a sheep run until well into the twentieth century.[71] Mama Kanani, a Ni'ihauan woman born in 1924, recalled that in her childhood shearing time was a busy period for Indigenous Ni'ihauans, the men shearing and the women cleaning and packing the wool into burlap bags for sale into the American market.[72] The island is still owned by descendants of the Sinclair family.

As with Ni'ihau, British capital spread sheep pastoralism beyond its formal empire to the extent that it has been called an "informal empire" with "virtual colonial tributaries" in the Pacific, the Atlantic, and Latin America.[73] Argentinean and Chilean examples are illuminating. The previously unpopulated Falkland/Malvinas islands of the South Atlantic Sea were run from 1851 as a giant sheep farm by the Falkland Islands Company, with the loosest of Argentinian sovereignty. Chile and Argentina battled for sovereignty over the vast area of Patagonia, including the islands of Tierra Del Fuego, which neither nation had the population nor capital to develop.[74] The Spanish, in their sixteenth-century conquests, had largely left Patagonia and its Indigenous populations in peace. But from the late 1870s "sheep, sheepmen and British capital was the actual occupying force" of Patagonia, catastrophically for Indigenous populations such as the Selknam people in Tierra del Fuego.[75] Rapa Nui (Easter Island) had a similar history of loose Chilean sovereignty from 1888. Williamson/Balfour, a large Scottish/Chilean shipping and trading company, ran the island as a sheep station from 1903 until the early 1950s. The Indigenous population, whose labor supported the station, was confined to a walled area on the island, while the sheep ran free.[76]

* * *

Over time, large-scale southern hemisphere sheep pastoralism was consolidated, and came to include Uruguay and the British colony of South Africa. Hitherto unimaginable quantities of fiber were sent to northern hemisphere factories that produced similarly phenomenal quantities of woolen fabrics. Wool was bought and sold differently in each nation, often by private treaty or individual company systems. Australia first introduced systems of raw wool preparation that enhanced wool's sale and manufacture as a global commodity. Wool began to be sold from the 1840s in city auction rooms, complemented by specialized wool stores (warehouses), whose top floor clerestories allowed buyers to view closely the wool they would later buy. New professions, and middlemen, emerged: wool classers in large shearing sheds sorted fleeces into different categories; wool buyers literally "did the bidding" for woolen mills and textile factories; wool brokers represented the pastoralists, and specialized shipping companies that transported wool across the world.

The long-established London auctions kept their advantage briefly after the introduction of steam-powered shipping in the 1860s. But with Australia the largest raw wool producer, wool markets began moving from London to Australia from the 1870s, aided by the newly laid telegraph cables that connected Australia's southeastern cities to Europe and the United States, and allowed wool buyers to communicate in close to real time with clients half a world away. Wool broking firms sent representatives, including Frederick Booth's father James, to visit large stations at shearing time to review the clip and encourage pastoralists to sell at local auctions. Melbourne's wool auctions initially dominated but by the 1920s Sydney hosted the world's largest wool auctions.[77] From about 1900, Sydney buyers also serviced auctions in Brisbane and other smaller cities. New Zealand developed its own, less centralized, system of wool auctions.

As wool textile production boomed in Britain, France, Germany, and America, sheep numbers in Europe and the UK declined significantly, while remaining relatively steady in the US.[78] European purchasers' share of Australian wool from auctions grew steadily from the 1880s, collectively exceeding British imports from 1891 and growing to 70 percent of the total in 1914.[79] Germany competed with Britain in wool textile manufacturing and also developed a substantial commercial shipping network. By 1907, 30 percent of Australian wool was taken away in German ships.[80]

By the end of the nineteenth century, the "sun never set" on fields of sheep across the globe, many of them on land that had been brutally usurped from indigenous peoples. British capital and direct and indirect colonization, served by two- and four-legged "agents of empire," were pivotal. First Nations peoples' labor enabled this huge colonial project: like the makers of the pituri bag, Indigenous peoples took what was useful—a blanket or a job—to survive and maintained and adapted their cultures in often hostile circumstances. Without the raw wool that emerged from these land wars feeding a newly industrialized woolen textile industry, perhaps the lengthy, mass, cold climate warfare of the twentieth century could not have occurred? But with both sheep and wool markets concentrated in southern hemisphere locales, textile manufacturers had extended supply lines that would be vulnerable in global wars. The rivalries and alliances—both industrial and political—that would emerge during World War I from wool as a strategic resource largely controlled by one nation had consequences that would outlive the war that engendered them.

CHAPTER 4

Sheep in High Places

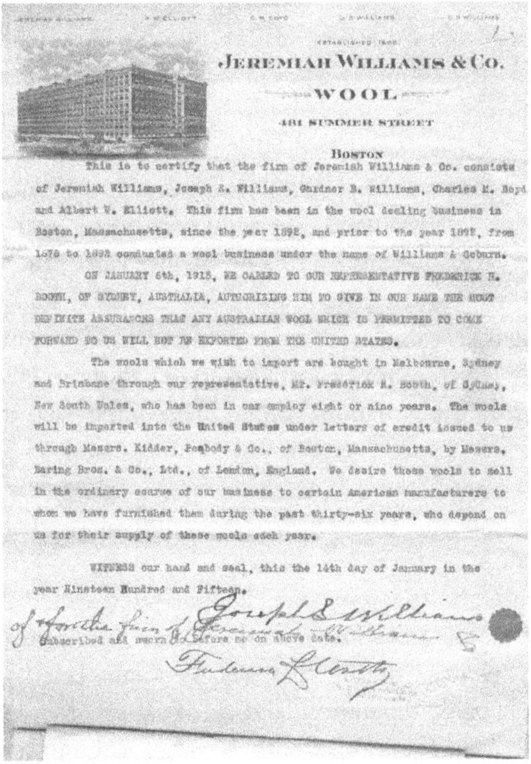

ESTABLISHED 1866

JEREMIAH WILLIAMS & CO.

WOOL

481 SUMMER STREET

BOSTON

This is to certify that the firm of Jeremiah Williams & Co. consists of Jeremiah Williams, Joseph S. Williams, Gardner B. Williams, Charles M. Boyd and Albert W. Elliott. This firm has been in the wool dealing business in Boston, Massachusetts, since the year 1892, and prior to the year 1892, from 1878 to 1892 conducted a wool business under the name of Williams & Coburn.

ON JANUARY 6th, 1915, WE CABLED TO OUR REPRESENTATIVE FREDERICK H. BOOTH, OF SYDNEY, AUSTRALIA, AUTHORIZING HIM TO GIVE IN OUR NAME THE MOST DEFINITE ASSURANCES THAT ANY AUSTRALIAN WOOL WHICH IS PERMITTED TO COME FORWARD TO US WILL NOT BE EXPORTED FROM THE UNITED STATES.

The wools which we wish to import are bought in Melbourne, Sydney and Brisbane through our representative, Mr. Frederick H. Booth, of Sydney, New South Wales, who has been in our employ eight or nine years. The wools will be imported into the United States under letters of credit issued to us through Messrs. Kidder, Peabody & Co., of Boston, Massachusetts, by Messrs. Baring Bros. & Co., Ltd., of London, England. We desire these wools to sell in the ordinary course of our business to certain American manufacturers to whom we have furnished them during the past thirty-six years, who depend on us for their supply of these wools each year.

WITNESS our hand and seal, this the 14th day of January in the year Nineteen Hundred and Fifteen.

Subscribed and sworn to before me on above date.

Official wool trade document, Jeremiah WIlliams & Co., Wool Buyers. Summer Street, Boston, January 14, 1915 (courtesy of the Booth Family Archive).

Chapter 4

> There never was a war in the history of the world, was there, when wool did not advance on the declaration of war?
>
> US Senator John W. Weeks
>
> I think not
>
> Colonel John P. Wood
>
> January 7, 1918[1]

Among the documents that remain from Australian wool buyer Frederick Booth's working life is one written in January 1915 by Joseph S. Williams, on behalf of Jeremiah Williams & Co., his family's wool-buying firm. Booth had begun working for Williams in 1907, toward the end of his three-year sojourn in England and the United States learning the wool business. Since 1878, Jeremiah Williams & Co. had been buying and selling wool on a commission basis for manufacturers around New England. The company's grand warehouse and offices on Summer Street in Boston, the center of American wool-buying, proclaimed wool's value in the economy and Williams' stature within the business.

Wool became valuable because the July 1914 assassination of the Austrian Archduke Ferdinand by a Serbian national set in motion diplomatic dominos that drew much of Europe into war within a month. The alliances that arrayed the UK, France, and Russia against Germany and Austria-Hungary counted wool as strategic: militarily, economically, and diplomatically. Even before shortages arose, efforts to control international trade and protect national economies complicated the global wool trade. The ability to outfit the massive armies involved in World War I rested squarely on the nineteenth-century industrialization of wool textile production and the concurrent growth of southern hemisphere sheep pastoralism.

This document, its importance demonstrated by a red wax seal and the embossed stamp and signature of a Notary Public, relates to an early effort to control wool during that war. Williams briefly recounted his company's longevity, reputation, and financial security, then got to the heart of the matter: Frederick Booth, buying for the firm in Australia, is authorized to certify that any Australian wool they are allowed to buy, or products made from it, will not be trans-shipped to Germany or its allies, in accordance with the British Government's (controversial) imposition of this trade condition in December 1914. Two other signed and sealed documents accompanied the letter: one from the Massachusetts Secretary of State attesting to the firm's trustworthiness, and the other from the British Vice-Consul in Boston certifying that the Secretary of State's signature and seal were genuine—but cautiously refusing to confirm that anything written in the letters, apart from the signature, was true. Nevertheless, the documents succeeded in their purpose, and whenever British wartime regulations permitted, Jeremiah Williams & Co. did an excellent business in British Empire wool, assisted in Australia by Frederick Booth.

These documents introduced us to the fraught relationships among Australia, the United States, the UK, and Germany around the sale of wool in World War I, and to how vital international personal and business relationships were to the wool business. They highlight how the political economy of wool in wartime touched almost every continent and the peoples of many nations, including those in "high places." The exchange quoted at the head of this chapter took place during a US Senate inquiry into the War Department's failure to requisition American wool once the United States had entered the war. Together, Colonel Wood's testimony and the Williams document epitomize wool as the Golden Fleece, not that it would necessarily feel like that to the soldiers literally on and in the ground. The challenge of keeping a world warm that was mired in conflict would involve diplomatic and logistic maneuvering on a scale commensurate with the war itself.

* * *

The 2022 film version of German writer Erich Maria Remarque's classic novel of World War I, *All Quiet on the Western Front*, contains scenes of uniforms being stripped from dead soldiers, the blood and mud washed out, and repairs made, culminating in a new recruit, Paul Bäumer, being issued a uniform with another man's name tag inside. In his innocence he points out the mistake, the supply officer tears out the tag, saying it probably had not fitted the man, and tosses it to the floor, joining many others. When war was declared in August 1914, there was no immediate panic over wool supplies. Both Germany and the UK had stockpiles, and anyway the war was supposed to be over by Christmas. But by 1917, when the fictional teen-aged Bäumer joined the German Army, a different reality reigned.

Although wool had been a staple for military uniforms and blankets for centuries, the scale of demand for it from 1914–1918, as the war of attrition on the Western Front called more and more men to arms, was new. Also new was how dependent the wool manufacturing centers of Europe, the UK, and the United States had become on imports of their preferred fine merino and medium crossbred clothing wools from the southern hemisphere, particularly British colonies, with 22 percent, and South America, with 19 percent. The British Empire controlled about a third of the world's total wool, but between its northern and southern hemisphere dominions, it controlled about half the clothing wools. The rest of the world produced an uneven mix of some fine, more crossbred, and even more coarse or carpet wools.[2]

Whether a nation was already at war, edging toward war, or determinedly neutral and hoping to avoid war, it would be affected by the amount of wool necessary to outfit the various military forces being raised, the new competitors entering the export trade, and the need to keep one eye firmly on the post-war economy. Britain's own woolen textile manufacturers were described in January 1915 as "dependent upon external sources for five-sixths of their raw supplies, relying on other countries for the purchase of more than half their production, and in close trading with all the belligerent countries."[3] This was true of many nations that imported wool.

What was all that wool for? The world's woolen textile manufacturers bought it to make wool tops (lengths of combed fiber ready for spinning); yarns for weaving, knitting, or embroidery; and woven, knitted, and felted cloth for clothing, furnishings, and industrial purposes. The UK and the United States consumed the most, with France and then Germany next in line. Austria-Hungary and Italy were distant also-rans, and the rest of the world hardly registered.[4] The European nations all manufactured both for domestic needs and for export, with the German export trade almost equaling Britain's by 1914.[5] In contrast, the US industry's export trade was insignificant. American-made woolen goods were almost entirely consumed in America.

That changed shortly after the war began. As the United States had learned during its Civil War (1861–1865), even nations with wool stocks in hand and functioning textile and garment industries need time to convert those industries to military production. When the call went out for volunteers to join the British Army in August 1914, a hundred thousand enlisted within a month. Another cohort followed immediately. The inevitable result was a dearth of standard-issue army uniforms to clothe them. So, just as the Civil War's first recruits had worn state militia uniforms until manufacturers caught up, Britain's new recruits trained in a motley collection of obsolete military uniforms, blue serge Post Office uniforms, and whatever overcoats the ready-to-wear trade could supply.[6] The War Office contracted with several of the largest Bradford woolen textile manufacturers, including Hainsworths, for delivery of "one million yards of khaki every ten weeks," necessitating subcontracting to smaller firms. Desperate to meet immediate demand, the government also ordered over a million uniforms and nearly as many overcoats from the United States and Canada.[7]

* * *

An almost unimaginable quantity of wool was consumed during World War I. As American journalist Frank Carpenter explained in early 1918,

> *for every 1,000,000 men we send over the ocean we must have 20,000,000 full-grown sheep here at home or in some other part of the world, and this is in addition to the vast amount of wool we need to clothe our own people.*[8]

Between 65 and 70 million men would serve in the combined armed forces of the combatant nations from August 1914 through November 1918. At 20 sheep per soldier, the world's 634 million sheep, even if they all produced the same weight of apparel quality wools, would clothe not quite 32 million soldiers once a year—and no civilians. Fortunately, not all those men served at the same time. Unfortunately, not all sheep produce clothing wool, and most combat soldiers needed more than one complete outfit per year. Factor in that many of the nations affected by the war either had to eat their sheep or starve, along with the effects of drought or flood or labor shortages on wool production, and the prospect of keeping those huge armies clothed in wool looked even worse.[9]

The US Army Quartermaster (QM) Corps's carefully recorded orders and deliveries of the goods required to mobilize millions of men. Between April 1917 and May 1918, the Army received:

131,000,000 pairs of wool socks
85,000,000 undershirts
22,000,000 blankets
22,000,000 uniform breeches
19,000,000 uniform jackets
9,000,000 overcoats.[10]

This for an Army that by November 1918 would comprise "only" four million men, about half of whom served overseas. The statistics don't include the 800,000 men who served in the Navy and Marines, as the Navy, then overseen by its own Cabinet department, had a separate procurement system.

The QM Corps figures included reserves in anticipation of demand—items received but not yet issued. The 3,000-mile ocean voyage between the source of supplies and the Army in France required maintaining a 90-day stock in a US warehouse; a second in transit across the ocean; and a third awaiting distribution in warehouses in France. Replacements for at least a couple of these were in the manufacturing pipeline. Britain's system was similar but not identical, as cross-channel shipping was much quicker. Certain items were replaced much more often than anticipated. Between June and November 1918, the replacement calculation for enlisted men was:

Slicker and Overcoat, 5 months.
Blanket, flannel shirt, and breeches, 2 months.
Coat or tunic, 79 days.
Shoes and puttees, 51 days.
Drawers and undershirt, 34 days.
Woolen socks, 23 days.[11]

Blankets, too, were consumed by the American military at a pace that in one year equaled those normally purchased by 100 million American civilians in just over two years. These statistics are relevant for other combatant nations, although likely not duplicated where resources were less abundant. Implicit in the reality of the wear and tear on soldiers' clothing is the physical toll on their bodies. Supporting their armed forces required considerable effort by the combatant nations to secure adequate supplies of wool.

* * *

That maneuvering began well before war was declared. Germany possessed a standing army much larger than Britain's, around a million men in 1914, and the uniform and equipment reserves to outfit them. The government had plans ready to mobilize the textile and garment industries for military work. Manufacturing capacity was ample. Germany's pre-war woolen textile industry had produced much more fabric than was consumed domestically. In 1913, for example, the Forstmann and Huffmann company in Werden an der Ruhr sold its officers' uniform cloth to the armies of Germany, Austria, Russia, Italy, Serbia, Bulgaria, Turkey, and Japan.[12] The raw material, though, was lacking: Germany imported about 93 percent of the raw wool that fed her industry. From 1912, Germany bought openly and heavily in the London, Australian, South African, and South American wool sales.[13] After war was declared, small amounts continued to arrive via neutral countries for a few months, including American wools—not previously an export commodity.[14] The German War Office also ordered the removal of all raw wool and other textile fibers from the areas its Army had occupied in Belgium, northern France, Poland, and Russia. The Australian trade journal *Dalgety's*

Review called this wholesale robbery.[15] It would be repeated with increasing rigor in all occupied territories until the war's end.

Britain took immediate steps to limit enemy access to wool and woolen goods. On August 20, 1914, the government declared that "Absolute" contraband of war included "clothing and equipment of a distinctly military character," while "clothing or fabrics for clothing suitable for military use" were considered "Conditional" contraband. Britain blockaded German ports, prohibiting passage of such cargoes to Germany, even seizing them from neutral ships. Two months later all exports of raw wool from the UK were forbidden. By November, Australia, New Zealand, and even the Falkland Islands were under export embargoes. South Africa and South America remained open markets, but shipping was scarce and British ships were forbidden to carry South American wool to the United States.[16]

By the end of 1914, the opposing armies on the Western Front were settled into trenches, dispelling the fantasy of a short war. In March 1915, Britain expanded its absolute contraband list to include raw wool and wool waste of all kinds, wool tops, woolen and worsted yarns, and sheepskins. The government's control of wool was not only about meeting its own wartime needs but also about keeping it out of enemy hands. Cornering the market while starving the competition would give British manufacturers a considerable business advantage when hostilities ceased.[17]

The UK's wool center in Bradford, Yorkshire, was taking on huge contracts from France and Russia, but capacity was still inadequate to demand. It diminished further as battalions of young Bradford men, skilled hands in the textile industry, joined the Army. With the woolen centers of Belgium and northern France in German hands, European customers turned to American manufacturers, who took on contracts while grumbling that Britain prevented them from buying the raw wool to fulfill them. After considerable lobbying by US woolen firms to the US State Department, and by Australian and New Zealand woolgrowers to their own politicians, the UK finally, in December 1914, granted temporary permits (including to Jeremiah Williams and Frederick Booth) for the United States to import some Empire wools, on guarantee that they would not find their way to Britain's enemies.

These initial settings and reversals of British policy foreshadowed a confusing, indeed dizzying, array of wartime wool trade regulations. Britain continually weighed strict control of wool against its need to earn hard currency and purchase woolen textile products from other nations. American manufacturing interests responded by banding together as the Textile Alliance, authorized in March 1915 by the UK Board of Trade to oversee American wool import licenses, although the British government selected the licensees. This renewed, if restricted, flow of wool was restricted to merino, too fine for most military purposes, and blackface sheep wool, conversely too coarse. From March 1915, Britain not only effectively controlled its Empire's raw wool, but, astoundingly, most of the world's trade in manufactured woolen goods as well.[18]

Despite this shifting business landscape, there was still evidently money to be made from wool. In June 1915, Frederick Booth was invited by A.W. Elliott, an executive at Jeremiah Williams & Co., to switch from a salary to a percentage of profits. Booth replied, "the profits last year must have been very high and any percentage I suggest would look like asking too much."[19] In the same letter Booth suggested that given the restrictions, he and Williams & Co. should concentrate on the "relatively cheaper and most neglected" wool categories—the only ones Britain was inclined to share.

* * *

Since the 1815 Congress of Vienna, at the end of the Napoleonic Wars, European protocols had allowed for trade in wartime to continue via neutral nations, a system that this war would sorely test and often breach.[20] Although Britain allowed neutrals to trade with her enemies in articles considered not of military value nearly until the end of the war, the ever-lengthening contraband lists made that less magnanimous than it sounds. In May 1918, for example, Sweden agreed, among a raft of other prohibitions, "to prohibit the export, directly or indirectly" to the Central Powers and their allies, of "all foodstuffs, animal and vegetable, and feeding-stuffs of any description except cranberries."[21]

Ever expanding contraband lists were not the only obstacle to trade. Wool prices were unsettled, as buyers from the United States, France, Italy, and Japan competed bitterly for the limited wool available in South Africa and South America. One of Jeremiah Williams's buyers, Thomas Trumbull, voyaged twice to South Africa in 1916 for the wool auctions. His September route from Boston crossed North America and then the Pacific Ocean, ending in Capetown via Hong Kong and Shanghai. He avoided German U-boats and investigated the Chinese wool market along the way.[22]

Buying the wool was only the first problem. Surface and submarine warfare added man-made dangers to the natural risks of long-distance ocean voyages. The German cruiser *Emden*, for example, had considerable success in the Pacific in late 1914, sinking ships judged to be carrying contraband and retrieving valuable cargoes to send home, including, on October 19, 2,000 bales of Australian wool from SS *Troilus*.[23] *Emden* was destroyed a few weeks later by the Australian cruiser HMAS *Sydney*, but other enemies lurked along the ocean routes. Shippers and insurers hiked rates on wool cargoes to compensate for the added risks.[24] New Zealand's Minister for Agriculture told attendees at a wool industry conference in November 1916, "you have only to look at the morning papers to see the number of ships that are going down daily by submarines. These ships are lost to the Empire."[25]

Lost ships and limited cargo space forced governments and shippers to juggle competing strategic cargoes. Britain had dominated merchant shipping for decades. Neutral and even British Empire nations tried to circumvent this. The US Shipping Board, established in 1916, chartered neutral-flag steam *and* sailing ships to carry home wool cargoes from South Africa and South America. The Australian government even bought ships to try to get its wool to Britain.

Opinions varied, of course, regarding the legality of both Britain's restrictions and neutral nation transactions. Complaints about deceptive British tactics, or *ruse de guerre* (false flags, disguising naval vessels as merchant ships, using commercial vessels as armed decoys, dressing soldiers on troop transports in civilian clothes), reading rather like a Horatio Hornblower or Jack Aubrey novel, take up pages of official

US government "Correspondence with Belligerent Governments" on the rights of neutrals.[26] Governments, politicians, the press, and even members of the public scrutinized the trade of neutral nations. A "Question" raised in the UK Parliament in November 1915 asked whether Australian wool shipped to Italy the previous May had been trans-shipped to Germany through Switzerland. Australia's Attorney General's office examined Italy's import and export records and textile production accounts, verifying that Italian firms had used all the wool for either their own army or the French.[27] On the other hand, in 1916 the US-based *Textile World Journal* openly lamented the loss of trading opportunities with the Central Powers. One valued trade route that had sent American wool and cotton to Austria via Cuba, Spain, and Italy had shut down in May 1915 after Italy declared war on Austria-Hungary, while in 1916 the strengthening British blockade curbed backdoor trading with Germany through neutral Norway.[28]

* * *

Meanwhile, Bradford's wool textile businesses were filling orders from both the UK and pre-war clients in neutral and Allied nations. They also courted customers formerly supplied by German and Austrian manufacturers, then fully occupied in outfitting their own armies, and also barred from exporting by the British blockade. Bradford also, of necessity, exported eight times more woolen textiles to France in 1915 than in 1914.[29] The French and Belgian woolen mills around Roubaix and Tourcoing, and contiguous Flanders, areas occupied by the German Army, were not simply out of reach, many no longer operated. Essential personnel had joined the armies, raw materials and equipment were seized and sent to German textile mills, and superfluous machinery melted down for armaments. Britain's overstretched woolen industry also faced having to replace the German distributors and banks that had been important intermediaries for exporting British goods, particularly to China and South America.[30]

Amidst the wartime pressures, agile businesspeople found opportunities. Meshe Osinky, a Lithuanian Jew who immigrated to Britain in 1900, aged 15, established a small business in Yorkshire making men's suits, changing his name to Montague Burton. By 1913, he owned five tailoring shops and during the war won sizable contracts to manufacture uniforms. Alexander Wilkie of Edinburgh opened a factory producing specially sized uniforms for the Scottish battalion known as the "Bantam Army," created early in 1915 for men under 5′3″ (160 cm). Wartime success would fuel the transformation of both businesses into retail empires. The war also brought Hainsworths out of a pre-war slump, in part, Hainsworth family lore relates, because when the Russian Revolution of October 1917 left the company with endless yardage of Russian blue uniform cloth, the newly established UK Royal Air Force was persuaded to choose that exact shade of blue for its uniforms![31] Trish also heard this story in relation to Salt's Mill, so whether it's apocryphal or a shared Bradford industry history we can't say. In any case, the two brothers who were then Hainsworth's managing directors built substantial mansions on wartime profits.

A fully employed textile industry achieved several ends for the British government. Stable earnings contributed to a compliant labor force, while taxes paid by businesses and individuals funded the war effort. Expanding exports generated income to pay for necessary imports and positioned Britain to retain its new customers after the war. But wars require manpower, which erodes the labor supply both of industry and the agricultural base that supports it. As a result, Britain needed to placate the American woolen industry and its enormous production capacity, while still ensuring its own supply of raw wool from its Dominions and guarding against the threat of the growing American woolen textile export business.

Germany also required foreign trade to fuel its war machine. Dyestuffs and pharmaceuticals, a near-monopoly for Germany, were particularly valuable in the United States, whose own dye industry was rudimentary. At the start of the war, with the United States officially neutral, Germany agreed to ship dyestuffs to the United States on American ships in return for American cotton. This worked until the British added both commodities to the contraband lists in March 1915. Panic ensued. Franklin Hobbs would recall of 1915's dye shortages that "even the ornamental cherry at the bottom of a famous American drink was threatened!"[32] The main threat, however, was not to cocktails but to clothing. Black dye was one of the few shades US firms made in quantity. Designers created black and white fabrics and garments in hundreds of styles, making a fashion statement of necessity. In Europe black more likely signified mourning for a loved one lost in the war.

One German response to the blockade, the brainchild of Alfred Lohmann, wool buyer and later President of the Bremen Chamber of Commerce, was a cargo submarine designed specifically to continue trade with the United States. Two subs were completed in 1916: one disappeared on its maiden voyage. The second, the *Deutschland*, made two successful and highly profitable runs, in July to Baltimore, Maryland, and in October to New London, Connecticut. The Germans brought dyes and dye chemicals (among other goods) to the color-starved textile, paper, and food processing industries. Plans for a third voyage were scuttled when the United States entered the war on the Allied side in April 1917; the submarine was turned over to the German Navy.[33]

The Bremen-based Lohmann family had much experience in international trade and shipping. Alfred's father Johann had managed North German Lloyd for 15 years from the 1870s and the family remained shareholders. In 1892, the same year the line bought its first fast steamship, Alfred arrived in Australia to learn the wool trade and secure a steady source of supply for the family's German mills. Based in Sydney, he established Weber, Lohmann & Co., wool buyers and mixed import/export traders, and rapidly became an eminent member of the trade. He returned to Germany in 1914, avoiding internment in Australia. The intersection in wartime of trade, national strategic interests, and the loyalties of citizens is both complicated and messy.

* * *

The year 1916 was a pivotal year for governments everywhere to truly comprehend wool's long-term strategic value. Drought in Australia and high meat prices in South America reduced wool production as flocks died or were sent to the slaughterhouse. Military contractors competed with civilian goods manufacturers for raw materials and workers. The resulting price and wage rises disrupted the UK Government's original scheme of paying manufacturers a "cost of production plus a reasonable profit" for requisitioned goods.[34] In response, in June 1916, the government designated UK wool manufacturing employees as "munitions workers," and announced the compulsory purchase, or commandeer, at a fixed price, of the entire UK wool clip. Australian Prime Minister Billy Hughes suggested Britain also commandeer Dominion wools, privately hoping it would not represent a "mere increase of Bradford profits at the expense of Australian wool growers."[35] The UK initially resisted this, while simultaneously demanding that Australia stop selling wool to the United States. Australia protested, but its wool sales to the United States in 1916 crashed to virtually zero from more than £8 million in 1915, although New Zealand's crossbred exports more than doubled. This allowed American manufacturers to continue exporting military-grade woolen cloth to the UK's allies, while preventing them from expanding into new civilian fine-wool markets.[36]

Wool trade pressures increased with the enormous casualties and wastage during the Battle of the Somme (July–November 1916). In November, Britain finally negotiated the compulsory purchase of the entire Australian and New Zealand clips, crossbred and merino, at a fixed average price of 15 pence per pound of wool. While this may sound simple, it involved complex and often acrimonious negotiations on purchase price and details of appraising, sorting, packing, storing, shipping, and payment. No formal agreement existed, just a series of cables between Britain and its two Antipodean Dominions, who were sometimes played off against each other.[37] Australia and New Zealand needed the income from wool sales to pay their own war bills. Both also suffered from the limited shipping available, so Britain's decision to pay upfront for the wool and its storage, whether it had been shipped to the northern hemisphere or not, sweetened the deal. Loyalty to Britain and the Empire led both Dominions to accept the scheme, with the caveat that local manufacturers could first take the wool they needed. Warehoused in Australia, wools owned but not used by Britain kept supplies out of both neutral and enemy mills. Shipments to the United States of wools already purchased by American buyers were halted, the stocks accumulating storage and insurance fees, the decision accumulating ill will.

Although the commandeer guaranteed payment to growers for their wool, the fixed price for that wool was contentious to begin with and became more so. Market prices for wool in late 1916 were 95 percent higher than pre-war rates, but the commandeer markup was only 55 percent. Although this was higher than the rate British growers had been paid in June, their price increased as the war continued, while for Australia and New Zealand it remained the same into 1920, through two renewals and an extension. Australian growers were also irate that within weeks of the agreement, Britain was re-selling Australian wool to allies for civilian uses at the commandeer cost, ignoring the provision that this kind of sale would charge the market price, profits to be shared between the British government and Australasian growers.[38]

A UK government-appointed Director of Wool Textile Production allocated the commandeered wools to the various British factories and determined which mill got which contract. Percy Reginald Gaunt, a Bradford industrialist and scion of the established Hainsworth and Gaunt wool dynasties, got the nod as Assistant Director. Other Bradford manufacturers accused Gaunt of giving too many contracts to the family company and other relatives, but Bradford's wool families were so interconnected that it might have been hard for Gaunt to avoid any nepotism.[39] By 1917, more than 50 percent of Bradford's looms were undertaking military work, compared with 5 percent before the war.[40] Colonial growers watched Bradford's textile manufacturers reap large profits, and believed the commandeer's fixed price cheated them of their own wartime wealth.

Other British Dominions were treated differently. India voluntarily agreed to ship its entire clip of the coarser wools used in army blankets to Britain, for distribution to manufacturers at a fixed price. South African wools remained in the open market. South African and South American wool producers enjoyed their increased competitiveness at rapidly escalating prices.

* * *

The US woolen industry was accustomed by 1916 to Britain's ambivalence about sharing Empire wool. Since America was functioning as a kind of department store for Britain and her allies, wool consumption was much higher than usual, but when in late 1914 the first orders for military cloth rolled in from the UK, France, and Russia, the United States was prepared. A change in US tariff law in December 1913 had removed the import duty on raw wool. Hedging against future rate rises, manufacturers had immediately invested in a stockpile. This, plus imports of 35 million pounds of South American and South African wools that would normally have been sold to France and Belgium, helped fulfill Allied orders through 1915. Profits were high. US manufacturers sold 35 million dollars' worth of woolen blankets, uniforms, and textiles to Britain, Russia, and France between July 1914 and June 1915. The previous year's exports had barely reached five million dollars. American civilians, finding few European imports available, also contributed to the US industry's profitability and hunger for wool.[41]

As Britain clamped down, however, the inadequacy of the American domestic clip and South American imports to meet the US industry's needs became clear. Disgruntled buyers wondered why the Textile Alliance rarely received advance information from the British regarding what wools would be made available. South African wools, they claimed, supposedly open market, were being cornered by English buyers, while the French dominated the Uruguay market. Wool and commercial circles speculated that the true point of British restrictions was to force US mills to suspend production or even close down, thus reducing American post-war competitiveness.[42] For their part, the British feared that American activity (and suspected German activity) in the South American and South African markets furthered German plans to revive its woolen industry after the war. Australasians feared that, in the post-war world, the customers they had turned away would decide to continue buying from their geographically closer wartime sources.[43]

Prompted by the shortages of wool for civilian purposes, the Philadelphia Wool and Textile Association began a "More Sheep, More Wool" campaign in 1916. The program targeted small farmers in the East and Middle West, offering them animals and the educational assistance necessary for them to thrive. Posters (*Join a Sheep Club!*), brochures, and publicity events such as Chicago's 1917 parade featuring fancy-dress shepherdesses leading sheep through the streets, broadened its appeal.[44] President Woodrow Wilson installed 40 sheep on the White House lawn in 1918, ostensibly to crop the grass, releasing gardeners for military service. The sheep were shorn, their wool sold to benefit the Red Cross and other charities.[45] Sheep in high places indeed.

Within a month of the commandeer, the United States had requested an allocation of Australian wool. Britain initially resisted, and terms were still being discussed in April 1917 when the United States entered the war. As the US Army then consisted of about 200,000 officers and enlisted men, one-twentieth of the four million who would eventually serve, it was clear that only an enormous and concerted industrial and logistical effort could outfit the new recruits. Britain still restricted import licenses of Empire wools throughout 1917, so between October 1916 and September 1917 the United States cobbled together 363 million pounds of wool from six South American countries, South Africa, China, and Spain.[46] Finally allocated 200,000 bales (roughly 45 million pounds) of Australian wool in October 1917, the United States requested that its own representatives select that wool, in Australia. Australia demurred, but the UK, desperately needing American military aid, agreed. Even so, only 100,000 bales were actually shipped in 1917, with a promise for 1918 that "tonnage will be promptly made available."[47] Frederick Booth found a path through these complexities, representing the US Quartermaster-General in selecting Australian wools for the American Army and Navy whenever that was allowed, while overseeing shipments of commandeered wool from New South Wales to Britain.

Germany's spring offensive of March 1918 spurred the British and French to urge the United States to shorten its timeline for getting troops to France. This transformed the US Army's relationship with its suppliers. The Quartermaster Corps was shocked when its spring 1918 procurement requests for woolen fabrics received no bids, as the necessary wools were simply not on the market—growers were reserving stocks, waiting for prices to rise. Shortly thereafter, the War Department requisitioned the entire wool supply in the United States, whether home grown or imported, to allocate as needed. Jeremiah Williams & Co., which had long been active in buying American-grown wools, was one of several Boston wool firms designated a "central dealer" in April 1918, earning a 3 or 4 percent commission selling American-grown wool directly to the US Army QM.[48] By mid-1918, more than half the nation's 1,000 woolen mills were working solely on US military orders. So little wool was available for civilians that a considerable portion of the industry's machinery sat idle.[49]

The US QM's Department of Wool, Top, and Yarn was headed from early 1918 by Albert W. Elliott, who had been Frederick Booth's contact at Jeremiah Williams. In this capacity Elliott likely drew on Booth's knowledge of and connections in buying Australasian wools.[50] The wool business in its heyday depended on close personal ties, both business and family, with regular international travel expected of wool buyers, dealers, brokers, and manufacturers.

* * *

These ties created significant tensions during World War I. Germany claimed that Britain was restricting the wool trade to cripple her two largest rivals, Germany and the United States. The sizable German-ancestry population of the United States was not wholly inclined to support Britain and France while the United States remained neutral, and the American woolen industry itself was split in its historical loyalties. Most of the older New England companies had English roots, while many of the firms organized from the 1880s in and around Passaic, New Jersey, were German-owned, founded in response to changes in US import tariff rates.[51] First to open was the Botany Worsted Mills, organized in 1889 by the Kammgarn Spinnerei (Worsted Spinning Mill), Augsburg, and Stöhr & Company, Leipzig. It was followed in 1904 by Forstmann & Huffmann, headed by Julius Forstmann. The men in charge of these new American mills encouraged skilled German textile workers and their families to emigrate for jobs in their mills.

Forstmann testified at Senate hearings in January 1918 on the quality of the cloth in US uniforms, drawing on his pre-war familiarity with the fine broadcloth that his family's firm in Germany wove for the officers of many European armies.[52] His comparisons did not flatter the American fabrics, which he faulted for durability and warmth. Forstmann & Huffmann, like its parent firm in Germany, manufactured fine woolens. In practical terms, this meant that most of the machinery used by the firm and its American competitors (such as Connecticut's Hockanum Mills, not German-connected), would require costly modifications to work on the coarser yarns and fabrics predominantly used by the military. Outside the woolen industry, the fact that such firms did not bid on every military contract was seen as a lack of patriotism, not technology. Forstmann defended his branch of the industry, stating that his firm lost money on the overcoat fabric he made for the army since the army contract price was below his cost of production. He also discussed shirting cloth his firm had offered to the US QM as superior to the government specifications and only slightly more expensive to produce, but which would enable him to utilize more of his machinery on military goods. Although the QM recommended the samples be adopted as new standards, the civilian committee overseeing military interactions with the textile industry chose instead to stay with the cheaper, lower-quality goods that could be manufactured by more companies. Forstmann and several other manufacturers maintained that high-quality cloth lasted longer and was therefore a better bargain.

Forstmann's constructive role in these hearings did not deter the growing anti-German hysteria, rapidly becoming synonymous with patriotism, from intruding on his business and personal lives. A vocal group of press, industry leaders, and politicians charged that the Passaic woolen industry was a hotbed of German sympathizers whose loyalties were extremely suspect. In March and April 1918 New York State's Attorney General convened hearings about supposed neutrality violations by members of the wool and dye industries of German descent, accusing them of ignoring British government restrictions on exports to Germany in 1915 and 1916. The hearing transcripts convey the contentious nature of the proceedings, and the muddle of evidence, innuendo, and rumor that conflated pre-war activities with wartime anxieties.[53] Questioners almost invariably doubted whether the defendants could be trusted to be loyal American citizens. Letters between German banking and wool-buying representatives, introduced in evidence, suggested that in 1915–1916, aware that getting wool through the blockade for immediate use was impossible, the German government wanted to ask German Americans in the wool industry to purchase and warehouse wool in neutral countries, for use after the war. Forstmann was among those named as someone to approach, but he denied knowledge of the scheme and no evidence that it was carried out was presented. Accused of disloyalty because of his assistance in February 1915 with shipping wool and cotton to Germany in return for dyes and pharmaceuticals, he countered with evidence that he had acted with the full approval of the US government. Just weeks before these accusations were made, Forstmann had been questioned about these dealings in the Senate hearings mentioned above and been supported in his answers by New Jersey Senator Joseph Frelinghuysen.

In a hasty maneuver seemingly inspired by the hearings, in April 1918 the Federal Alien Property Custodian (APC) took control of six German-connected woolen mills in Passaic—including Botany and Forstmann & Huffmann—operating them through surrogates. The *Textile World Journal* jingoistically declared this would "separate forever the woolen business in this country from the domination if not complete ownership of the woolen cartel of the German government."[54]

Several German American mill owners fought back against what they felt was unjust treatment from the APC. Forstmann and Thomas Prehn were vindicated in 1919 when a newly appointed APC reversed the 1918 decisions against them, and Forstmann won a libel lawsuit against his accusers, receiving a public exoneration and apology from New York's new Attorney General. Workers and mills of German origin in Bradford faced similar ostracism, and in Australia several wool buyers with German connections were interned for the duration of the war. Although the wool industry's international connections among growers, buyers, shippers, and manufacturers would survive this war, the precarious nature of the wool business had been driven home to all.

* * *

Japan was also scratching for access to British Empire wool during the war, and its wartime travails would reverberate through textile manufacturing and trade in the post-war world. The Meiji government began westernizing its military uniforms in the 1860s, and its Court dress and government service (police, mail, and railway) uniforms in the early 1870s.[55] To make western-style clothing the norm, Japan first had to acquire from the West either finished garments or the fabrics and unfamiliar tailoring skills (patternmaking, cutting, fitting) necessary to make them. Japan produced very little raw wool, and although its primary export, raw silk, had a ready market abroad, it could not balance Japan's new wool trade on its own.

In 1877, with self-sufficiency in mind but relying on German machinery and technical training, the government supported the country's first woolen mill, in Sonja, Tokyo, to weave cloth for the army. Other mills followed, at first filling the government's westernizing and military requirements, but by 1900 new versions of traditional fabrics, such as lightweight woolen kimono cloth, were popular. From Japan's first order of 187 bales of Australian wool, in 1890, the country slowly and steadily became one of Australia's best customers. Since Japan relied almost entirely on imported wool to support this new industry, it sat squarely among the have-not nations, a costly position during Japan's wars with China (1893–1894) and Russia (1905). Wool fiber and yarn imports more than doubled between 1903 and 1905, and imports of woolen fabrics and blankets increased sixfold.[56] Australia was Japan's preferred source for all wools, as the fiber was high quality and shipping between these Pacific Ocean neighbors was less costly. Once the war began and German wool buyers were excluded from Australian auctions, Japanese firms such as Kanematsu and Mitsu[sic]Bussan stepped up—until Britain began controlling her Empire's wool trade.[57]

Japan exploited the wartime absence of its European and American competitors to expand its cotton goods trade in African and Asian markets.[58] A long-lived diplomatic dance among Japan, the United States, and the UK around international trade in textile fibers, textiles, and finished products resulted. Japan purchased raw cotton from the British Empire (mostly India) and the United States, benefitting the cotton growers, while simultaneously selling cheap textiles that eroded those countries' manufacturing market share. The US silk industry, by 1910 the world's largest consumer of raw silk, much of it Japanese, was anxious to keep other commodities' tariff and territory squabbles from damaging that relationship. Economists and politicians struggled amid these conflicting interests to draw up palatable trade agreements and tariff laws.

Wool had a place in these negotiations. Even as an ally, its forces engaged against Germany in the Pacific and Indian Oceans, Japan's access to Empire wool was tightly controlled, and limited to poorer qualities, such as the September 1916 sale of "faulty" Australian crossbred wool for Japanese army uniforms.[59] Japan's privately owned woolen mills also made a low-quality army cloth for Russia, mixing only 20 percent Australian wool with the cheapest wools from New Zealand and China and wool waste from Japanese spinning mills.[60] It was clear to the Japanese, and the other nations trying to make do with the dregs of the wool market, that Britain's stringent control kept cash flowing into the Empire's trade coffers, while preserving the best quality wools for Britain's purposes.

Chief among them, of course, were Germany and Austria. Their wool stockpiles long gone by 1916, both nations were hurting, although their propaganda made light of this. One German source bragged in January 1916 that there were enough raw materials on hand to keep fighting "for years."[61] This was bluster. Together the two nations harbored fewer than 20 million sheep. Without imports the 20 sheep to one soldier trope suggests they could outfit an army of perhaps one million men, leaving nothing for civilian use. Yet in total from 1914–1918 their collective armed forces numbered nearly 23 million. Again, not all of them fought, they did not all serve at once, and the pre-war stockpiles of uniforms and wool had been significant. Even so, both countries experienced desperate shortages.

A US Army intelligence report submitted shortly after the Armistice stated that German occupiers in France had received "recent order[s]" to seize "blankets, wool from the mattresses, and even shoddy cloth."[62] The Germans, however, had been confiscating textiles and textile fibers for years. In mid-1915 the German Ministry of War had reported that daily shipments of "large quantities of rubber, wool, cotton, flax, hemp, yarn, hides, and leather" were received from occupied Antwerp,

Ostend, and Bruges, although British sources thought this was exaggerated.[63] Film footage from 1917 taken in St. Quentin, on the French side of the French-Belgian border, shows a group of German soldiers maneuvering a horse-drawn cart full of mattresses through the streets. Other occupied regions suffered similarly, documented in photographs of Romanian civilians packing wool for shipping to Germany under the watchful eyes of German soldiers, and of Serbian villagers showing off bags of wool they had hidden from the Germans during the war.[64]

* * *

Since new wool was in such short supply, it's clear that, whether the re-used uniform movie scene described earlier embodied or exaggerated reality, everyone had to recycle in some manner to meet demand. On the home fronts, civilians mended and reworked garments, while cloth and clothing that could not be repaired was gathered for recycling. In the United States, many chapters of the American Red Cross assisted with this work.[65] In camps and on battlefields, Military Salvage units recovered damaged and abandoned garments. The Central Powers' salvage efforts have eluded us, but among the Allied nations, battlefield salvage was an important and carefully organized activity. From mid-1915 the British army implemented a comprehensive salvage system in its own and in its Empire forces. The Americans followed suit upon arrival in France in 1917, a QM report pointing out that keeping its million-plus-man army in France clothed "would be impossible . . . unless some system of saving and reconstruction were adopted."[66]

Three levels of clothing salvage operated: minor repairs that returned clothing to the original user; more extensive reworking that sent items to the supply depots for re-issue; and sending unusable fabric away to have the fiber recovered. Both the British and US services claimed that salvaged materials stained with blood were burned. Repairs for the British Army were handled by tailors attached to each unit. Remaking was done by a mix of private French firms, army-operated depots in France, such as the Depot at Quay de Javel, Paris, and in Britain at either the main Royal Army Clothing Depot in Pimlico, London, or branch depots scattered around the country. The United States had salvage and reclamation depots in the United States and in France. The first depot in France opened in January 1918 at St. Pierre des Corps, staffed by four officers, five enlisted men, and six local women employees. By war's end, the US salvage service in France ran 20 storage and distribution depots with 11,000 dedicated personnel. An additional field force of soldiers fluctuating between 2,000 and 12,000, "according to the exigencies of the service" roamed the battlefields retrieving usable items.[67] French workrooms and depots serving the French, British, and American militaries employed thousands of French and Belgian women, who repaired millions of garments.

Recycled uniforms *were* distributed to men in the field. In its US camps, the American Army reclaimed trainees' damaged or lice-infested uniforms for sterilizing, repair, and re-issue to new recruits. In Europe, repaired "good as new" replacements were issued to American soldiers at delousing stations behind the lines. US uniforms unsuitable for re-issue were dyed green and distributed to prisoners of war.[68] Similar efforts operated in the British and French armies. The best recycled stock was reissued, the remainder was re-dyed distinctive shades for use by prisoners of war or by support services, such as the British Army's Indian, Chinese, and Egyptian Labor Corps.[69]

A striking photograph taken near Bapaume, France, shows seven soldiers in a bleak, muddy landscape, next to stacks of rifles and helmets, and sprawling piles of overcoats.[70] Wool was a high priority in the recycling scheme, specifically because of its ability to be reworked into new yarns if it was past reusing as a garment or textile. The textile industry technical term for reworked wool was "shoddy." Shoddy, one of the first substitutes for new wool, would not be the last, and the shortages even of shoddy during this war would force the exploration of alternatives.

* * *

Throughout 1918, governments promoted raising more wool and conserving existing supplies. Meanwhile Britain continued to turn the tap of American access to Australasian wool on and off. In January 1918, wool manufacturers lamented that the UK was again "forbidding licenses for shipment of English and Colonial wools."[71] Australasian woolgrowers bitterly resented the effects on their incomes of the commandeer's fixed price, wartime inflation, and lower than expected receipts for sales of commandeered wool to Allies and neutrals. In March, Australia's Central Wool Committee requested that Britain suppress US press reports of the Boston wool sales, given the high prices compared with what Australian growers were receiving. Britain countered that the information should instead be censored in Australia. Soon afterward the UK agreed to Americans using Empire wool for whatever purposes they chose, military or not.[72]

The entire wool industry—growers, buyers, and textile manufacturers—continued to produce as if the war would last forever. Just days before the Armistice took effect on November 11, 1918, the United States placed a huge order for Australian wool with Britain. Behind the scenes, though, governments and just about everyone in the wool business fretted about wool stockpiles and how to liquidate surplus fiber and fabric without damaging post-war prices. The Armistice made those stockpiles extraneous and added the costs of storage and disposal to the war-premium purchase prices. In late 1918, the United States estimated it had on hand raw wool valued at $324 million, blankets at $5.5 million, and underwear at $10 million. In May 1919, the United States cancelled the outstanding balance of its November 1918 wool order.[73]

Lessons from the supply and deployment of wool in World War I would last well beyond the war. The United States, Japan, and Germany learned at great cost what happened when their extended supply chains were disrupted. Neutral nations around the globe shared the pain, as the war disrupted their agricultural, commercial, and industrial activities, which depended on imports of foreign products and exports of their own. Australia and New Zealand found their key commodities removed from their control, while Britain tested its power over the Empire. Governments everywhere lost income from import tariffs and domestic taxation, for as war industries boomed, peacetime products went bust. The war's economic disruptions allowed countries which had been reliable consumers of European goods to establish or increase their own manufacturing capacities. As one Canadian analyst put it, "Western Europe found that it was no longer the world's factory."[74]

The war that Joseph Williams, Julius Forstmann, and Alfred Lohmann lived through from 1914 to 1918 foreshadowed the future for nations and industries whose expanded production potential was hampered by long, treacherous, and costly supply chains, and contrived shortages of the raw materials necessary to fuel that production. Frederick Booth, in Australia, invested some of his wartime wool profits in a new home. While he would again experience good business conditions in future wars, the circumstances surrounding wool in this war had unleashed forces that would eventually destroy his family business. The red wax seals attesting to Jeremiah Williams & Company's willingness to accede to British trade demands in 1915 can be viewed as one of a series of little goads that—internationally—stimulated research into new sources and new materials. War, and the peace that followed, created winners and losers in unexpected ways.

Chapter 5

Ersatz and All That

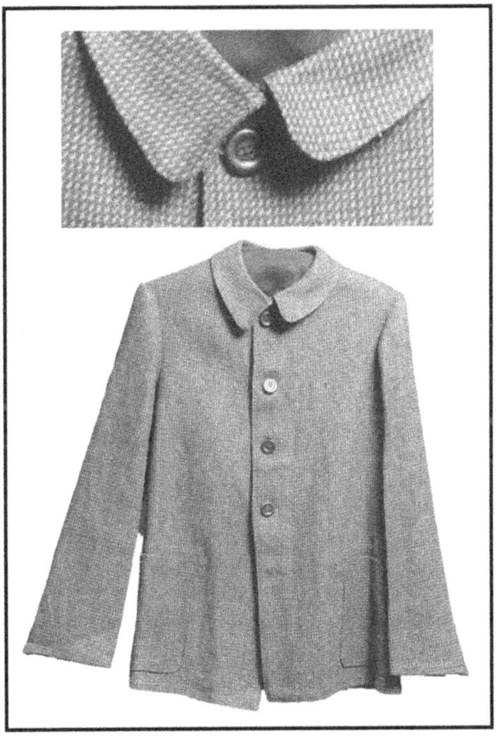

Jacket and collar detail from man's two-piece suit of spun paper yarns, Germany, circa 1918. Gift of A. Price Dillont, 1926 (courtesy of the Newark Museum, Newark, New Jersey, USA).

Chapter 5

> Inventions from the war may play an important role in the markets of the world after peace has been established.
>
> US Consular Reports on Textile Trade in Germany[1]

Madelyn grew up knowing the meaning of the German word *ersatz*. Her maternal grandmother, Angela Baer, emigrated to the United States from Germany in 1926, a year after her husband, with her two small daughters and a younger brother in tow. She never shared memories with her family either of her life or her parents' deaths in Germany during World War I, but her wartime experiences cast a long shadow. A number of things commonly consumed in America during the 1950s and 1960s, such as instant coffee, margarine, and rayon, she contemptuously labelled as *ersatz*. They were emphatically unwelcome in the Baer home. Turnips and beets, not in themselves *ersatz* but the primary ingredient in many wartime *ersatz* foods, notably bread and coffee, were also *verboten*. Her dislike was not an affectation. Real suffering resulted from the dire shortages of food and textiles that affected civilians in the Central Powers during the war and for some time after, as the blockade preventing imports into Germany was only lifted after the Treaty of Versailles was finally signed, in July 1919. Civilians in the regions occupied during the war by the Central Powers suffered for even longer, and often more cruelly, as their resources and economies were looted to bolster the occupiers' homelands.

In 1923 and 1926, two different donors gave suits made from paper yarns to New Jersey's Newark Museum, in the heart of the state's large textile manufacturing region. Each had acquired his suit in Germany, but did not say when.[2] As we've seen, wool had been in great and often unfulfilled demand. Cloth woven from paper yarn, and made into dozens of necessary objects, was one of several vital wartime substitutes, particularly in Germany, where the process had first been patented. The donor of the suit seen here was a paper company executive; he may have visited Germany specifically to explore this technology.[3]

Yarns spun from strips of paper cut from long rolls had been in use in Germany since about 1895, primarily for sacking and floor coverings. War demanded new uses for paper, from fine screening to heavy cargo nets, and all kinds of clothing. Cloth woven from paper yarns was inexpensive, surprisingly flexible, and easy to dye. Germany had an abundance of trees, and additional supplies of cellulose pulp from Swedish forests were closer to hand than American cotton or Australian wool.

Today, the suit reminds us that although Germany had bought a great deal of wool fiber in the years leading up to war, and ruthlessly commandeered any fiber and finished cloth they found in occupied territories, the scale and ferocity of this war overwhelmed them nonetheless. Substitutes were a necessity, and many different types were exploited during and after the war, as Germany's economic recovery was slowed by Allied occupation of certain industrial areas, rampant inflation, and war reparations payments. Only desperation could have forced millions of people to wear paper clothes several years after the war's end.

The need to replace wool during World War I was not confined to the Central Powers. Shortages of wool occurred for many reasons in many places, spanning consumption, production, and transportation. Substitutes—*ersatz*—were essential. Paper was just one of the alternatives that the contorted politics of wool in wartime made a necessity. This chapter explores these alternatives and how their shortcomings set up the dedicated goal to replace wool itself after the war.

* * *

From the early nineteenth century, textile manufacturers sought ways to extend their supplies of wool. Essential for cost-cutting in peacetime, it took on even greater importance in wartime, when using wool wasn't just about affordability, but access. For the have-not nations, substitutes and adulterants were one answer, and for a time, until the sizes of armies reached unimaginable heights, they filled the gap reasonably well. The earliest substitute, to this day immensely important to the textile industry, was "shoddy."

The word "shoddy" is actually the standard nineteenth-century textile industry term for recycled wool fiber, also known as reprocessed, recovered, or rag wool. Before the start of the American Civil War (1861–1865), the word had a relatively benign meaning within the textile industry, and virtually no recognition outside it. A small amount of shoddy, shorter and less resilient than new wool fiber, could be mixed with new wool and re-spun into new yarn, decreasing the fabric's cost without seriously impairing its looks or strength. Although shoddy fiber couldn't be used to spin yarn on its own, a yarn containing it was defined by its presence, and was also called shoddy. The proportion of shoddy to new wool in a yarn was supremely important in calculating both the price of a textile or finished garment and its durability. Shoddy yarns were primarily used in the weft (crosswise) direction of woven cloth, as they couldn't withstand the constant changes of tension which the warp (lengthwise) yarns undergo during weaving. They were, however, suitable for use in hand knitting and some machine knitting.

The shoddy trade began in England in about 1813, around the towns of Batley and Dewsbury in West Yorkshire. Woolen rags from garments and textiles that had been used, and tailors' clippings (remnants of unused cloth left over from cutting out garment pieces) were sorted by color and fiber content. Machines called pickers and grinders shredded the rags and clippings back into fiber for sale to yarn spinners. Unused remnants made the highest grade of shoddy, called mungo. Rags that were only part wool first had to undergo additional processing to remove the other fiber so that the wool could be recycled. Shoddy manufacture proved vital to the growth of industrialized woolen textile production. Commonly used in cheap cloth, it also found its way into better grades when wool prices were high.

Shoddy was originally touted as a boon to the working poor, but until the 1860s, the cheapest grade of British-made blankets and yard goods for clothing, woven with a cotton warp and shoddy weft, were also exported in quantity to plantations in the Caribbean, South America, and the American slave states. American shoddy mills began to open in the 1840s, allowing US textile manufacturers to incorporate it into their own low-priced goods for laborers and the enslaved. Charles Noska, a weaver in Manayunk, Pennsylvania, an important center of American woolen textile production, began a sample book in 1860 of the kinds of cloth he needed to know how to weave. It included several swatches of coarse striped cloth with cotton warps and shoddy wefts, manufactured by "A Cambles [sic] Mill."[4] Archibald Campbell operated two

Manayunk mills, specializing in cotton and cotton/wool mixed goods for sale to the "slave cloth" markets.[5]

Shoddy gained notoriety, and a new meaning, during the first year of the American Civil War. The US (Union) Army expanded from under 18,000 in December 1860 to nearly 200,000 in July 1861. The Union's quartermaster and individual state militias struggled to outfit those tens of thousands of incoming soldiers. Manufacturers who took army contracts for cloth, uniforms, and blankets found that there was simply not enough wool in the country to meet demand. In the months before wools purchased overseas could be received, many manufacturers resorted to using a larger proportion of shoddy to new wool than customary, hoping the resulting yarn would make cloth strong enough to satisfy the contracts. They were wrong.

Complaints concerning the quality of some uniforms and blankets began to surface in May 1861. One cartoon depicted Pennsylvania soldiers, recipients of sub-standard uniforms, standing face outward in little circles around their camp, so as not to reveal their nearly naked posteriors to visiting ladies.[6] State legislatures in New York, Pennsylvania, Vermont, and Connecticut began to investigate, as did the federal government. A Congressional Select Committee held hearings from June 1861 in 12 cities, interviewing hundreds of witnesses. Actual shoddy, in the textile industry meaning of the term, rarely surfaced in the reports, although during the testimony of the deputy US Quartermaster General regarding a delivery of blankets, he described a federal investigator examining one blanket as having "pulled out of it a piece of an old nightcap, which had happened to escape being chopped up fine. It was an inch and a half long."[7] It is unlikely that any garment could be identified from a tiny fragment, but hyperbole reigned in all public proceedings about this scandal. For the most part the investigations found that militia uniforms, instead of being regulation all-wool broadcloth or kersey, were made of cheaper, less durable fabrics such as satinet or jean cloth, with a mix of cotton and wool fibers that might also include shoddy. The word shoddy—usually misunderstood and badly defined, in one instance as old rags glued together to make new cloth—took on a new politically charged meaning that would become universally accepted: deliberately deceptive and of inferior quality.

In fact, shoddy had legitimate military uses. Several extant Union water canteens sport striped cloth coverings with a shoddy weft, resembling the samples from Archibald Campbell's mill. Union and Confederate quartermasters and officers complained bitterly, often, and at length about how profligate soldiers were with blankets and overcoats—jettisoning them on long marches in hot weather, retreats, and routs, or simply shipping them home if the opportunity arose.[8] An exasperated Confederate quartermaster in 1864 outlined a scheme for a blanket mill in South Carolina that would use shoddy yarns, thus saving the Confederacy from having to buy such blankets from Britain and then run the cargoes through the federal naval blockade of southern ports. It could, he wrote, employ "3 skilled hands bal[ance] negro labor and disabled soldiers. . . . The shoddy can be made of any kind of rags from the Clothing Depots . . . woolen rags will supply the extracted wool at cost of 3 cts a lb. Cost of manufacturing shoddy 1 ct a lb."[9] Both sides agreed that blankets needed to be replaced so often that purchasing best quality pure new wool ones was wasteful.

Pleading frugality did not save the government from denunciations over using shoddy in military goods. The *New York Times* asserted that "instead of buying in England the best [blankets] the market could offer—such as is used in the British and French armies—our Government agents have bought the very poorest, meanest and cheapest they could find" and quoted a Liverpool wool broker as saying that in blankets, "a little wool goes a long way, and shoddy, waste and low noils are largely drawn upon."[10] Cartoons and popular songs ("Sal Jones sells no more fish, She goes not near her stall; A contract made her rich, She's at the Shoddy Ball") of the period reinforced both the new popular understanding of the term and the stereotypes of war profiteers.[11]

* * *

Public dismay at the use of shoddy survived the war. In September 1865, John Hayes, the secretary of the National Association of Wool Manufacturers, gave a speech on the state of the industry. In praise of wool, he said, "The existence of 'shoddy,' that term of reproach to the woolen manufacturers, is the strongest proof of the excellence and indestructibility of its original fiber." He continued, however:

sixty-five million pounds of shoddy are annually consumed in England, a greater quantity than the whole wool product in the United States, estimated at 60,264,913 pounds by the census of 1860! It is one of the advantages of depending upon foreign importation for our goods, that we are in blissful ignorance of their origins, and are not shocked with the consciousness of being clad in the cast-off habiliments of a Polish Jew or an Italian beggar.[12]

Hayes's insinuation that dirty and possibly diseased rags from unsavory foreigners ended up in the goods English woolen manufacturers sold to unsuspecting American consumers illustrates how shoddy became the repository for bigotry and bias inspired more by issues of race, religion, and class than by any soldier's potential or actual suffering. The textile remnants we call rags were (and remain) a fact of life anywhere people wore clothes, hung curtains, or slept under sheets and blankets. The rag man collecting castoff clothes and textiles for recycling (cotton and linen into paper, wool into shoddy) was a common neighborhood sight in Europe and the United States, well into the twentieth century.

Stigmatizing the use of shoddy for military purposes was largely political theater. Cheap to produce, relatively easy to acquire, and versatile, it was widely used in the woolen industries. Until truth-in-labeling laws were passed in the mid-twentieth century, almost no one outside the textile industry was the wiser, although "manufacturers' success and reputation depended upon judging a fine balance between price and quality."[13] By the 1880s, refinements in the grinding machinery that reduced the fabric pieces to fiber allowed a blend as high as 85 percent shoddy in cheaper lines of civilian textiles. As the number of shoddy mills grew in wool manufacturing nations, many governments quietly kept down the cost of military overcoats and blankets by accepting up to 35 percent of shoddy in the fiber mix. US Census records in 1910 listed 88 shoddy mills. It was a booming business. Textile industry trade journals routinely discussed prices of imported and domestic rags, and the selling prices of shoddy extracted from those rags, both to US manufacturers and abroad, primarily to the English wool trade. Competition between civilian and military buyers made shoddy a hot commodity in the woolen markets, supported by a flourishing international rag business carrying at least a hundred different categories of rags.

Periodically the US Congress investigated the woolen industry's use of shoddy, sometimes in civilian textiles and sometimes to reassure the public—however insincerely—that shoddy did not taint US military goods. Never quite resolved, the topic arose in committee hearings and as the subject of bills introduced in Congress in 1901, 1909, and from 1912 through 1914. Even so, using shoddy in certain military fabrics was condoned when price and availability made it an efficient use of resources.

* * *

British manufacturers were the recognized masters of knowing just how much shoddy they could get away with using. This made it doubly important to wartime woolen textile production in the UK, which although it controlled much of the world's wool, faced the same shipping problems as every other nation. The British Army's Salvage units operated everywhere, sending "old uniforms, hosiery articles, etc." to the Government Rag Depot, Dewsbury, Yorkshire. There they were shredded back into fiber and sold to textile mills, to be reworked into new fabrics.[14] One report listed "45 million separate items of clothing—jackets, trousers, greatcoats, breeches, puttees, shirts, caps, cardigan jackets, socks, drawers" as having been received at the Dewsbury Depot by late 1917, including 18 million wool socks.[15]

Roger Hainsworth, who bought wool for his family's Yorkshire woolen firm for 30 years from the 1980s, recounted family lore regarding the use of shoddy in World War I from a business perspective:

> *You couldn't give a soldier a second-hand greatcoat that had a bullet-hole in the heart of it, no one would get over the top of the trenches would they? They'd get the old greatcoat back and ... grind it all up with as little new wool as you could get away with. These army greatcoats weren't ceremonial, they were very cheaply made uniforms, using lots of mungo or shoddy.*[16]

Except in cases of extreme need, morale issues as well as functional ones kept shoddy from being used in military garments worn next to the skin, such as underwear and shirts. Otherwise, it was ubiquitous. In August 1915, American companies filling Italian orders for uniform cloth bought up South American lambswool, because "shoddy and wastes are so scarce and high that it is proving cheaper to increase the quantity of [new] wool used."[17]

From 1917, the US Quartermaster's Operations Base Section Plant in New York City housed a sorting, laundering/dry cleaning, repair, and re-issue service for US-based and repatriated troops. Photographs and a short silent film exist of the work carried out here.[18] Men unloading overcoats checked the pockets "for matches" and other sundries; a stray match struck during processing might have ignited the dust endemic in such a facility. Large, bustling workrooms were staffed by male and female workers, mostly civilians, including a few African American men. Uniforms were unloaded and examined; unusable ones were sent to the rag sorters. Groups of four men loaded bales of recyclable materials larger than themselves onto trucks for transport to the shoddy mills of America.

One facet of the January 1918 US Senate hearings into how the War Department was equipping its much-enlarged armed forces arose from what one witness called the "apprehended scarcity" of wool when the United States entered World War I in April 1917.[19] By then the industry had replaced the scorned word shoddy with the less culturally loaded term "reworked wool." The government's civilian advisory Committee on Supplies, anxious, perhaps even a little panicky, about wool supplies due to Britain's rigid licensing system, changed the fiber specifications for certain army cloths. Overcoats, for example, had been 75 percent wool and 25 percent cotton; with cotton also in short supply, this was altered to 65 percent wool and 35 percent shoddy. The Paymaster General of the Navy, whose responsibilities included the purchase of clothing and most other equipment, boasted to the Senate that the Navy absolutely did not allow shoddy in its fabrics. He backtracked the following day, having been corrected by a subordinate: 35 percent of "high-grade shoddy" had been approved and accepted, as the contracts calling for 100 percent new wool had received no bids—new wool being either unavailable or priced so high that no profit could be made on the contract as originally written.[20]

Philadelphia Depot QM cloth inspector Col. Elmer Lindsley testified at these hearings about the quality of some cloths woven to the new, wool-conserving standards. He began:

> *I expect to get a regiment of my own some day and I do not want them to take a shot at me the first time I get in front of them, if they found out I had something to do with buying the clothes they wear.*

Lindsley complained that the new standards did not specify the acceptable grade of reworked wool, so manufacturers often chose the lowest priced shoddy, producing cloth both less durable and less wind- and water-resistant. In agreement with Julius Forstmann's testimony at the same hearings, he observed "it costs just as much to make a suit of clothes out of poor cloth as it does out of good cloth. It costs just as much to transport the goods, just as much congestion, both on the railroads and on the steamers going over."[21] The logistics of wool supplies in wartime were much like fuzzy woolen yarns: inconvenient factors of access, quality, cost, and transportation stuck out at all angles. The process was anything but smooth.

Just a few months after these hearings ended, the National Association of Wool Manufacturers reassured readers that "the soldiers are now sufficiently supplied with clothing to be kept warm and comfortable. No shoddy or wool substitutes are used in the . . . uniforms." Overcoats and blankets, however, were mixed shoddy and new wool.[22] To forestall having to increase shoddy in military garments, civilians were asked to reduce the amount of wool they consumed, and manufacturers added more shoddy to the woolen cloth they made for the civilian market. Rags, after all, had to come from somewhere, and the import/export rag trade, like the raw wool trade, was large and international, a disadvantage in wartime. So even as shoddy crept further into military textiles, the search for wool substitutes continued as armies grew larger, trade routes more hazardous, and wool supplies harder to access.

* * *

Recycled wool fiber was just the first in a long line of substitutes. Up through World War I, these were confined primarily to adaptations of natural fibers. Since the US produced less raw wool than needed to meet domestic demand for woolen yarns and cloth, American manufacturers were adept at adulterating wool. A shocking fraud to those—especially Australasians—for whom the word "merino" describes a particular breed of sheep and its wool, was the common American practice, from the late nineteenth into the twentieth centuries, of using merino to designate a yarn blended from wool and Aspero cotton, a strain of strong, crimped, long staple cotton fiber from Peru.[23] Manufacturers maintained that consumers couldn't tell the difference between the blended yarn and one of 100 per cent wool.

During the war, however, cotton of all types was also at a premium, both in supply and availability of shipping. The only fibers that saw limited military use were silk and the specialty "hair" fibers such as mohair (from the Angora goat) and the camelids (alpaca, llama, and of course, camel), which were either expensive or of limited availability and/or usefulness.

Mohair was readily available in the United States. Herds of goats had been established in the late nineteenth century to support manufacturing of imitation furs and upholstery velvet and plush for furniture and railway seating. Mohair plush found a wartime use as a lining for aviators' winter overalls, and when in 1918 government regulations prohibited using either cotton or wool for civilian home knitting, Pennsylvania yarn manufacturer S.B. & B.W. Fleisher, Inc., introduced a mohair and silk blend "Conservation Yarn." In contrast, the knitting yarns Fleisher made in US Army and Navy shades were all wool and came with instructions for home knitters to make regulation socks, gloves, chest protectors, and other "comforts" for the services.[24]

While shipping raw silk from China and Japan to the United States escaped most hazards of naval warfare, the military had only two specialty uses for silk. Parachutes, which required fine silk, were not yet standard issue to aviators, and the Air Services in any case were still quite small. Artillery shell powder bags were woven of low-grade spun silk, which left no combustible residue inside the guns. That left the American silk industry, by production volume the largest in the world, to capitalize on wartime restrictions to wrest civilian market share from cotton and wool. Companies rushed to develop new ranges of highly textured "Sport Silks" and heavier fabrics suitable for men's and women's suits and cold weather wear. These helped Americans conserve wool and cotton, and brought silk into the realm of wearability for all seasons, around the clock, and across the class divide, when it had traditionally been reserved either for the upper classes or for "best."[25] Post-war, consumers' new comfort with silk would open the door to the widespread use of artificial silk, which would have its own consequences for the woolen industry.

Once the United States entered the war, conservation shifted from merely commendable to a patriotic duty. Placards at the Connecticut State Council of Defense exhibition in October 1918 scolded viewers: "Women, Wake Up!," "Only one farm in seven in the United States has any sheep—Conserve Wool!," "The United States is only raising enough wool to make one suit for each inhabitant every four years. Our Army needs the wool this year." Ideas for remodeling and patterns for cutting down worn but serviceable adult garments for children adorned the walls.[26] Newspapers, women's magazines, and government departments all reinforced this message.

Textile chemists and engineers, particularly in the United States and Germany, were by 1915 experimenting with, in some cases actively using, other natural materials as wool alternatives, including ramie (a bast, or plant stem fiber), jute, stinging nettle, milkweed, and seaweed. Ramie and its close cousin China Grass are derived from a variety of stingless nettle found in India, China, and Africa. A US manufacturer, the Superior Thread and Yarn Company, claimed its "Stycos Wool Substitute" ramie fiber was "suitable for mixing with the best 3/8 blood stock" (crossbred sheep with three merino ancestors of eight).[27] It takes complicated chemical processing to separate ramie's usable fibers from the plant stem, which made it a fairly costly substitute and reduced demand. The United States also tested typha fiber, derived from the cattail plant, and the silky fiber from the seed pod of the milkweed plant. Neither proved practical.

The Germans investigated many substitutes, some in development before the war, but put to new uses after 1914. Typha fiber, as in the United States, was not a success. Sources also mention experiments, but not success, with peat fiber, willow bark, pine needles, cornstalks, and even asparagus![28] Stinging nettle, however, became a mainstay. Cousin to ramie but native to northern Europe, nettle had a long history across that continent before cotton began its rise to the top of the plant-derived fiber heap in the eighteenth century. The plant grew wild and was also cultivated; the resulting cloth was rather like linen. German women and children were exhorted to harvest the wild plant. Posters exclaimed "*Sammelt Brennessel! Wenn ihr Kleidung und Faden wollt!* (Collect stinging nettles if you want clothing and thread!), and "*Sammelt Brennesseln, die deutsche Baumwolle!*" (Collect stinging nettles, the German cotton!).[29]

The American textile industry took notice. In February 1917 a US trade publication warned that nettle fiber might make Austria, Hungary, and Germany independent of American cotton. About a year later an American Commerce report stated that the German military was taking all the nettle cloth that could be produced.[30] In Britain, articles for the public tended to portray German *ersatz* as proof that the nation's morale was suffering, while the textile industry, as in the United States, followed developments with great interest.

The Deutsche Faserstoffe-Gesellschaft ("DFG," German Fiber Material Co.) of Fuerstenberg, manufactured three other important plant-derived fibers: from a marine plant, from China Grass or ramie, and from jute. The company began operations in 1912 with "marine fiber," derived from Posidonia australis, a sea grass found in large beds along the coast of South Australia and around New Guinea (then under German control). Like linen from flax, the outer sheath of the leaves must be rotted away to release the usable fibers, and since the rotting happened in the ocean, the fibers were essentially mined from the seabed. The plant is slow-growing, so harvesting the fiber was not a sustainable business, but that was not a concern in 1912, for either the Australians or the Germans. Marine fiber, which cost half as much per pound as shoddy, was blended with wool or shoddy to make yarn. Germany used up its pre-war supplies of the raw material very early in the war, however, and, barred from importing more from Australia, also found it too difficult to transport it from New Guinea.[31]

Solidonia, on the other hand, was a bast fiber similar to the American Stycos ramie. China Grass, as it is also known, does not only grow in China. Germany's source for it was said to be Africa, perhaps from its colonies there. Solidonia was in demand in Germany for table linens and knitted garments before the war and was for sale in the Unites States by 1914. An American official investigating German textile industries post-war claimed that German uniform cloth had been blended at a ratio of 25 percent solidonia and 75 percent wool, and in civilian garments solidonia and shoddy were blended 50–50.[32] DFG also successfully "woolenized" jute fiber by treating it with caustic soda, making the jute fine and soft enough to mix with wool. The mixture of wool and jute eventually reached as much as 60 percent jute, possibly for uniform cloth but certainly for civilian goods. Whether uniforms of jute or ramie mixed with wool were durable, comfortable, or warm is debatable. Jute is commonly used to make twine and rope, and fabrics like burlap for sacking: millions of jute sandbags lined the trenches of the Western Front during World War I. Jute was also primarily a product of British-controlled India and the islands of the East Indies, so Germany and her allies, needing what jute they had to eke out wool supplies, had to find another substitute for sacking.[33]

Europe's fiber research was scrutinized by the US textile industry. At that time one of the economy's most important sectors, textiles employed more than 915,000 workers (about one-tenth of the nation's industrial workforce) in over 5,300 establishments, and contributed products valued at more than a billion and a half dollars to the economy.[34] The Smithsonian's National Museum housed a curatorial department that collected all things textile-related and an exhibit hall dedicated to displaying them. Because textiles were big business, American Consular officers and Commerce Department officials submitted regular reports to the Commerce and State Departments on developments overseas, including new fibers and technologies, keeping manufacturers apprised not only of what their competition was up to but of potential new areas of research and supply. This was not just an exercise in curiosity or competitiveness.

It was vital to the industry's stability and growth, because America's own sources of many fibers, particularly wool, were so uncertain.

* * *

In 1907 one of those Consular officers, Carl Bailey Hurst, had sent boxes of an inventive new textile commodity back to the Commerce Department from Plauen, Germany: spun paper yarns, called Xylolin or Textilose. His written report on the industry accompanied samples of yarns and matting.[35] Factories in Saxony (Germany), Bohemia (then a part of the Austro-Hungarian Empire), and England, Hurst said, were turning out inexpensive but durable paper yarns for sacking, "outing hats," canvas shoes and slippers, wall hangings, towels, and for a variety of floor coverings, "clean and fresh, and particularly suited to summer houses and verandas." The garment trade was using the yarns, dyed blue or brown, for workmen's jackets and overalls, and also in lightweight men's suits, either for "outings" or "the tropics."[36]

This was not the first use of paper in the textile world. Twisted paper parcel twine was in common use around the world, and Japan had long been making clothing from hand-spun and hand-woven yarns from the inner bark of the paper mulberry tree. The German paper yarns aroused excitement because the mechanized production processes encouraged new and varied uses. Emil Claviez, an entrepreneur and inventor working in the textile field in Chemnitz, Germany, patented his first machines for automating and therefore speeding up the spinning of the paper strips into yarn in 1895, and immediately began manufacturing yarns. Success in Germany led him to patent his invention across Europe, as well as India, Brazil, Chile, and the United States, by 1898. Three competing processes were patented by others.[37]

The process began with cellulose pulp (preferably from Swedish or Canadian pine trees), processed into a wide roll resembling kraft paper. The paper roll passed through a machine that cut it into strips, of whatever width was necessary for the finished product, from a few millimeters for screening to a few centimeters for hammock cord. A second machine twisted the strips into yarns. These were treated to increase water resistance and then woven into cloth, often combined with yarns of other fibers. By 1907, the initial product range of sacking and floor coverings had grown into the various utilitarian and decorative products described by Consul Hurst. Machine-made lace companies in and around Plauen also took up paper yarns—these would find an unexpected use in wartime.

It is difficult to pinpoint when paper textiles became the most important wartime substitute in the Central Powers. Arthur Kuffler, president of Austria's War Association of Cotton Spinners downplayed it, telling an American journalist in 1916 that only flour bags and twine were made of paper in the Central Powers, owing to the blockade cutting out US cotton. Kuffler claimed the new material would give the United States stiff competition for its cotton trade in the post-war world.[38] He warned American readers that this newfound technology would replace the foreign trade that had been essential to Germany and Austria pre-war, especially with nations that had been unhelpful during the war.

Other observers had more expansive views of the Central Powers' use of paper. The *Berliner Boersen-Zeitung*, a German financial newspaper, estimated that in 1916 German mills manufactured 66 million pounds of paper yarn, with new products such as cordage, industrial belting, tent and sail canvas, aprons, and surgical bandages joining the product list already known from 1907.[39] An Australian newspaper in April 1917 claimed that German soldiers were "clothed in" paper and cotton, with a bit of shoddy. While this was, perhaps, propaganda to counter the bad news of heavy Allied casualties at Arras and Vimy Ridge, it is possible that the clothing referred to was underwear. The same month, New Zealand soldiers had taken photographs comparing their own woolen underwear with a German prisoner's undershirt and drawers, described as being "like sacking"—which may well have been paper cloth.[40] By late 1917, many German jute and cotton spinning mills had adapted their machinery to paper to meet the increasing demand for all the forms this substitute could take, including the government decree that from May 1917 all burial shrouds must be made of paper cloth.[41]

In March 1918 an industrial exhibition in Chemnitz, Germany, displayed a huge array of paper products over two exhibit halls: knitting yarns, hosiery and underwear, gloves, cravats, and suspenders, children's clothes, and women's purses.[42] Scattered examples of these civilian products, besides the Newark Museum's suits and the Smithsonian's 1907 Consular samples, exist in museums around the world, such as the UK's Imperial War Museum collection of German, Austrian, and Swiss-made paper garments, including a boy's knitted knickers, men's jackets and trousers, and a woman's nightdress, chemise, and underdrawers trimmed with paper lace. These seem to have been donated by the UK Government's Department of War Trade Intelligence, whose existence tells us a lot about the value of commodities and commerce in wartime.[43]

Considering how much of it was made, it is surprising how few museum collections contain civilian paper garments. Even more surprising, however, is the extent to which paper textiles were in common use by the German military—a situation they tried very hard to conceal. In mid-1918, an article republished in two Australian newspapers reported that in a Berlin exhibition of paper goods, prepared by the Imperial Clothing Office, "The military section displayed paper saddles and harness (for export rather than for use in the German army), paper sandbags, towels," while "paper oilskins for submarine crews" were also mentioned.[44] But a huge range of German military equipment made of paper yarns exists in four museums in the UK, the United States, New Zealand, and Australia.

In addition to its civilian goods, the Imperial War Museum has sacking and sandbags, rope and twine, bandages, a burial shroud, a cartridge pouch, field cable (paper-twine wrapped metal wire), mail bag, puttees, a gas curtain, shoe liners, a towel, and an entrenching tool and water bottles with woven paper covers. The 53 objects at the Smithsonian's National Museum of American History include truck covers, sheaths for tools and weapons, a saddle bag, a knotted cargo sling, braided horse trappings, and feed buckets for horses, all collected as military salvage by the US Army, and toured around the United States after the war as, essentially, victory trophies. In 1923, the Smithsonian's textile curator, Frederick Lewton, accessioned the paper items, aware that American anxiety over textile shortages and supply chains remained high, and that despite its shortcomings as a wearable, paper was an important US industry, and easily convertible to this technology should the need arise.[45]

Another cache resides at the Tāmaki Paenga Hira Auckland War Memorial Museum, brought back to New Zealand by soldiers and medical staff. Items include a palliasse, or rectangular bag to be stuffed with straw or leaves as a mattress; a flat-woven bath towel; and swatches of different weights and weaves of paper textiles, each with a gummed label giving its purpose (palliasse stuff, stuff for driving belts, covering for blankets, railway carriage upholstery, etc.). Rolls of woven paper bandages in several different widths and weights speak to the depths of Germany's textile shortages, and rolls of paper lace, also in various widths, may have been pressed into service for binding bandages, splints, or packages.[46] The Australian War Memorial holds two other haunting relics. One, an artificial leg, its woven paper puttee still in place, was removed from a German pilot, killed when his plane was shot down in France in May 1918. Another, all-too-familiar item to frontline soldiers, called jumping off tape, guided troops to their stations before an attack. In Germany even that was made of paper yarn.[47]

Capt. Pollard, whose report on the Berlin exhibition was quoted above, ended his recitation of Germany's paper on a derogatory note:

> *the paper fiber industry has advanced wonderfully, paying enormous dividends—on paper. After the war, there is no doubt that there will be an attempt to flood the world's markets with these undesirable substitutes for good natural wool, silks, and cotton goods; but for the present, there is ample demand for them in Germany—where any woven material that will cover the nakedness of the people is badly needed.*[48]

Considering the sheer number of uses to which Germany put its paper textiles, civilian and military, we wonder how long their use allowed Germany and her allies to continue fighting, beyond the point when the lack of raw materials might have been expected to force them to stop.

The British and Americans certainly took paper textiles seriously. US Commerce Department observers noted in 1917 that "a definite effort is being made to emancipate the trade from foreign patents and processes," and in 1918 and 1919 documented British paper technology in depth.[49] A British firm, Textilite Engineering Co., exhibited its spinning machines and products at the August 1918 British Scientific Products Exhibition at King's College, London.[50] Wartime uses in these nations were confined to a few industrial and household uses, but if the war had lasted another year or two, paper clothes might have been a welcome addition to war-shabby Allied wardrobes as well.

Indeed, paper textiles and clothing continued to be manufactured for several years after the war, and not just in the defeated Central Powers. In Frankfurt, in December 1918, a US newspaper correspondent "saw woolen suits at $200, others in shoddy cotton at $75, and still others of paper at $12."[51] In February 1921, paper clothing was still being manufactured and worn in "Argentina, Austria, Germany, Great Britain, Italy, and Turkey," whose economies had not yet recovered from the war. Paper garments then cost much less than woolen: the equivalent of 59 cents for a workman's outfit; $1.40 for a man's suit; and 47 cents for a shop coat worn by workmen and artisans.[52] The Textilite Engineering Co. manufactured its yarns and fabrics and patented machinery improvements at least through 1922. While we can readily imagine paper's shortcomings—which are not much discussed apart from Allied propaganda—it filled an enormous gap during these years.

Certainly, the hyperinflation Germany experienced from 1921 would have made purchasing woolen clothing nearly impossible. The year 1923 in which Germany's inflation peaked and the fabled "wheelbarrow full of money" wouldn't buy a loaf of bread, was the year Angela and Willi Baer, who married in 1922, began to plan their emigration to the United States. Willi, a merchant seaman, was also no stranger to deprivation. He had been serving on a ship docked in a Finnish port when war was declared. He and the other Germans on board were removed to a prison camp in Siberia, where he stayed until news of the Russian Revolution reached the camp, and the guards all disappeared. The prisoners followed suit, and Willi finally reached Germany sometime after the Armistice. Just a few years later he, his wife and children were en route to America, and the hope of a future in a nation with greater self-sufficiency and less *ersatz*.

* * *

The textile genie that stirred in World War I would not be content with resurrecting long-disused natural fibers, or hunting on land and sea for new ones. It would also deliver new textile resources, with the aid of chemistry. Specifically, the fiber we now call rayon.

Rayon, originally known as artificial silk and conceived as a silk alternative, has some mid-nineteenth-century roots, but commercially it dates to 1889 and 1891, when Hilaire de Chardonnet patented, and then began commercial production of his nitrocellulose-based process for an artificial silk filament, an extremely long fiber, smoother and more uniform than silkworm silk. Not until about 1910 did the industry become commercially viable. Along the way, additional processes were invented and refined: Viscose (which became the most common, patented originally in 1892), Cuprammonium (also in production from about 1892), and Acetate (the latecomer, about 1924). The term "rayon" would be made up in 1924 by an American trade association, the National Retail Dry Goods Association. In the interests of simplicity, we will use the term "rayon" even though (like wool) the nomenclature is complicated.

Technically, rayon is a regenerated cellulose fiber. It was initially called artificial or man-made; current terminology dubs it a semi-synthetic. It is not fully synthetic because the raw material it's made from is naturally occurring cellulose, but the cellulose is chemically and physically modified. The readily available cellulose pulp that made the paper textiles of World War I an object of universal interest among resource-starved nations was also the basis for this new fiber. The best quality of rayon started with wood from Sweden and Canada, or cotton linters (the short, waste fibers left after the spinnable cotton was ginned from the seeds), mostly from US mills. Other sources of cellulose, such as beech trees (Germany), reeds (Italy) and soybean stems (Japan) were used when access to the preferred woods was difficult, as it was for those nations when hard currency issues or war interfered. The cellulose-bearing plant material is reduced to pulp, then treated with a chemical cocktail that turns it into a jelly-like solution. The jelly becomes a filament by forcing (extruding) it at high speed through something like a shower head, called a spinneret, after which the filaments pass through an air chamber or another solution that hardens them up. The chemicals involved in the various processes can include caustic soda, sulfuric acid, nitric acid, alcohol, ether, ammonium sulfate, acetic acid, formaldehyde, and copper sulfate or hydroxide. The filaments are then spun or twisted together with others to make a thread or yarn suitable for weaving, knitting, etc.[53]

Initially, this new technology, which was both research and capital intensive, was wielded by a few companies which had enough of the latter to fund the former and hoped for freedom from the vagaries of the raw silk trade. These included the British silk manufacturer Courtaulds (making rayon from 1906), and two European companies created specifically to exploit this new fiber: Vereiningte Glanzstoff-Fabriken (VGF) in Germany and Comptoir des Textiles Artificiels (CTA) in France.[54] Courtaulds' US subsidiary, American Viscose Co., produced small quantities of rayon from 1910. In 1912, the Smithsonian Institution acquired a range of fabrics made in the United States, utilizing rayon, for display in the National Museum's Textile Hall, as examples of innovative technology.

During the war, Germany was forced to experiment with artificial silk as a mixer, among the other adulterants and substitutes we've mentioned.[55] German mills either gathered the waste fiber from spinning rayon yarns for civilian uses or used those yarns, cutting the material into short lengths, called *stapelfaser*, for blending with cotton or wool fiber in the spinning process, just as they used wool shoddy or their woolenized jute. The resulting yarns were considered crude and had limited use. As a conservation measure this was marginally successful, and far behind paper yarns in both utility and usage. But the door to textile innovation had opened.

* * *

The supply and deployment of wool in World War I would have lasting repercussions. Those who hadn't been forced to use substitutes still watched carefully the advances and failures in the nations that had. Shoddy, the best available substitute for new wool, was, after all, a wool by-product, subject to the same supply chain problems. Most of the other natural fiber substitutes had been found wanting, either for reasons of availability or technical challenges. The single most important substitute for the Central Powers had been the textiles made from spun paper yarns. Yet these, too, although they seem to have kept Germany and her allies in the fight, were not a long-term solution: they were inexpensive, yes, but not truly durable, or warm.

Every manufacturing nation in the interwar period took these lessons to heart. Better substitutes were needed for the raw materials that another war would again put out of reach. The readily available cellulose that had been the basis for the paper textiles was also the basis for rayon, and in that form was a more efficient use of the raw material, cutting out the intermediary paper-making step. The countries that had faced the worst of the shortages of wool, and to a lesser degree, of cotton, having reviewed their strategic commodity needs for the next war, would build on the research, experiments, successes (few), and failures (many) of their wartime expediencies in their search for substitutes and synthetic alternatives.

Oddly enough, many interwar developments in new fiber technologies would result from international cooperation among industrialists and the scientists they employed. But would these new materials suffice to replace wool? Or were they to be a kind of tip of the iceberg, their own limitations and deficiencies inspiring new avenues of research? And, vitally, how would the wool industry—from growers to manufacturers to marketers—respond to this threat? The next two chapters explore the interwar period from two different points of view: how wool fiber fared once its markets were again private, and how its new competitor rayon developed.

Chapter 6

Life on the Edge

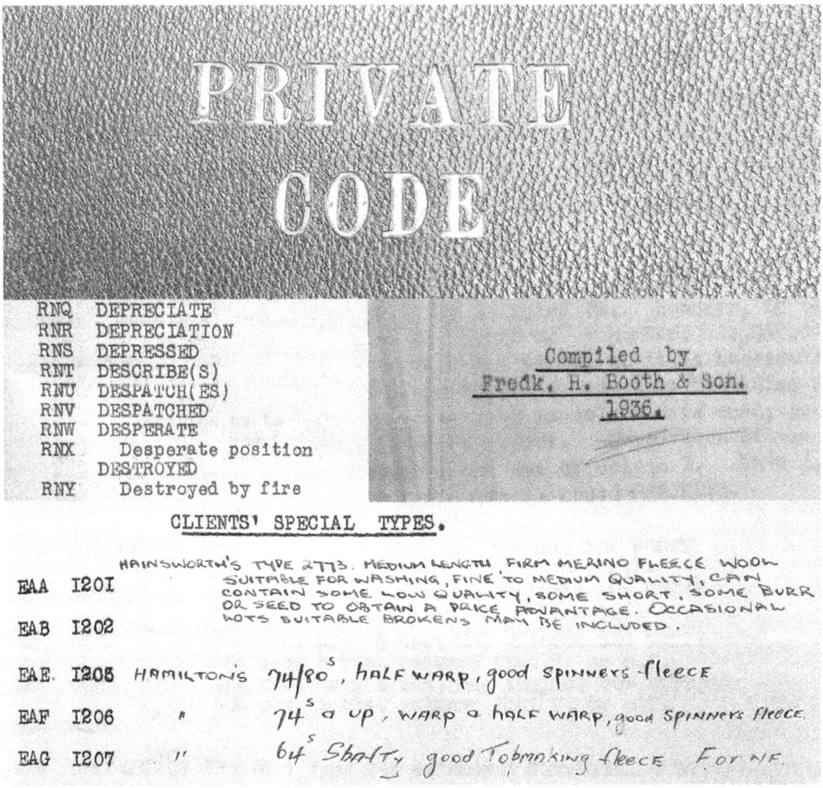
PRIVATE
CODE
RNQ DEPRECIATE
RNR DEPRECIATION
RNS DEPRESSED
RNT DESCRIBE(S)
RNU DESPATCH(ES)
RNV DESPATCHED
RNW DESPERATE
RNX Desperate position
DESTROYED
RNY Destroyed by fire
Compiled by
Fredk. H. Booth & Son.
1936.
CLIENTS' SPECIAL TYPES.
HAINSWORTH'S TYPE 2773. MEDIUM LENGTH, FIRM MERINO FLEECE WOOL SUITABLE FOR WASHING, FINE TO MEDIUM QUALITY, CAN CONTAIN SOME LOW QUALITY, SOME SHORT, SOME BURR OR SEED TO OBTAIN A PRICE ADVANTAGE. OCCASIONAL LOTS SUITABLE BROKENS MAY BE INCLUDED.
EAA I201
EAB I202
EAE. I205 HAMILTON'S 74/80s, half warp, good spinners fleece
EAF I206 " 74s & up, warp & half warp, good spinners fleece.
EAG I207 " 64s Shafty good Topmaking fleece For NF.

Collage of pages from the 1936 Private Telegraph Code Book of Fredk. H. Booth & Son, Sydney, NSW, Australia (courtesy of the Mitchell Library, Sydney, NSW, Australia).

> Sydney Royal Exchange is the largest wool selling center in the world. To every true Australian there is something inspiring in this spectacle ... for with the progress of the great wool industry is bound the progress of Australia. ... In the city the great wool stores are crammed with bale after bale of "white wealth."[1]
>
> Voiceover, *Just Wool*—British Pathé newsreel, 1933

A young man in the second row of a Sydney wool auction, writing studiously in his notebook as others leap to their feet to bid, appears in a scene in the newsreel *Just Wool.* He is James Booth (b. 1907), a member of his father's wool buying firm, Fredk. H. Booth & Son. The auction room is full of buyers, all male, from all over the world. So full that some are sitting or standing in the aisles. No telephones are visible: the buyers are reliant on their own knowledge of wool and its current market.

Wool buyers were typically experienced world travelers, making annual trips back to the northern hemisphere to communicate in person with the manufacturers they served. In the heat of the auction season, however, before telephone communication was common, communicating with clients telegraphically and confidentially was an essential component of a wool buyer's toolkit. The telegraphic code book collaged at the head of this chapter was one of several used by Fredk. H Booth & Son in buying Australian wool for the northern hemisphere textile trade in the 1920s and 1930s.

Telegraphy and its codes developed from naval semaphore, which used line-of-sight flags and hand movements to send coded messages, such as NF4, meaning "Land the Troops," or NFE, "troops to land with one day's provisions cooked." Telegraphy itself used combinations of electronic dots and dashes in the alphabetic Morse code, enabling messaging beyond line-of-sight. Early telegraphy was extremely expensive; in 1866 sending a 20-word message cost $100.[2]

Compressed telegraphic codes made confidential business communications possible and cheaper. Code books specific to wool auctions allowed buyers and the mills they bought for, half a world away, to give and take information and instructions in a matter of hours or days, not weeks or months. Despite Australia and New Zealand producing much of the world's apparel wool, it's unlikely that the shift from London to Australia by the world's biggest wool auctions in the 1880s would have happened without these communications advances.

Buyers from dozens of nations came to purchase wool in Australia, fostering in the collective combinations and permutations of code a kind of "sheep Latin." The earliest extant wool code books use one word for each concept. In an 1880s example, the word "Plodding" stood for "other purchases are within limits" while "Ploughman" meant "You have exceeded credit by . . . bales for account of . . . ."[3] Perhaps not surprisingly, these books are very large, and both coding and decoding required a formidable memory and a secure space in which to work.

Frederick Booth's 1926 code book was unique to his company and his principal American client in Boston, Massachusetts, Jeremiah Williams and Company. In this code whole phrases are represented by combinations of capital letters with no intrinsic meaning. Many are about money:

EZTOP—We can buy cheaper in Boston
JOHZO—Keen competition among American buyers for all classes of suitable wools
ODCEL—Market excited and it is impossible to buy at limits

Other codes condensed information about the amount and quality of wool to be bought, its ultimate destination, itinerary, and shipping logistics.

Booth's business expanded considerably in the interwar years, probably stimulated by his prominent roles during 1914–1918. Based in Sydney, the company also bought at auctions in Brisbane, Geelong and Melbourne. The first section of his 1936 code book lists 44 different clients, most of them in the UK, including A.W. Hainsworth and Sons. One code, which combines letters and numbers, efficiently conveys extraordinarily specific detail:

EAA 1201—Hainsworths Type 2773 Medium Length, Firm Merino Fleece, Wool Suitable for Washing, Fine to Medium Quality, can contain some low quality, some short, some burr or seed to obtain a price advantage. Occasional lots suitable brokens may be included.

Booth used the second and substantially larger section of the 1936 book for a code unique to his then biggest client: the Arlington Mills, whose factory complex in Lawrence, Massachusetts, occupied 75 acres by 1925. Arlington had supplied the US Army Quartermaster (QM) with quantities of woolen textiles during the war, and Booth had probably met Arlington executive Franklin Hobbs during his wartime work representing the QM in buying Australian wools. Hobbs and his son Marland were close business associates of Booth's for several decades. We don't know why this American client required secrecy, while code sharing was fine for British firms.

Although the codes suggest that the open wool market was again flourishing by the mid-1920s, there were signs of vulnerability. The 1936 book offered:

QAZ—Come home next boat
WFN—The Boston market is bare and you must ship as much as you can by next Pacific coast mail boat
YIE—We expect the President to Veto

These attest to both new tensions and remembered crises. One code, "KBJ—Absurd," written in by hand, implies a wool market indeed on edge during those turbulent years.

This chapter explores the wool business and its vicissitudes in the interwar years, primarily through people, events, and politics in Australia, its economy then absolutely centered on exporting wool. Twining within and around the Australian wool business were opportunities and difficulties faced by individuals and companies in many different nations, shaped by wool's vital strategic role during the prior war. Even in times of apparent peace, the military aspects of wool profoundly influenced its destiny.

* * *

The Armistice of November 11, 1918, dramatically changed immediate demand for wool and forecasts of same. A month earlier, at the urging of Australian woolgrowers, the UK government had extended its commandeer of Australasian wool until June 1920. Britain already owned a stockpile of more than two million Australian bales, more than a normal year's clip, and three quarters of a million New Zealand bales, about eighteen months' worth.[4] Much of the commandeered wool remained stored in Australasia, with few ships available to get it to Europe. Wool prices were expected to plummet immediately post-war because of these stockpiles, causing disparate approaches to wool among various interested nations, manufacturers, workers, and producers. With the benefit of hindsight, an American government official would argue that the UK stockpile gave its post-war woolen textile industry a significant edge over its competitors.[5]

In fact, the US government, in May 1919, cancelled the balance of a huge order of wool that it had pushed hard for just before the war ended, feeling that peacetime military needs could be met by existing stockpiles of raw wool and cloth. These could be dribbled onto the market so as not to undercut prices and upset either the growers or the normal buying habits of the American industry. Surplus blankets could always be used, ditto uniforms if the styles were not changed—and American uniforms remained largely the same until the 1930s. The raw wool stockpile was cleared at auctions with a fixed minimum price, even though sales were suspended between July and November 1919 to allow the new domestic clip to be sold without competition. The US woolen industry easily met the immediate post-war demand by civilians who had done without and by returning soldiers—including Marland Hobbs, a Lieutenant in the American Expeditionary Force, released from a German prisoner of war camp on December 4, 1918.[6]

Simultaneously, uncertain demand and an abundance of available labor from returning soldiers encouraged mill owners to impose wage reductions in some parts of the industry. A successful strike in the Lawrence, Massachusetts, mills in early 1919 pitted low-skill immigrant workers against not only the mill owners but also high-skill workers, amidst a lot of vicious anti-immigrant rhetoric and activity.[7] It would not be the only strike American woolen mills faced in the interwar period, contributing to the precarious nature of the overall trade.

Manufacturers feared competition from restarted European competitors, particularly since enormous war debt had depreciated the currencies of the UK, France, Belgium, and Germany. This directly decreased labor costs and made their fabrics cheaper than American-made goods.[8] In May 1920, the market for domestic wools essentially collapsed, with very limited demand for all grades of wool and American range wools almost unsellable. Textile manufacturers cancelled wool orders, and the 200 or so wool-buying and brokerage firms in Boston, including Jeremiah Williams, found that "there was for several months hardly enough trading in wool to establish a scale of prices."[9]

In response, the US Tariff Commission began to rethink tariff levels. Julius Forstmann advocated for protection of woolen and worsted manufacturers (the New England sector of which was again experiencing labor troubles after slashing wages), during the 1922 Congressional wool tariff hearings.[10] Forstmann had emerged from his wartime troubles a very wealthy man, investing some of that wealth in building a mansion on East 71st Street in New York. He also purchased a controlling interest in his family firm in Werden, whether capitalizing on Germany's financial woes or assisting his family by infusing cash into a troubled firm, or both, is unclear.

* * *

British-Australasian relations over wool remained contentious immediately following the war, particularly regarding the clause of the commandeer that promised growers half the profits of requisitioned wools resold for civilian use. With military needs suddenly minimal, this essentially described the whole stockpile. Yet during 1919 the British government sold 450,000 bales to Bradford mills, and 250,000 bales to Allied governments, at *less* than the commandeer price, rather than at a current market price honoring the profit clause.

Although Bradford wool manufacturers were portrayed as collectively profiteering from the wartime wool commandeer, internal conflicts were rife. Percy Gaunt, the Assistant Director of Wool Textile Production, did not receive the knighthood he had expected for his wartime service due to vocal opposition by his Bradford peers, citing his favoritism to relatives in the industry. One relative, W. C. (Billy) Gaunt, had sold the British government a million yards of woolen khaki cloth every ten weeks during the war. Immediately after the war he secured much of the stockpile stored in Britain at commandeer prices for just a 1 percent deposit. His competitors felt cheated upon discovering that the rest of the stockpile, stored in Australia, would remain there until ships were available for transport.[11]

Despite fears of a glut, wool sold at 1919 auctions in London and elsewhere for much more than the commandeer fixed price, and by April 1920 at almost double. Australians were obviously losing money from the continued commandeer, and Prime Minister Billy Hughes complained in 1919 about "a course which puts millions into the pockets of the British manufacturer at the expense of the Australian woolgrower."[12] Neither Australia nor New Zealand knew who was buying their wool, prompting suspicion about any profits and their division. For Australia, heavily indebted to British capital for financing its own war effort, money from selling wool was critical to servicing that debt. The British government's suggestion that any profit directly pay war loans' interest was emphatically and successfully rejected by the Australian government and woolgrowers. Profits would first return to Australian woolgrowers, who would pay income tax, which would then pay the interest.[13]

Discord also developed over how quickly to sell the stockpile and whether to prioritize its sale or that of the fresh wool clips of 1920–1921. The former meant only a half share of any profits on top of the original commandeer would come to Australia. The latter meant much more export income for the Australian economy. Another big sale of wool by the UK to France in March 1920 at the commandeer price sparked such fury in Australia that the sale quantity was cut by 20 percent.[14] Fierce debates continued as the June 1920 end of the commandeer agreement approached. Australian wool auctions prepared to reopen in October, while Australian woolgrowers still awaited payment for their share of the profits of the resold stockpile wools. The London sales of the wool stockpile paused for several months in late 1920 and early 1921 to support restarting the Australian auctions, but auction prices were depressed.[15]

Only the best wools sold, and at a fraction of the prices pertaining a year earlier. Buyers held back, expecting an avalanche of cheap stockpiled wool to hit the market.

A new joint Australian/British bureaucracy found a way out of this morass. Early in 1921 the BAWRA (British Australian Wool Realisation Association) was established, led by John Higgins, who had run the Australian Central Wool Committee during the war. BAWRA also oversaw the sale of New Zealand's stockpile and most of South Africa's.[16] Although Australia pushed for BAWRA, the organization's founding documents required it to protect the interests of British consumers and to sell the stockpile as quickly as the market allowed. Australian Senator James Guthrie feared that the British population's pressing post-war need for warm clothing would mean the whole stockpile being dumped on the market at once.[17]

In the end the stockpile was cleared faster and with fewer negative impacts than was feared, although the Australian fine merino wools sold faster than the mainly New Zealand crossbred wools, which had seen strong wartime demand. Drought and labor shortages had interrupted sheep pastoralism in Australia during the war, and war itself had interrupted wool growing in France, Germany, Turkey, and the UK.[18] US wool production had decreased from its war-induced peak in 1919, dropping slightly below pre-war levels due to a drought in the western ranges in 1919, and the price panic of 1920–1921. By the end of 1921, worldwide demand for wool outstripped production, fueled in part by Germany and Japan again purchasing on the global wool market.[19] The Australian and New Zealand stockpiles were cleared by 1924, with BAWRA credited for this success.

* * *

The interwar wool trade, however, was anything but consistent. In late 1924, wool prices were again booming. In 1923, the NSW Minister for Agriculture, speaking at the Sydney Sheep Show, had referred to "financially Australians riding on the sheep's back."[20] The phrase quickly entered the vernacular as a kind of mantra for Australia's economic security, but from the outset there were those who questioned the certainty of that ride. When in 1925 wool prices again fell sharply for no apparent reason, the nation was said to have "come a cropper" from said back.[21] "The rapid development and use of artificial silk and other substitutes for wool" were identified as a possible culprit for the dip, the earliest such warning we are aware of.[22] To R. W. Thompson, a young British man who worked on an Australian sheep station in the late 1920s, the phrase represented "stupendous conceit and self-satisfaction."[23]

Julius Forstmann's interwar businesses were affected by the general instability. In 1925, he transferred ownership of his family firm in Germany to a larger concern, Augsburger Kammgarn Spinnerei, and received in return a seat on the Board of Directors and shares in the merged and renamed Werdener Feintuchwerke AG. Back in New Jersey, several of the Passaic woolen mills cut wages and/or hours, sparking a bitter strike spanning several months in 1926–1927. Forstmann & Huffmann shut down its mills in response to the strike, holding out against the workers' demands after other mills had reached resolution. Although labor activists decried Forstmann's eventual offer to work with employees to build an in-house union as paternalistic, the strike was finally ended in February 1927.[24] In 1929, Forstmann faced new recriminations for embarking shortly after the stock market crash on a seven-month-long round the world cruise with family and friends on his new 330-foot-long private yacht, the *Orion*, built in the Krupp shipyard in Kiel, Germany.[25]

Meanwhile employment in the US woolen textile industry had declined steadily since its peak in 1917. In mid-1929, the Botany Mills, Passaic's largest employer, cut its workforce by about half, down to 3,300, just months before the shattering effects of the Great Depression began to overtake the entire US textile industry.[26] Another casualty of the Depression was Bradford's Billy Gaunt, who went bankrupt in 1929, unable to service the debts he accrued a decade earlier by buying up commandeered wool. Like many in the 1920s and 1930s, he had lived a "life on the edge."[27]

Australian woolgrowers too were on a roller coaster ride through the 1920s and 1930s, their incomes varying hugely by location and across time. Alexander Mackay's descendants were able to ride the vagaries relatively easily, their land experiencing a moderate range of temperatures and rainfall. Alexander's son, Kenneth, had been a soldier in the Boer War and a military administrator in World War I, rising to the rank of Major General. He also served in the New South Wales Parliament and owned Wallendbeen Station and a smaller holding, Wallendoon. Given his responsibilities beyond the day-to-day management of a sheep station it was lucky that his daughter Annie married Aldred Baldry, a station employee who became a manager focusing on growing fine wool.[28]

Sheep pastoralism was much tougher in the parts of Australia with erratic climates, especially for those with less land and capital. Helen Close (nee Barnes), grew up on Rivoli Downs in Western Queensland in the 1930s. Her father won a 99-year lease in 1924, in a general ballot (land lottery) held as part of the continuing process of breaking up Australia's big sheep stations. He had grazing experience but minimal capital and had to borrow money from a wool broker to establish his sheep station. Loan in hand, he proposed marriage to Helen's mother, saying that he had "four thousand pounds and needed help to spend it." This ongoing family debt gave the wool broker great power, so much that at age 90 Helen would not name the firm because "it's dangerous!"[29]

Cyclical droughts about every fourth year meant that the land could regularly not carry sheep. Added to this, economic depression after 1929 meant a very tough time for Helen's family. When conditions became dire in 1935, Helen's father moved the family to Brisbane for several years and paid for the family's sheep to graze better land closer to the coast. When rains came in the late 1930s, Helen's parents used a bequest her mother had received to buy another neighbor's land. The neighbor, a returned serviceman on a soldier selection (allotment), had exhausted his finances. Helen's family bought his 17,000 acres for a paltry £1,400.[30] This more than doubled their grazing land, but they still lived on the edge of viability.[31]

Helen's young life was luxurious compared to James Edward Cain, Mary Jane Cain's son and Tup Bateman's grandfather. Cain had been a laborer tending sheep around Coonabarabran NSW before joining the Australian Light Horse and Camel Corps, serving in Palestine from 1917. Aboriginal servicemen received equal pay to other soldiers during wartime, but on their return to civilian life were not eligible to enter soldier settler ballots. Cain was shut out of the opportunity to acquire a landholding of his own.[32] He had returned from war shell-shocked but married in 1920 and had three children, including Tup's mother Violet. His illness made it hard for him to hold down a job, and eventually the marriage broke down. Violet was raised by one of James's sisters and grew up to work primarily as a shearer's cook.

American woolgrowers also experienced a wide variety of environmental and economic conditions between the wars. The Great Depression resulted in closures and reduced operations in the textile industry and therefore in the market for wool, but in late 1933 Franklin Roosevelt's New Deal economic program created the Commodity Credit Corporation to support farmers across the country with loans and other aids to ensure commodity prices held and that farmers wouldn't lose their land. High tariffs on imported merino and crossbred wools also kept US growers in business. Overall, US wool production held up, growing strongly in the 1920s and rising slightly in the 1930s to 426 million pounds in 1939, placing the United States fifth in the world in wool production. It was all for domestic consumption, but imports were also necessary to feed the nation's woolen textile industry.[33]

* * *

Germany wanted and needed wool as it attempted to recover economically from the war. Until August 1922, Germany was prohibited from accessing Australian wool, although in 1921 rumors and some evidence suggested that the German government was buying Australian wool via third parties, even amid hyperinflation.[34] Restrictions on Germans entering Australia were lifted in 1925. Georg Waldthausen (Alfred Lohmann's nephew), returned that year from his wartime sojourn in Germany, and reopened Lohmann and Co. in Sydney. He would recall the period of the Weimar Republic as a time of excellent business.[35]

Historically, Germany's need for wool meant its overall imports from Australia were much greater than its exports, by a factor of three in the early 1930s.[36] The punishing reparations Germany had to pay under the Versailles Treaty pressured their government to change this. From the 1880s, there had been talk of a German Chamber of Commerce in Australia, but it was only established in Sydney in 1929, just weeks before the Wall Street crash which sparked a global depression. Its primary aim was to increase German exports, but this was nigh on impossible after the 1932 Ottawa Agreement between Britain and its colonies, which allowed free trade within the Empire, but erected high tariff walls against imports from other nations.

The Chamber of Commerce made little headway until after Hitler assumed dictatorial powers in Germany following the Reichstag fire in February 1933. From June 1933, German textile companies were required to buy wool from German sources wherever possible and were financially compensated for this.[37] In March 1934, Germany explicitly outlawed importing textiles or other raw materials unless the exporting nation bought equivalent German exports. A complex new bureaucracy (ASKI) was established to apply this legislation. Wool could only be bought when there was equal credit for German exports, so the wool-buying firms had to remake themselves as import/export companies. To bypass ASKI rules, barter transactions were explored. In 1936, a suggestion by the Australian arm of the American company General Motors to swap wool for a German car assembly line was rejected by the Australian government, protecting British car makers' privileged status in Australia.[38]

With wool scarce in the early 1930s, Germany began to focus on self-sufficiency in textile fibers, encouraging greater production of its semi-synthetic fabrics: Vistra (viscose rayon), Wollstra (Vistra mixed with wool), and Zellwolle (rayon staple). Even the Werdener Feintuchwerke, which had subsumed the Forstmann family woolen company, brought Zellwolle into its yarns and cloth. In late 1934, the German Foreign Office hosted a lunch in Sydney to showcase Wollstra, hinting that if Australia would not accept more exports from Germany, German textile innovation might damage Australian exports. Behind the scenes the German government cautioned that "attempts by Australians to rip the material and suchlike must be avoided . . . or counter propaganda could be developed."[39] A pamphlet published in Sydney in 1935 by "An Economist" (possibly the German-Australian Chamber of Commerce) warned Australian woolgrowers that unless Germany was allowed to barter its industrial products for Australian wool, bypassing hard currency exchange, they would suffer.

> *Sixty million Germans . . . cannot be expected to go naked. They must have clothes. If they cannot get wool, they must find a substitute for wool. . . . The urgent question for Australians is this—will the Germans be forced to make synthetic wool?*[40]

Much press coverage denigrated Wollstra's qualities. The *Sydney Truth* proclaimed, "the rattling of the sabre did not do Germany much good in the bad old days, the rattling of a skein of Wollstra is not going to do Germany much good in these days."[41] Others understood its threat: a trade representative sent to explore German Wollstra factories and textile markets reported back to Australia that German wool imports were likely to decline sharply.[42]

Amid these trade impediments, the German Chamber of Commerce urged its members to socialize with Australian woolgrowers and politicians, hoping to promote a German-Australian bilateral trade deal.[43] Within this strained political climate, a friendship developed between Eberhard Noltenius, a German wool buyer, and the Mackay family of Wallendbeen Station. Noltenius, born in 1908, was a relative by marriage of the Lohmann and Waldthausen families. He came to Australia in 1931 to work for Lohmann & Co. A series of letters from Noltenius to Agnes Mackay (born 1898), daughter of Major General Kenneth Mackay, provide a window into a relationship born of the global wool trade that reveals the inner workings of that business. Eberhard and Agnes first crossed paths in October 1931, shortly after he met her father. He was soon regularly buying Wallendbeen Station wool via her brother-in-law, Aldred Baldry.

Despite the global depression, Eberhard socialized with wool buyers from other nations, including Japan: attending parties, horseback riding, and playing tennis. His letters to Agnes in 1932 and early 1933 attest to Germany's active wool buying: "We have been extremely busy all last week," "Baldry wool has got the best prices in the market and is headed for Germany," and "the world seems more unsettled than ever, but here the people are mad after wool."[44] But as the Nazi government's rules began to bite, Eberhard complained "in spite of the good wool prices, business is very difficult for us."[45] Germany had been buying about 13 percent of the Australian wool clip, but in early 1934 imports crashed to barely a third of that.[46] German wool imports were lower for several years in the mid-1930s, and German exports to Australia rose, but despite German lobbying, a free-trade agreement never materialized. While no letters between Agnes and Eberhard survive from 1934 and 1935, her passport and subsequent correspondence show that she visited Germany for more than two months in the second half of 1935, and met Eberhard in Berlin during that time, presumably while he was spending the northern hemisphere summer in Germany consulting with Lohmann's clients.

* * *

Rising geopolitical tensions in the 1930s affected other Australian wool trade relationships. Japan's use of raw wool more than tripled between 1923 and 1932, placing Japan second only to Britain as a client for Australian wool, and wool second only to cotton in Japan's raw material imports.[47] Despite getting only the dregs of Australian wool during World War I, Japan was a rising client. *Just Wool*, the 1933 newsreel, featured several Japanese wool buyers, and noted that "sheep running in an Australian paddock today may furnish next winter's overcoat for a merchant in Manchester or a tailor in Tokyo."[48] Japan's invasion of Manchuria in 1931 and the increasing tendency of Japanese men to wear European-style business suits drove this trade.

Japan encouraged sheep raising in the occupied zone of its puppet state of Manchukuo. In 1934, the Australian government started negotiating a treaty of "Friendship, Commerce and Navigation" with Japan, sending foreign minister J. G. Latham with a delegation to explore Japan's wool industry. Latham's report described Manchukuo wool as "almost resembling a hemp fiber," often adulterated with sand and rocks, and unlikely to threaten Australia's wool primacy.[49] Ian Clunies Ross, a Japanese-speaking Australian scientist, reported back from his (quite openly intelligence-gathering) 1936 trip to China, Manchukuo, Korea, and Japan that Manchukuo wasn't suited climatically to sheep, nor were the indigenous people interested in becoming sheep herders.[50] This was good news to the Australians, who felt their Japanese wool market was thus assured.

But as with Germany, trade, political, and eventually military tensions bedeviled this market. Japan had been producing cotton at prices well below those of Manchester, UK—the traditional center of cotton textiles—from the 1920s, becoming the world's largest cotton fabric exporter. By the mid-1930s, Japan had also moved decisively into rayon production. Its exports of cotton and rayon to Australia more than tripled between 1932 and 1935, despite the tariffs Australia imposed under the Ottawa agreement. The Latham report was confident that wool exports ensured a favorable trade balance with Japan, but Britain's expectation of controlling its Dominions' trade complicated matters. In 1933, the UK government asked Australia to restrict imports of Japanese rayon and cotton, to protect British textile exports. Australia resisted until 1936, when Britain threatened to curb imports of Australian beef.

Tensions over commodities and territories collided, disrupting the wool trade. Another of Ian Clunies Ross's 1936 observations was that wool was everywhere replacing cotton and silk for both traditional and western style clothing. Of Manchukuo, he wrote, "In the capital, Hsingking, today one sees civil servants, police, and soldiers, all wearing woolen uniforms, whereas prior to the establishment of the present regime cotton or silk garments were almost universally worn."[51] Perhaps encouraged by this report, in May 1936, Australia demanded that Japan halve its exports of cotton and rayon. Despite its need for wool, Japan refused, and Australia substantially hiked tariffs on Japanese cotton and rayon. Japan responded by prohibiting imports of Australian wool and wheat and barring its wool buyers from Australian auctions. As the Australian wool auction season of 1936–1937 began, Eberhard told Agnes, "We are all very anxious to know what the Japanese are going to do and how it will affect the prices. It appears now that they won't be buying the first two month [sic]."[52]

Australian woolgrowers lobbied hard to protect their market, arguing against their government's tariffs. A confidential pamphlet distributed to woolgrowers quoted Melbourne University economics professor L. F. Giblin that "high prices for wool would not be nearly so effective in encouraging substitutes as the passionate national sentiment of a people devoted to taking each and every means to overcome their dependence on wool." Giblin also suggested that it was a poor time to pick a fight with Japan given that Australia was still so poorly defended. Graziers feared that Japanese buyers' absence from the wool auctions could drive down prices by as much as 20 percent. Foreshadowing an independent nationalism to come they also argued that Britain should be making its own industries more efficient "before Australians are required to place their staple industries in jeopardy."[53] Meanwhile, Clunies Ross engaged in "private diplomacy" with Shigeyoshi Hirodo, head of the Sydney branch of wool-buying firm Kanematsu, Ltd. At least one conversation, he wrote, was facilitated by "a very adequate dinner when both his utterances and my perception may have been slightly blurred."[54]

The Japanese embargo on Australian wool did not lower global wool prices because in the build-up again to war, wool was in demand. Japan bought its wool in South America and South Africa, but Germany and Britain bought heavily in Australia and overall prices held steady. Early in 1937, Eberhard noted "Prices for wool seem to rise higher and higher, making business very difficult for the buyers and very pleasant for the growers."[55] Eleven days earlier, Australia and Japan had reached a settlement whereby Japan agreed to buy more than 500,000 bales of wool each year in return for Australia dropping the harsh 1936 tariffs on Japanese rayon and cotton exports.[56] With the dispute resolved, in 1937 Australian Senator Guthrie told an international conference that he expected Australia to soon be exporting a million bales of wool annually to Japan.[57] This was never to be.

Japan invaded China the same year (the Second Sino-Japanese War) and, as woolgrowers had feared, Japan responded to wool supply chain problems by blending its own staple rayon with wool to stretch supplies. In early 1938, Japan sought to dial *down* expectations of how much Australian wool it needed, partly because of pressure from South Africa and South America to balance trade with them by buying wool. In a new trade agreement, Japan guaranteed to import at least 350,000 bales of Australian wool annually, in return for Australia taking an equivalent quantity of heavier weight staple rayon fiber.[58] Trade resumed on a slightly smaller scale than in the past, but in 1939 there were still more than 50 Japanese wool-trading houses operating across several Australian cities.

* * *

Sharp fluctuations in wool prices resulted in repeated discussions about coordinated wool marketing. Proposals for establishment of a joint wool board to help mitigate sharp fluctuations in wool prices received significant support from the smaller woolgrowers at both a 1925 international graziers' convention in Melbourne, Australia, and the 1931 Empire Wool Conference. Both were defeated, however, by coalitions of big graziers, wool buyers, wool brokers, banks, and most Bradford wool manufacturers.[59] In 1932 however, with wool prices so low that sales did not cover the cost of producing crossbred wool, the Australian federal government set up an Australian Wool Inquiry Committee. It recommended a government wool stockpile and limiting exports but was thwarted by the same coalition. After a short rally early in 1933, at about the time the *Just Wool* film was shot, prices again went steeply south. The Australian Woolgrowers' Council held back more than 200,000 bales from that year's clip from auctions to support prices.

Finding consensus about marketing wool to civilians was easier than manipulating its price, especially as the specter of rayon undercutting wool took shape alarmingly in the 1930s. The NSW graziers had set up a global "Use More Wool" campaign in May 1929, funded by a levy on woolgrowers and brokers.[60] By the mid-1930s, Australia, New Zealand, and South Africa each had national bodies working on improving wool's characteristics through research and its reach through marketing.[61] In 1937, these nations established an International Wool Publicity and Research Secretariat (IWS), based in London, chaired by Ian Clunies Ross, and funded by a levy on woolgrowers. Bradford manufacturers never joined the IWS, collectively wary that their raw wool supplies would rise in price. Instead, they were talking to Courtaulds UK about producing blended fabrics of rayon and wool.[62]

Despite its name, the IWS emphasized science and research more than publicity, partly because wool was massively outgunned by rayon interests in terms of advertising dollars. Researching improvements to wool fiber, addressing its susceptibility to shrinkage and moth damage, took place in a laboratory near Leeds in the UK. Accurate labelling was a key focus, so that labels such as "all wool" and "wool" could only be used when minimally blended with other fibers. It was probably lucky that the IWS did not focus too much on marketing wool fashions. With the drums of war again beating, fashion's part of wool's position in the panoply of global textiles would soon be sidelined, with civilians again asked to accept austerity and "making do and mending."[63] To add insult to injury, once war began, and despite strenuous objections from the IWS, the British Board of Trade allowed up to 85 percent of non-wool fibers in fabrics marketed to civilians as "wool." But the full impact of the rise of rayon, along with the first appearance of fully synthetic fibers, was masked by a great surge of demand for wool caused by impending war.

* * *

As war approached wool sales boomed. Although in 1936–1937 Japanese wool manufacturers had ventured into the US market, sending sample menswear fabrics for sale to the garment trade, ultimately Japan's war with China made wool too important domestically to invest in expanding its export markets.[64] Germany, Japan, and the United States were all buying crossbred medium wools as heavily as possible, both in New Zealand and in South America, with Uruguay and Argentina again the most prolific producers. German buyers were also active in South Africa, buying up about 40 percent of that country's raw wool from the 1938–1939 season.[65]

Paradoxically, while wool sales boomed, in many nations—notably the United States—rapidly increasing populations were actually using *less* wool per person. The fluctuating American market responded to changing tariff laws and new standards of living, including central heating. This translated into the overall quantity of wool used in the United States remaining fairly static, but decreasing imports of fine wools, now finding competition from substitutes. This decline greatly concerned Australian woolgrowers. Australia's Trade Commissioner in Canada sent a very comprehensive and confidential report to the Canberra government in March 1938 recommending that "in view of the importance of wool to Australia, it may be worthy of consideration for the Commonwealth Government to establish a close official unobtrusive surveillance through the New York Office just as the interests of the Australian dried fruit industry are 'observed' in Canada."[66] For a nation "riding the sheep's back" wool-related espionage was becoming essential.

Woolgrowers were right to be anxious. In March 1939, an American woolen industry journal reported that manufacturers were requesting that Depression-era wage controls be reviewed, and the minimum wage in woolen mills be reduced to that offered in cotton and rayon mills. They argued that lower foreign wages were making American cloth less competitive in price, with competition also coming "from rayon, the consumption of which has exceeded the use of apparel wool for three years."[67] Equally distressing was the rapid growth of ready-made clothing, which was changing the dynamics of the textile trade. Instead of appealing directly to consumers, including "small tailors and dressmakers," textile manufacturers were becoming beholden to the garment trades, who "almost appear to issue mandates" regarding pricing and materials.[68]

At the same time, the Bradford, Yorkshire, wool buyers and mills were being shut out of the South American markets, with one industry observer noting "we, with an Empire producing the bulk of the world's wool, have found access to it remarkably difficult."[69] The fear that Yorkshire's mills would be idle for lack of raw material while other nations took over Britain's textile export trade had influenced the UK's actions regarding wool during World War I. It would arouse similar responses in the late 1930s.

In 1937–1938, Frederick Booth built a nine-story modernist building in central Sydney, close to Reiby Place where the city's wool auctions were then held, and to Circular Quay from where wool was exported. The building accommodated his company offices along with wool buyers from myriad nations. Its shower rooms allowed wool buyers who spent mornings inspecting the bales of greasy, dirty wool they would later bid for, to change into suits, refreshed, for the afternoon auctions. At the building's opening the head of the NSW wool buyers paid tribute to

Booth, his optimism, and "the enterprise displayed . . . when the wool trade seemed to be surrounded by impenetrable gloom."[70]

Globally, despite increasing consumer demand for new clothing as the Depression eased, wool's recovery was largely due to military contracts using crossbred wools. French woolen manufacturers were already busy with army contracts in early 1939. Civilian production, and demand for fine wools, languished.[71] A new wartime product line emerged during 1939, as the import of aerial bombing campaigns in Spain, Ethiopia, and China was absorbed: black woolen fabrics suitable for blackout blinds and curtains.[72] In June of that year, America's First Lady Eleanor Roosevelt and Britain's Queen Elizabeth met in Washington, DC, each clothed in a dress of special lightweight "Thermos Wool" fabric: the Queen's made by English designer Norman Hartnell of Forstmann Woolen Co. cloth, given by American woolgrowers; Mrs. Roosevelt's by American designer Clare Potter from fabric woven by John Emsley, Bradford, of wool from Australia, New Zealand, South Africa, and Canada.[73] The promotional value of this exchange, highlighting wool's value in comfortably transitioning from the summer heat of Washington to the air-conditioned White House, was overshadowed by politics: not until mid-August did the news make its way to Australasian newspapers.[74]

In the later 1930s, Germany bought huge quantities of Australian wool, shifting the balance of trade back toward Australia.[75] The Noltenius-Mackay correspondence reflected the quickening pace and sharpening tensions of the wool trade. In May 1937, Eberhard reported that "I never worked so hard in my life before . . . because Germany decided to buy an enormous quantity of wool." One of his old bosses from Lohmann's tried to help but had heart attacks from the stress.[76] In July Eberhard reported a month of hugely busy sales in Brisbane, in September volatile prices, and observed that "nobody seems to know what will happen with the unsettled state of the world."[77]

New technologies lightened his "extremely busy" workload. Early in 1938, in Brisbane for the wool auctions, Eberhard reported "we are the biggest buyer this sale."[78] He had bought his first car in Sydney and in March 1938 flew to Brisbane rather than catch a train. Flying to a wool auction nearly a thousand kilometers north of Sydney made Eberhard an early but not the earliest adopter. The year before, a small Stinson airplane had crashed into jungle on the border of NSW and Queensland. Several passengers died but the survivors included Joseph Binstead, a wool buyer flying between Sydney and Brisbane—under a pseudonym because his wife did not trust plane travel.[79]

Later that year Eberhard wrote that "political events . . . did not leave too much the life comfortable [sic] . . . and I had a few nasty experiences." He thought he would soon be required to return to Germany on Lohmann and Co. business and wanted to fly; his employer preferred him to catch the usual leisurely steamship. That trip was postponed, and he was sent instead to India on unexplained company business, possibly related to the pressure on Lohmann's to build German export income. In October 1938, just after the Munich crisis, he "never in my life before felt so miserable," until British Prime Minister Neville Chamberlain announced, "Peace in our time" with Hitler, and Eberhard professed his "greatest admiration."[80] The world hurtled toward trouble; Eberhard's personal and professional lives would never be the same.

The lengths that Germany would go to get wool, echoing the previous war, were displayed in late 1938. Germany forcibly annexed Czechoslovakia's Sudetenland, defining all Sudeten stocks of "wool and cotton commodities" as "installations" and transferring them to German ownership. The Czechs disagreed that textile stocks were permanent installations. Britain offered some support but ultimately deferred to the decision of the "International Commission formed to give effect to the Munich agreement."[81] In the end it was a moot point. Hitler abrogated the Munich Agreement, occupying the remainder of Czechoslovakia in March 1939, thus acquiring that nation's formidable manufacturing capacity *and* its textile stocks.

In Agnes and Eberhard's early correspondence, there are occasional intimations of romance but from November 1937 his are a suitor's letters, ending "I am yours; Ever; Eberhard."[82] By March 1939 Eberhard knew he would soon sail to Europe on Lohmann company business, believing it "will be an unpleasant trip from a business perspective" and "nobody seems to see better prospects for the near future."[83] He left for Europe in April, clearly feeling divided loyalties. He never explained his "unpleasant" business but between May and July 1939 he visited Italy, Sweden, France, Belgium, and London and Bradford in England for Lohmann, traveling quickly by car and by airplane. Eberhard's close ties to the family were clear when he told Agnes, "Unfortunately I had no time to see Kenneth." Agnes's nephew, Kenneth Baldry, was then in England training for the Royal Air Force. The pressures of business compromised Eberhard's health and a Bremen doctor advised "something drastic for my intestines." He spent three weeks in a sanitarium in the Bavarian alps at Berchtesgaden, Germany,[84] coincidentally the mountain eyrie associated with Hitler and Eva Braun.

Eberhard was determined to get back to Australia and to Agnes before war broke out, despite knowing the likely consequences of his imminent enemy alien status. He flew to Australia in late August 1939 on an eight-day trip via Batavia, Indonesia, arriving just before war was declared between Australia and Germany, September 1, 1939.[85] He was arrested three days later, and, as he fully expected, interned.

* * *

Wool was critical to British Empire victory in 1914–1918, but forces unleashed in that war continued to erode wool's place in the market so that the fiber lost the peace of the interwar period. Wool manufacturers and buyers such as Julius Forstmann, Frederick Booth, and Eberhard Noltenius rode the highs and lows of the interwar market, but theirs was a business on edge. Despite the rapid communications offered by telegraph and private business codes, and then by motorcars and airplanes, there was more happening in the world of textiles than anyone could readily keep track of.

Diplomatic relationships limited market growth when wool could have been consolidating its standing as a valuable textile. Woolgrowers formed an international organization representing their interests, but efforts to market the benefits of wool and to overcome its shortcomings were too little, too late. Wild fluctuations in the price of wool hampered both wool producers and textile manufacturers but helped substitutes for wool to gain ground as serious alternatives. Textile manufacturers, especially but not only in the wool "have not" nations, wanted continuous access to their raw material and saw possibilities in blending wool with other fibers. By the late 1930s, impending war meant that the wool market was again strong, but it had lost civilian market share to substantially cheaper semi-synthetic fibers that were not necessarily seen as inferior. Given the flaws of various substitutes for wool in the previous war, it's important to understand how rayon and especially its staple version came to threaten wool in the period between the two World Wars. That is where we will take you next.

Chapter 7

"Mary has two new dresses!"

Wally Lanagan, Dalby, Queensland, Australia, with a Japanese airman's flying suit brought home by his uncles as a war souvenir from New Guinea, 1945 (courtesy of Wally Lanagan and the Pioneer Park Museum, Dalby, Queensland, Australia).

Chapter 7

> It is nonsense to say or assume that artificial fibers do not compete with wool. They do and will to a very serious degree. Science does not stand still.
>
> Senator J. F. Guthrie, in a speech to the Geelong (Australia) Legacy Club[1]

In May 2019, on a research trip to western Queensland, we stopped at the Dalby Pioneer Park Museum to consult with one of the local historians about some land in the area with a long-ago family connection for Trish. Once there, however, we pottered about the sprawling compound, finally making our way into what was called the Military Shed. And lucky that we did. From the jumble of artifacts in the shed, most of them Australian military uniforms with minimal labeling, one piece drew us in. A deep green flying suit was draped on a rattan coat hanger, a sheet of paper with some typed donor information clipped to the front. A Japanese airman's coverall, lent to the museum in the early 2000s by the nephew of two Australian infantrymen who brought it home from New Guinea as a souvenir at the end of World War II. Even behind the dusty glass of the display case we noticed the fabric had an odd sheen that begged examination.

The caretaker/manager graciously unlocked the case and allowed us to remove the suit. We opened it gingerly, not expecting a handy "Fiber Content" label inside, but the textile's sheen and its smooth but not slick surface suggested that it was a blend of rayon and wool, and probably a fine merino wool, at that. A cloth label affixed inside the front chest was printed with Japanese characters.[2]

Why was the suit a blend, we wondered? Especially a blend with rayon? Wouldn't a flight suit need to be warmer and more flame-resistant than rayon? A teaser of an object, one that would introduce us to the concept and place of "Autarchy" in both the global wool trade and wool's increasingly popular competitor, rayon. A dictionary synonym for autocracy and absolutism, autarchy in the context of 1930s authoritarian governments meant economic nationalism: a nation's ability to create products from its own resources rather than depending on international supply chains, which were (and are) a feature of the textile industries. Autarchy was not just about textiles, but textiles, particularly rayon, were significant to its development in Italy, Germany, and Japan. A similar, but rather less strident, philosophy emerged in nations such as the United States and France, conjured by the lingering memory of wartime wool shortages, heightened by the economic dislocation of the Great Depression. While rebuilding tariff walls on imports to protect their own industries, and workers, from competition, they explored blends with natural fibers such as wool.

The fact that the suit was clearly partially made of wool, although wool was not among Japan's primary products, did not surprise us. We knew that Japan's initial government-supported 1880s mill had by 1924 become 42 mills operated by private industry. This had reduced Japan's reliance on imports of woolen textiles, but vastly increased Japan's reliance on Australia for raw wool.[3] In fact, in an interview with Wally Lanagan shortly after we had first seen the flying suit in Dalby, he told us that "Dad always said that 'it's made out of Australian wool'" although Wally added, "and I thought that was just a joke because you couldn't see how the Japanese would get hold of Australian wool during the war."[4]

The other fiber that we presumed to be used in the suit, rayon, was increasingly in common civilian use internationally in the 1920s and 1930s. Until the mid-1930s, rayon was mostly considered a threat to silk; indeed, one chapter in the 1929 book *Labor & Silk*, by labor and women's rights activist Grace Hutchins is devoted to rayon. Hutchins and her life partner Anna Rochester had visited textile mills across Europe and in the Soviet Union in 1927. She was so impressed by the Soviet mills that she became a staunch Communist, her labor activism having thoroughly soured her opinion of capitalism. A chart included in her book shows a spaghetti-tangle of lines indicating cross-linked transnational ownership among rayon companies.[5] When the Japanese flying suit came to our attention, we began to wonder how those relationships functioned—or didn't—in the 1930s and during World War II.

So, while we were aware that rayon was in production and use around the world by the 1930s, neither of us knew when we visited Dalby the extent to which Germany, Italy, and Japan—the Axis powers of World

War II—had incorporated rayon into their standard military textiles, and worked to make rayon/wool and rayon/cotton mixed fabrics the norm for civilian use. The Japanese flying suit led us to the answer to one big question: since the substitutes used in World War I were acknowledged as failures, and access to wool was *still* a problem, either due to a troubled peace or a new war, then what? Well, technology did not stand still during the 1920s and 1930s. Rayon, particularly in its "staple" form, became the most important milestone in those decades along the path of synthetic fibers' eventual triumph in the marketplace, and the not entirely coincidental triumph of fast fashion.

Rayon, as we've seen, had begun to find its place in the civilian textile fiber market just before World War I, but played a vanishingly small military role in that war. Not until post-war did the industry become a major player in the textile world, partly because in both its manufacturing processes and finished forms, rayon had its growing pains. In addition, the industry was patent-reliant and tightly controlled by international—and interconnected—capital. While the wool industry, both in its raw material and manufacturing phases, was a creature of close international family and business relationships, rayon was much less a family affair, its operations more corporate and anonymous. To give rayon its rightful place as a threat to wool, we'll first continue our look at its development, then move to the structure of the industry and its place in international trade.

* * *

Of the four different manufacturing processes that each make a slightly different version of the regenerated cellulose fiber we call rayon—Viscose, Cuprammonium, Acetate, and Nitrocellulose—only the first three survived the economic chaos of 1914–1918 ready to test the interwar market. Nitrocellulose had the distinct disadvantage of being very flammable. Efforts to "de-nitrate" it, in addition to making it less flammable also made it weaker. Unsurprisingly, it was rarely produced by the 1920s.[6]

Because rayon can be used as it comes from the mill, without any of the preparatory processes necessary with natural fibers, it was not only cheaper as a raw material, it lowered labor costs downstream for the yarn and textile manufacturers who used it. Global rayon production grew, from 40 million pounds in 1919 to 285 million pounds in 1928.[7] In its original slick, shiny filament form, however, when woven or knitted and made up into clothing, the fabric tended to slip and pull open at seams, and fray when cut. Rayon had less than half the strength of real silk when dry and was even weaker wet—about one-fifth the strength. It was subject to stretching or shrinkage when laundered or dry-cleaned, and it wrinkled easily. So, until the later 1920s it was used mostly as a secondary fiber in fabrics where shine was an asset: the pile in a woman's velvet evening wrap, a stripe or geometric pattern in a man's cotton shirt, a jacquard-woven figure in a light woolen cloth for an afternoon frock. For rayon to become a serious competitor, as a stand-alone textile, its problems had to be solved.

What made the problem-solving worthwhile? Although in the early days it was not significantly less expensive than silk, locally produced rayon removed those nasty supply chain worries about shipping raw silk from Asia, or bad weather affecting the silkworms and the mulberry trees that fed them, and therefore the quantity and quality of the silk filaments produced. By the mid-1920s prices started to come down, and as that trend continued, when shine and slickness were not liabilities, rayon began to be woven or knitted into fabric on its own, primarily imitating silk.

Until about 1927, when chemists figured out how to dim the luster and give the yarns a matte finish—albeit not yet permanently—rayon wasn't a threat to wool or cotton. By 1930, though, rayon staple, also called staple fiber, had entered the market. The term staple refers to fiber length, which in wool and cotton are measured in inches or centimeters rather than in tens or hundreds of yards or meters. Rayon staple was simply rayon filaments, cut to a customer's specification, then spun into yarns more closely resembling cotton or wool, or mixed with those fibers during spinning. The matte-finish yarns could also be woven or knitted together with cotton or wool yarns. Adding rayon to other fibers lessened the cost of production and was not always detrimental to the fabric or deliberately fraudulent. But the practice was also not necessarily highlighted in advertising. Rayon's drawbacks continued to loom large.

Those problems were not confined to its physical properties. Rayon mills profited greatly from the fact that its manufacturing processes required less skilled labor than other fibers. In the United States, since the industry was new and its facilities purpose-built, the rayon mills tended to be in states hostile both to labor unions and to government regulation of working conditions such as daily or weekly hour limits, overtime pay, and child labor. Several rayon companies followed silk textile industry analyst James Chittick's 1913 advice to companies that could function without high-skills labor: to seek out locations for new mills in coal mining areas such as Pennsylvania and West Virginia, where male employment was precarious and miners' wives and children were eager for any work, no matter how wretchedly paid.[8]

Grace Hutchins penned another pamphlet, *Women Who Work* in 1932, at the height of the Great Depression. She cited statistics claiming that 50 to 60 percent of US rayon workers were women, many of them younger than 20, and in the southern and Appalachian mills, the low wages they earned dragged down men's wages too. Working conditions were abysmal, both in terms of safety and in terms of what's known as "speed-up" or "stretching-out" in manufacturing, whereby employees were given higher quotas and/or more machines to tend, while still having their pay docked for flaws in the product or stoppages to fix problems with the machinery.[9]

Piling misery on misery, the rayon manufacturing processes, particularly for viscose, relied (and still relies) on chemicals poisonous both to workers and the environment. Workers suffered from vision and respiratory problems, headaches, fainting spells, and a host of other neurological symptoms. This was known by the mid-1920s, but largely suppressed and ignored. Efforts by occupational medicine specialist Dr. Alice Hamilton in the 1930s to hold US viscose manufacturing firms to account for the serious health problems facing many of their workers were largely smothered by big profits and the lure of self-sufficiency.[10] During World War II, Germany's rayon industry relied heavily on enslaved labor. Agnès Humbert's 2004 memoir, *Resistance Memoirs of Occupied France,* detailed her wartime forced labor and the total disregard for workers' health in the Phrix rayon factory (Phrix Uerdingen) in Krefeld, Germany. Phrix was a subsidiary of a Dutch-German rayon cartel that linked Dutch Enka and German VGF. German wartime experiments with formaldehyde-based finishes for rayon fabric to limit shrinkage and wrinkling may also have contributed to workers' health problems.[11]

All of this was buried beneath relentless positive public relations campaigns, funded by and on behalf of manufacturers, and in the overtly autarchic countries by government agencies as well. The abiding conceit was that rayons were not inferior silks, but wonderful new, modern, fibers, fully as useful as any other.[12] Manufacturers knew this was not actually true. Textile industry trade journals regularly detailed rayon's flaws and how to try and fix them, even as rayon fiber and textile companies were promising consumers that their products were, to quote Mary Poppins, "practically perfect in every way." Mills found that machinery couldn't always be run at full speed: rayon yarns might develop flaws called "shiners" under too much tension on the loom. The first "delustering" processes were ephemeral, vanishing with the touch of an iron or cleaning fluid. Another ubiquitous trade journal advertiser, the Onyx Oil & Chemical Company, promoted its "Fiba-Weld" resin finish from mid-1937 to solve common complaints about rayon fabrics: seams pulling apart, cut edges fraying, excessive creasing or shrinkage, and spotting in the rain. (Contemporary textile trade journals still carry advertisements for new corrective finishes for rayon yarns and fabrics.)

Complaints about rayon did not feature prominently in English-language newspapers and popular magazines of the 1920s and 1930s, which earned significant advertising revenue from the fashion industries.[13] One prescient article, though, is uncannily relevant to how we have learned to consume fashion. "False Bargains Betray Us," written by Earnest Elmo Calkins (1868–1964), an advertising executive known as an innovator in the field, chided consumers for choosing price over quality: "We sowed the wind of careless shopping; we are reaping the whirlwind of shoddy goods." He gave three examples of the "vocabulary of aspersion" about clothing and textiles: shoddy (in its post-Civil War meaning of poor quality) for "fabrics mysteriously manipulated to make them seem better than they are," while "dreck" and "schlag" describe women's and men's clothing of poor materials, skimpily cut, and poorly sewn, "Made to sell rather than wear."[14] We couldn't have said it better ourselves.

In 1931, the American Viscose Company, maker of Crown Rayon, lauded the efforts of the United States's National Retail Dry Goods Association (NRDGA) to establish "scientific retail buying" through quality testing, saying that 52 percent of dress returns were due to "fabric faults [of] fading, shrinking, stretching, bleeding, splitting and slipping" rather than garment faults.[15] Just a year later, American Viscose offered its own "Crown Rayon Tested Quality" label to users of its yarns whose products passed the tests the NRDGA proposed, a plan applauded by E. E. Calkins. Five years later, Courtaulds, North American Rayon, and American Bemberg followed suit. Opposing them was British Celanese, which tersely called fabric testing pointless, for "if economic conditions are such that the public demand light and cheap fabric qualities . . . then this demand must be met by British manufacturers, or the necessary goods will be obtained from abroad."[16] It seems that while rayon yarns and products differed widely in quality, even the best wasn't perfect.

Perhaps one real danger in using 100 percent rayon fabrics, with no tempering addition of wool, was being suppressed. In February 1939, Edith E. Cox of Cleethorpes, England, wrote to Australia's Prime Minister, enclosing her appeal to the UK Parliament in favor of clothing made of wool over clothing made of rayon. She asked for "your kindness to pass to Australian woolgrowers associations the enclosure." She stressed the flammability hazards of rayon, saying "Women and woolgrowers need mutual support," and that giving women back their woolen dresses "would save many a life in peace time and should war come, grave disaster."[17] Rayon, like other cellulose fibers, is flammable, acetate rayon especially so. Scientists had been experimenting with flameproofing fabrics from the early nineteenth century, when open flames for heating and lighting made this a rather urgent priority. Progress was slow, however, especially for clothing fabrics. Where open fires had not been replaced by central heating, rayon clothing that would previously have been made from wool might have increased the risk of burn injuries, though our searches in online newspaper archives have not so far unearthed such stories.

With Rayon 101 under our belts, we can look at the entwined corporate and national histories that made rayon the first link in the decline of natural fibers after the rest of World War I's myriad substitutes faded away.

* * *

As early in rayon's development as 1910 manufacturers, not just in Britain and the United States, but also Germany, France, Belgium, and Switzerland, were working quite cozily together, across national borders. A corporate history of Courtaulds from 1941 boasted that "chemistry is a brotherhood that knows no boundaries of nationality." This notion was epitomized by the industry's formal "consortium of viscose yarn spinners" organized in 1911, to "facilitate exchanges of visits and technical information, the pooling of markets, and other projects."[18] A cartel, or medium for price-fixing and restricting competition, in all but name.

This cozy collaboration largely evaporated when war was declared in August 1914. Courtaulds' Russian subsidiary "disappeared" during the war and subsequent revolution. Its UK plants faced the same wartime problems as the rest of the textile industry: male workers (perhaps most importantly machinery repair technicians) becoming soldiers, female workers leaving to replace men in other jobs, and limited supplies of the machine parts and chemicals necessary to make the fiber. The same applied on the European continent, magnified by the devastation of warfare and occupation.

In the United States, however, insulated from wartime problems first by its neutrality, and after it entered the war in 1917 by its self-sufficiency in cellulose and certain chemicals, American Viscose Co. did not suffer. On the contrary, as the nation's sole rayon manufacturer, it earned record profits selling artificial silk to the civilian market, where it was used in combination with silk, cotton, and wool.[19] This released larger supplies of those fibers for the essential military textiles that American industry was supplying to both the United States and the Allies.

No nation in 1914–1918 considered sending soldiers to war clad in fabric made solely, or even partly, from shiny, slick, clammy rayon, although the Central Powers experimented with blending small amounts of it with other fibers. But since during those years pretty much the whole industrialized world had felt the effects of textile fiber shortages and trade disruptions, in the early 1920s companies in the UK, the United States, Europe, and Japan committed enormous resources to the chemistry of man-made fibers to minimize future problems, whether there was a war or not.[20]

After the war, the rayon industry immediately reverted to its roots: big international capital and interlocking ownership, convoluted enough to make your head spin. When the first viscose process patents expired in 1920, new American companies were organized and British Celanese (whose owners were Swiss), Germany's VGF and Bemberg, and Dutch Enka all opened American subsidiaries. Courtaulds' and VGF together bought a controlling interest in Italy's Snia Viscosa. Germany's chemical and dye industry giant, I.G. Farben, invested in VGF and Bemberg. E.I. DuPont de Nemours' Fibersilk subsidiary, operational in 1921, was an international player by the late 1920s with ties to Japan's Mitsui Corporation.

In 1927, the management of Courtaulds, VGF, Snia Viscosa, Enka, and some French firms came to a formal agreement to control prices, markets, and research. This layered spider web of investors/partners and companies collectively produced between 80 and 90 percent of the world's rayon.[21] One economist observed in 1930 that

> *Rayon is a man-machine-made fiber and its production may be controlled even from day to day. . . . Further the production of rayon is centered in the hands of relatively very few producers. . . . Rayon production, then, is susceptible to the closest production control of any of the major textile fibers.*[22]

The rayon industry was among those studied for a US Department of Commerce report on international cartels in 1928—along with the chemical industry, with which rayon was "closely allied."[23]

Despite its many flaws, rayon fibers, yarns, and fabrics increased production and market share every year. By 1934, Celanese could advertise a "Permanently Dull Yarn," recommending it for use with wool, since it didn't need "piece delustering" after weaving to make the rayon surface match the woolen one, a chemical process that damaged the wool.[24] At the same time, of course, the new finish made it harder to tell if a fabric sold as "wool" also contained rayon. Demand for staple rayon pushed world production from under 10 million pounds in 1931 to 134 million pounds in 1935. That would triple by 1939, led by Italian, German, Japanese, and American firms.[25] Rayon was a very lucrative product, not only for the fiber manufacturer but for the fabric manufacturer who could use it to cut costs without sharing that information with consumers.

As rayon output increased and its price continued to drop, some woolgrowers began to pay attention. One persistent voice, Australian Senator, woolgrower, and advocate J. F. Guthrie, often admonished the wool industry for its complacence. He was dedicated to supporting Australia's pastoral industry, and to promoting the use of wool worldwide. His letters and opinion pieces appeared in trade journals and newspapers in Australia, the United States, and the UK. One pamphlet, titled *Sniafil's Challenge to Wool,* probably from about 1927, essentially told woolgrowers "ignore rayon at your peril."[26] In 1930, Harold Thorby, Australian Minister of Agriculture, exhibited skeins of "wood fiber" in the Commonwealth Legislative Assembly, saying that "you cannot tell it from wool tops." A member of the legislature objected, saying "there is no warmth in it," to which Thorby sounded an exasperated warning, "No, but it is being utilised on an extensive scale in the making of fabrics."[27]

* * *

As international tensions rose again in the 1920s and 1930s, textiles and politics were again increasingly overtly intertwined. Economic sanctions against Italy and Japan followed their respective incursions into Ethiopia and China. Germany was still struggling with reparations payments, currency instability, and lack of export commodities. Rayon supplied these countries' textile and garment manufacturers with stable—both in price and availability—supplies of cheap raw materials. But this was cloaked in the rhetoric of patriotism: rayon's use in the country it was made in conserved hard currency and encouraged self-sufficiency: the much to be desired state of autarchy.

Italy was the first proponent of autarchy as it emerged from the economic rubble of World War I. Mussolini, in power in Italy from 1922, said in 1930 "an Italian style in furnishings, interior decoration and clothing . . . must come into existence now."[28] This push for economic self-sufficiency was extended to many products and spheres in addition to textiles and design, including architecture, minerals, and fuels. Man-made fibers, primarily rayon made from Italian reeds and imported wood or wood pulp, became central to both the economy and the design culture of the nation.

The Società di Navigazione Italo-Americana (SNIA) was founded in 1917 as a shipping company but transformed in the 1920s to become Società nazionale industria e applicazioni, with viscose rayon its main product. From 1926, the company introduced "Sniafil" branded dull-finished rayon filament as a substitute for wool. An Australian wool man visiting Europe that year disparaged the effort, reporting that "the fiber has not the characteristics of real wool—it is merely artificial silk without its lustre."[29] In 1927, the firm faced bankruptcy and was bought up by two foreign competitiors, Courtaulds and VGF, which shared technology with the Italian firm but also controlled its output and pricing. The fascist regime initially approved the takeover, coveting the technical knowhow, but decided in 1930 that SNIA's management should be Italian, even if ownership was not. A neon sign, "Autarchia," hung over the company's main factory building in the 1930s. Demonstrating the Mussolini regime's keen interest in rayon, from 1933 the Italian government owned Châtillon, a small domestic rayon producer.[30]

Italy's low wage rates supported development of a middling-quality rayon export trade, primarily to India and China. SNIA remained the main Italian rayon exporter, in 1935 introducing Sniaflocco, a dull-finished staple rayon to mix with cotton or wool. The domestic market for rayon was small until Italy's invasion of Ethiopia (1935–1937) required reducing imports to conserve hard currency, and reserving cotton and wool for the military.

Getting Italian consumers to embrace rayon, however, required assiduous marketing. The Italian government set up the Ente Nazionale della Moda (National Fashion Corporation) to extol rayon's Autarchic virtues throughout the country. In May 1934, a convoy of trucks emblazoned with the word Rayon and equipped with loudspeakers set off on a tour of Italy, blaring poems such as this one by a futurist poet, Luciano Folgore:

Hercules one day became obsessed
Because in Nessus' hairshirt he was dressed
yet if his tunic had been rayon instead
With envy he would have knocked 'em dead.[31]

At each destination the trucks transformed into an exhibition hall for rayon products, while Modernist visions of rayon fashions were projected onto a screen. At the same time newspapers began to carry full-page advertisements such as one from December 1935: "All-Italian products strengthen our resistance: Rayon is an Italian textile." The fact that the underlying cellulose was likely imported from Scandinavia was not mentioned.[32]

Italy's other semi-synthetic Autarchic fiber, Lanital, was, like rayon, man-made from a naturally occurring substance. The name combines *Lana* (wool) and *Italia*. Chemically derived from the milk protein casein, it was, like rayon, mechanically extruded in a process patented in 1935 by Antonio Ferretti. An Irish newspaper, about a year later, gave a tongue-in-cheek report on this, "Unable to export her gorgonzola cheese owing to sanctions. Italy is converting the casein in her surplus milk into a substitute for wool."[33] The article continued that tests were going to be conducted by UK textile scientists, but there was doubt as to whether Lanital was actually a threat to British Empire wool. And indeed, Lanital had problems: it was weak and, rather unfortunately, smelled like sour milk when it got wet.

Propaganda efforts increased as war loomed. In 1936, the national government mandated blending rayon with natural fibers in fabrics for civilians. In 1938, the Italian National Textile Exhibition focused on *Autarchia Tessile*. Marinetti—the futurist leader who had helped to draft the Italian fascist manifesto—wrote florid illustrated poems for Snia Viscosa exalting Lanital, rayon, and viscose rayon's manufacturing process as nature improved. In 1940, he published the three poems together, lauding the "dynamism, autonomy and creativity of the SNIA VISCOSA Corporation . . . dedicated to the uniqueness of Imperial Fascist Italy."[34] Advertisments repeated this theme in endless variations.

* * *

The other European proponent of autarchy, Germany, had, as mentioned earlier, experimented with regenerated cellulose during World War I. The German word for cotton is "baumwolle"—literally, tree wool—while its word for staple rayon was "Zellwolle"—literally cell(ulose) wool. This can be read as evidence of the importance of sheep's wool in the history of German textile consumption, since everything coming after is compared to it, but between the two World Wars it also indicates how the Germans tried to sell staple rayon as a wool replacement, regardless of its actual properties. Filament rayon continued to be called artificial silk.

For several years after the 1918 Armistice, Germans were still able to buy the suits and other clothes and textiles made from the spun paper yarns that had been their last resort during the war. The economy was in disarray and consumer goods were scarce and costly, pushing German chemical and textile companies to intensify their research into man-made fiber technologies. Some advances were made in the 1920s, as I.G. Farben gobbled up competitors, incorporating their research into its own products. But perhaps because of the nature of the international rayon cartels, Germany's real splash in the international markets came about after 1933, when the Nazis came to power. The government's 1934 National Fiber Program imposed a huge increase in staple rayon production on the industry, more than 10 times previous levels. This too was in service of autarchy, since Germany imported all its cotton and much of its wool. Domestically produced rayon staple could replace these expensive imports, saving foreign exchange for the materials needed for war. In 1935, the government tried to impose restrictions on both imports and exports to conserve hard currency. Germany's two largest rayon producers, I.G. Farben and Glanzstoff, each with strong international ties, resisted these barriers to their international trade. As a result, the government began to support smaller, so-called regional rayon factories, at first in Germany, and eventually in Austria (annexed in 1938) and

Poland (occupied in 1939). These rapidly became a kind of domestic cartel, sharing researchers and research and company officers.[35]

As in Italy, the German government and textile industry put a lot of energy into persuading German consumers of the quality of Zellwolle. In one of those amazing instances of serendipity that have graced this project like confetti at a wedding, one of Trish's colleagues at Griffith University, Professor Regina Ganter, an eminent German-Australian historian who has helped us with translations from German documents, found a page from the newspaper *Der Führer*, dated January 21, 1938, lining a drawer in her mother's childhood home. At the very top of the page, an article titled "Truths and Falsehoods about Zellwolle" reported on a radio broadcast by the head of the department for raw materials and resources, President Kehrl. Just as in other countries whose consumers were not thrilled at having rayon thrust upon them in mandated blends with the natural fibers they knew and preferred, Germans, he said, held "wrong and senseless opinions" about Zellwolle, that he wished to correct. It was not "a desperate solution offered by German chemists in response to shortages of import materials." Rather, Zellwolle had been around since the late nineteenth century and German companies had been working constantly to improve it. Kehrl declared that Zellwolle was "as stable as wool, although not as stable as cotton," and that the recent government instructions on laundering were not targeting Zellwolle, they were "merely issued under the motto of 'war on wastage' so that any laundry items, whether cotton or linen, are treated correctly." He chided those who spread "ill-intentioned rumours to worry the populace," and reproached his listeners, saying that "all users, sales assistants and manufacturers should make it a point of honour to participate in the popularisation of a raw material which significantly contributes to German raw material freedom."[36]

It was not just propaganda. German chemists were hard at work in the field of man-made fibers. A 1937 textbook for the German industry, *Zellwolle: Kunstspinnfasern*, listed twelve different names (some of them foreign company brands, like Courtauld's Fibro and Snia Viscosa's Sniafiocco) for staple rayon then in use and production: Vistra, Flox, Cuprama, Phrix, Merinova, Telusa, Zehlawo, Aceta-Rhodia-Faser,

Drawinella, Sniafiocco, Fibro, Rayon Staple Fiber—and ended its list with an "etc." to show that this list was not all-encompassing.[37] Sample fabrics blending Tiolan, Germany's version of Italy's Lanital, with either wool or rayon staple in spinning yarns, were entering the marketplace. Skim milk, the raw material for extracting casein, was abundant in Germany and primarily used for animal feed.[38]

In the mid-1930s, the German press campaign selling its branded viscose-process staple rayon products Vistra and Woolstra became of great and general concern in the UK, Australia, New Zealand, and the United States. Starting in about 1934, articles with headlines like "Menace of Wool Substitutes" appeared in newspapers as disparate as the Lahore, India, *Civil & Military Gazette*; Britain's *Bradford Observer, Coventry Evening Telegram,* and *Caerphilly Journal;* Australia's *Sydney Morning Herald* and *Shepperton Advertiser;* New Zealand's *The Press*; and in the United States the *Boston Globe* and *La Opinion* in Los Angeles. At the same time, Australia's J.F. Guthrie's travels on wool industry business and his well-crafted speeches at meetings large and small, in rural Australia and cosmopolitan Paris and London, assured that he was constantly interviewed or quoted by journalists. Guthrie warned that although the new fibers could not match wool, wool's few but important shortcomings for the modern consumer (shrinkage and clothes moths) *must* be addressed for the continued health of the industry. He also recommended increased advertising to counteract the rayon cartel.[39] American rayon manufacturers spent the equivalent of £5 million a year on research and publicity during the 1930s, and Courtaulds UK spent about half a million in its much smaller market. Collectively the wool industry spent only in the tens of thousands of pounds.[40] Slowly but surely, advertising, price-cutting, and the cartel's cooperation on market share pushed rayon to the top of the fiber heap.

And so we circle back to Japan, and how the rayon in that flying suit in Dalby got there.

* * *

During and just after World War I, Japan had rapidly expanded into the global cotton textile trade and tested the markets for woolen textiles. The government had negotiated successfully for the necessary imports of cotton from the United States or India, and wool from the British Empire or South America, but the costs had been high and supplies uncertain and often of poor quality. The country's industrial giants (*Zaibatsu* or "enterprise groups"), notably Suzuki, Asahi, Mitsui, and Mitsubishi, responded by adding rayon production to their textile enterprises. Suzuki had been an early investor in 1915, but the early product was poor, and the rayon subsidiary, then named Teikoku Jinzo Kenshi Co., Ltd., only became profitable in 1923. German and British expertise and equipment assisted the others in entering the field in the later 1920s and early 1930s. By 1935, Japan was one of the top four rayon-producing nations, focusing on staple fiber.[41] By 1937, it had overtaken the United States as a producer and exporter of rayon yarns and fabrics, its international competitive advantage supported by the very low wages in Japan's textile industry. In 1935, this aroused Grace Hutchins, outraged by Japanese imperialism in China (and as a committed Communist, fearful of Japanese designs on Soviet territory in the Far East) to write another pamphlet, *Japan's Drive for Conquest.* It mentioned a possible strike by Japan's rayon workers, hoping to raise wages in the face of industry-wide poverty and the tight control exerted by the government and big industrialists.[42]

The trade in textiles was not the least of the tensions between Japan and the western nations in the 1930s. The United States increased tariffs on Japanese products in 1929 to protect its own industries; Japan had to work hard to replace that revenue. Japan's successive invasions of Manchuria in 1931, North China in 1933, and Eastern Manchuria in 1935 sharpened its need for hard currency from new export markets to purchase raw materials for its military expansion. Rayon was essential to this program, with about half the country's production exported. For one under-the-radar example, Canada's rayon textile imports from Japan rose from 273,000 yards in 1935 (about 10 percent of total rayon imports) to 2,964,000 yards in 1937 (about 36 percent of the total).[43] Japan was poor in textile fiber resources other than silk, so feeding rayon exports required raw material imports. Occupied Manchuria was touted as a potentially valuable source of cotton, wool, and cellulose pulp for both domestic and export textiles, but this never materialized.

Japan-Australia trade relations were quite the roller coaster ride during the 1930s. Japan's need to equip its expanded military for the war in China required both exporting its rayon *to* and importing wool *from* Australia. Australia in turn had to satisfy British textile manufacturers that their products would not suffer from Japanese competition. It refused to allow imports of rayon staple textiles that would compete with, or lessen consumer interest in wool, its most important export. Japan argued that it would have to replace Australian wool imports with its own staple rayons—or what might be worse, buy the required wool from Australia's competitors: South Africa and South America. In 1938, each side gave a little on the quotas they wanted, and the two nations adopted a "Textile/Wool Arrangement."[44] The year before, Japanese consumers, like their Italian and German counterparts not eager to adopt rayon, finally had no choice: the Japanese government mandated that varying percentages of rayon be added to all wool and cotton cloth. The percentage of rayon would increase over the next few years.[45]

* * *

Rayon had a different consumption arc in the United States, perhaps because the fiercely competitive US textile industry—with some notable exceptions—was largely geared to manufacturers making small profits on large quantities of middle-market goods. Woolen industry competition had often resulted in cost-cutting by the "adulteration" of virgin wool with either cheaper recycled wool (shoddy) or cotton, so the concept was established before rayon came along. Once the ready-to-wear clothing industry became dominant in the 1920s, however, textile manufacturers faced the challenge of new market forces: the ready-made clothing manufacturers and the large retail establishments that catered to mass market consumers. Instead of women buying fabric for a dress or suit from the textile hall in their local department store, then taking it to their local dressmaker to be made up, they were buying the garment ready-made from that same store. From the point of view of garment manufacturers and retailers, "styles in textiles are as perishable as vegetables" and they shied away from the kinds of large advance purchases that had previously sustained the textile industry.[46]

Newly important retail intermediaries edged the textile companies away from any direct relationship with the ultimate consumers of their goods. Retailers pressured clothing companies to reduce prices, and clothing companies forced down fabric prices, making cost-cutting in the textile industry a recurring cycle. As early as 1912, silk textile manufacturers had begun using rayon in their lines to reduce the stress of the roller-coaster raw-silk market. The stock market crash in October 1929 forced many of them to cut costs further by incorporating more rayon into their fabrics or even converting to rayon altogether. Once rayon staple emerged in 1930, cotton and wool manufacturers found themselves in the same boat as their silk counterparts. Both the rayon and ready-to-wear industries had expansive and well-funded public relations machines and used them relentlessly in the print media to promote the new fibers and fabrics. While the well-heeled might be able to demand and afford pure wool or pure silk fabrics, most consumers settled for the offerings in their price range. Rayon was introduced almost simultaneously into the least and most expensive textiles and clothing, and in everything in between, replacing or augmenting natural fibers.[47] Famed Paris couturiers appeared in magazine ads alongside their rayon creations, courtesy of the rayon yarn manufacturers, like Courtaulds, or Tubize, or Celanese, or DuPont. The ads don't reveal whether the couturiers were paid for their endorsements.

DuPont first entered the rayon field in 1921 when it opened its Fibersilk subsidiary. The company's enormous profits from its primary product, explosives, easily funded the years of research that went into developing new technologies and products, including fibers and dyes. Wallace Carothers led the company's polymer science research, beginning in 1928, with no particular end product in mind. This resulted first, in 1932, in neoprene, a synthetic rubber. After the 1934 publication of the book *Merchants of Death*, which inspired a US Senate investigation into munitions profiteers in World War I, DuPont embarked on a rebranding exercise, placing applied chemistry and textile fibers at the heart of its business plan.[48]

DuPont was not, as we've seen, the only US rayon manufacturer. American Viscose, the Courtaulds' auxiliary, was the largest in number of plants and output. But American Bemberg and Celanese Corporation of America—both European offshoots producing "other than viscose" rayon, were active and profitable, both in filament and staple forms. Not all US rayon firms were in the non-union, low regulation states. The New Bedford (Massachusetts) Rayon Company reported in 1937 that its high-quality fabrics, high production volume, closeness to its customers, and skillful advertising made it successful in spite of "unfavorable taxation, higher labor costs and many burdens such as restriction of hours competitively, higher fuel and power costs, and such drawbacks as are created by climatic conditions."[49] In the late 1930s seventeen different US rayon companies operated 29 plants.

The National Rayon Weavers Association created an educational filmstrip in 1937 to help department store salespeople answer consumers' questions about rayon fabrics and clothing—specifically on the "advantages of rayon."[50] Since the United States had plenty of cotton and a reasonable, if not entirely adequate, supply of wool, its use of rayon in the apparel field tended to be either to replace cotton or silk purely for cost, or to mix with varying quantities of wool for lighter weight clothing "that was more comfortable and cost less."[51] Even companies that did not make textiles themselves but supplied that industry got on the bandwagon. General Electric, for example, whose motors drove machinery in many mills, advertised in 1937 that "Mary has two new dresses," which cost less and were better made than the one dress her mother could afford 20 years prior, because "research engineers have worked effectively to improve processes and to give the public more for its money. More goods for more people—at less cost."[52]

On April 30, 1939, the New York World's Fair opened after four years of planning and construction, highlighting the role of American innovation and business in the recovery from the Great Depression. Two of its buildings encapsulate the pre-World War II triumph of rayon in the consumer culture of the day: the Hall of Fashion, or Fashion & Textiles Building, and the DuPont building. The original plans for the 1939 Hall of Fashion included sections for wool, rayon, and cotton textile manufacturers to show their wares, alongside clothing manufacturers. A 1938 memo from the Fair's President to the Director of Exhibits began without any niceties, straight to "it is essential to sell the Textile building, [and] that rayon take the lead in arranging for a large amount of exhibit space." This was not to be: the rayon exhibitors wouldn't commit to the square footage expected of them. Eventually, and briefly, the industry was represented by some of the biggest names—American Viscose, Celanese, North American Rayon, American Bemberg, and Tubize Chatillon—but *not* DuPont, which declined to participate in the joint display.[53]

Where was DuPont? In its own building, "The Wonder World of Chemistry," a highlight of the "Production and Distribution Zone." Designed by Walter Dorwin Teague, famed American industrial designer, it featured a tall "Tower of Research" simulating a bubbling distillation unit. DuPont's rayon was the subject of one of the pavilion's many exhibit spaces—the company also featured its paints and dyes, plastics like Lucite, its Cellophane film, Neoprene rubber substitute, and Fabrikoid coated fabrics. Most importantly, it introduced the new, first fully synthetic polymer fiber, nylon, to the public, in a display featuring nylon stockings being knitted and shaped, with a white-coated chemist at the end showing the dyeing and finishing processes. DuPont's patent for nylon was issued in 1938, with product prototypes introduced in 1939, but the manufacturing facility was not fully functioning until 1940.

As part of its rebranding in 1935, DuPont had adopted the slogan "Better Things for Better Living Through Chemistry." For the Fair, artist John W. McCoy (whose father and brother were DuPont executives) painted a huge mural, reputedly on DuPont's imitation leather, Fabrikoid, depicting how "Chemistry" (a male figure holding aloft a chemical beaker) brought humanity forward from the drudgery of pre-industrial life to the modern enjoyment of leisure and clean work. The brochure for the 1940 season dubbed the building a "cavalcade of chemistry." Like the Fair as a whole, the building promoted corporate science and chemistry, describing the value of research in terms of consumer economics: "a picture of new and virtually limitless economic vistas opened up by chemical research . . . new discoveries spreading out like ripples on a pond, creating new jobs, new circulation of wealth, new opportunities for the taking."[54]

The word autarchy was not, to our knowledge, used by DuPont or its competitors in marketing. But in 1939, the company's president, Lammot Du Pont, characterized the American industrial exhibits at the New York World's Fair as

> *evidence of a new economic freedom, a new security. Beyond any possible doubt, this nation is provided today with the means to supply its every reasonable need. This is in contrast with a very few years ago. To illustrate, the United States then was dependent upon foreign lands for such vital materials as rubber, fertilizers, dyestuffs and fine chemicals, among many other things. Now this country has all of them through the ingenuity of man.*[55]

Most of the items mentioned were DuPont products, so the ingenuity might reasonably have been attributed to a specific group of highly trained research chemists working in the DuPont laboratories rather than a generic "man." Central to the company's marketing, not only of its textile fibers, but certainly of immense significance in the public's acceptance of them, was a redemptive narrative of how modern science had not created mere substitutes, but the promise of a utopian future enabled through chemistry. Nylon, the first fully synthetic, chemically produced, fossil fuel-derived polymer fiber would lead the way in the synthetic textile revolution.

But not right away. The Fair's first season closed almost two months after Europe went to war, again, in September 1939. Nylon was not yet ready for prime time: its first success was replacing silk and rayon in hosiery, and animal hair in brush bristles, and during the war nylon would replace silk for parachute cloth. But rayon still held sway, and staple rayon would have an outsized influence on the course of the war. The Japanese flying suit in the Dalby Museum is one example of rayon's military role in World War II, a role made possible by the nationalist-inspired research and development of rayon to civilians in the lead-up to the war. Although wartime rationing would limit Mary's ability to continue buying two new dresses, wartime mandates for blended fabrics for civilians would smooth the road for post-war civilian consumption of clothing made of cheaper, partly or wholly synthetic fabrics, prioritizing ease of care and trendiness over durability and remodeling.[56]

And what of wool? Britain would again requisition its Empire's wool, but, having learned its lesson, right from day one of this war. Neutrals and enemies alike would evaluate their wartime plans accordingly, and their decisions would have long-lasting consequences for the wool business, the textile industries, and consumers around the globe. Like wool, rayon was an international commodity, with international capital. Yet it allowed individual nations to feel that they controlled their own destiny, without supply chains for raw materials that straggled across half the globe. Dalby's Japanese flying suit points us toward the new "coping mechanisms" for supply chain shortages that would surface in many nations during World War II, the Korean War, and the Cold War that followed.

Chapter 8

Wool Bubbles and Better Living

Advertisement for Deering, Milliken "Lorette" fabric, made from 55 percent DuPont Orlon and 45 percent wool. *American Fabrics* magazine, No. 24, Winter 1952–1953 (private collection).

> Another in the Series of Famous Milliken Magic Fabrics . . . Like All Wool? You'll like washable LORETTE even better . . . the unduplicated Orlon/Wool, with all-wool's fine qualities amplified, plus astonishing talents of its own.
>
> "LORETTE by Milliken" advertisement
> *American Fabrics*, No. 24 (Winter 1952–1953)

Thirteen years from the start of World War II, the threat that synthetic alternatives posed to wool was mainstream. The decades of research by DuPont chemists and engineers that led to the release of nylon, the world's first fully synthetic textile, in 1939, had continued unabated. The advertisement at the head of this chapter showcases a new fabric, 55 percent DuPont Orlon and 45 percent wool, trademarked as Lorette. The manufacturer, Deering Milliken, was founded in 1865 as a sales agent for New England woolen mills, moving to manufacturing only in 1944. The company focused on innovation, such as Lorette's "Milliken Magic" of washability and permanent pleating. Advertising was critical to the steady market share gains for synthetic textiles after World War II.

A skirt with cinched waist and copious pleats might appear little connected to the exigencies of textiles in wartime. But Lorette and its kindred blends can be considered the culmination of a politics of wool (and to a lesser extent other natural fibers) that had, as we've shown, been brewing for decades and was turbocharged in World War II and the early 1950s. Unreferenced in this advertisement, the Korean War was stumbling to its "hot war" conclusion as this ad was published. It represented the zenith of wool prices—a brief bubble—and the death knell for wool as the cold-climate textile of everyday choice for Americans. Even in 1952 Deering Milliken used half of DuPont's Orlon production in its fabrics.[1] Ironically, the "Cold War" that was just then emerging would support the wool market for a few more decades, in ways you might not suspect.

In 1941, DuPont, alongside selling gunpowder to Allied nations, began working on Fiber A, the first acrylic fiber, ultimately trademarked as Orlon. Development continued throughout the war, and a pilot Fiber A factory opened in 1944. As with nylon, DuPont poured huge resources into marketing as well as laboratory research. A 1948 press release touted the continuous-filament version of Orlon as a silk replacement "while 'Orlon' staple is the most wool-like we know."[2] Still, Orlon could only accept dye from 1952, making Lorette one of Orlon's first market successes. In contrast to the ad's promised fabric magic, DuPont's internal communication shows keen awareness of Orlon's continued limitations, detailing myriad problems with "uniformity of dyeing," "glazing," "fuzzing," and "flammability" along with a "disappointing resilience." Researchers recommended blending it with wool rather than considering it for stand-alone use.[3] But a significant advantage of fully synthetic fibers was that chemists and corporations could continue to tinker with different formulas to achieve DuPont's mantra of "better living."

The forerunner of what today is known as polyester—the most common synthetic textile in the contemporary world—also arose during World War II. Building on the pre-war research of DuPont's Wallace Carothers, British chemists brought together an acid and an alcohol to patent "polyethylene terephthalate" or PET, that as a fiber called Terylene was manufactured by Britain's ICI (Imperial Chemical Industries) from 1941.[4]

But Orlon and other synthetic textiles, either alone or in blends, offered no immediate knockout punch for wool as the preferred cold climate textile. Rather, synthetic fiber manufacturers launched a series of incremental assaults. This chapter explores the staged triumph of synthetic fibers over wool, both in fashion and for military use. First, however, we need to consider World War II as a catalyst for change.

* * *

On September 1, 1939, the same day that Germany invaded Poland and triggered a declaration of war, Britain passed the "Control of Wool Order" forbidding wool trading and setting a maximum price for UK wool.[5] Economic warfare followed patterns from the previous war: Britain imposed a blockade and contraband lists; Germany replied with a counter blockade. A new Australian Central Wool Committee (CWC) was established, headed by Norman Yeo, experienced in its World War

I equivalent. With war imminent, Australia had already postponed its wool auction season. Negotiations began for the UK to commandeer Australian and New Zealand wool for the duration of the war plus one year.[6] Just over a month after Australia joined the UK in a declaration of war and even before a commandeer price had been agreed on, ships full of Australian wool were en route to the UK.[7]

Although a wool commandeer by Britain had been discussed at the time of the Sudetenland crisis in 1938, no price had then been fixed. In 1939, Australia was negotiating from a position of weakness. A year of drought had produced poor-quality wool and low prices, and the government accepted a fixed average price of 10 ¾ British pence per pound of wool, less than two-thirds the World War I price.[8] After much messy negotiation with a new Labor government after October 1941, Britain agreed to raise the Dominions' commandeer price. By mid-1942 the price was increased to the World War I level but as before, wartime inflation ate away at its value.[9]

Although the pricing agreement shared profits from commandeered wool sold outside the UK with growers, it also allowed the UK government to sell commandeered wool to Bradford manufacturers for civilian purposes without further payment.[10] Disgruntled Australasian woolgrowers complained that newspapers would not critique the deal; that wool was "being seized and sold under war enforcement without the grower being consulted," and of "powerful Bradford combines . . . having secured a wonderful wool bargain."[11] South Africa had joined the scheme in August 1940, receiving a somewhat better deal: the same price as Australia minus the compulsory commandeer, and retaining the right to sell certain wools on the open market. In practice, Australian and New Zealand wool was also sold to many countries, but only with UK permission.

As in the previous war, neutral nations struggled to get the wool they needed. Britain again promised some supplies to those that committed not to trans-ship to Germany. Japan, still formally neutral, had reduced its imports of Australian wool in the late 1930s, but immediately after Britain and Germany declared war, requested 300,000 bales. This was contentious, as in 1936, 1937, and 1940 Japan, Germany, and Italy had formalized their alliance, termed the Axis powers. Frederick Booth later claimed that the CWC managed "the sale and shipment of wool to Japan [so] that no remonstrances would be provoked from that potential enemy and yet she would obtain little or no advantage in case of war."[12] But conflict between the UK and Australia on this point is apparent in contemporary accounts. Australian woolgrowers and their advocate, Ian Clunies Ross, pushed for continuing the trade with Japan, hoping to squelch competition from rayon and other wool-producing nations. Others argued that providing wool to Japan could dissuade it from waging war against the Allies. But Britain's Ministry of Economic Warfare insisted that limiting Japan's wool access was a better strategy and imposed a monthly wool allowance to minimize the risk of Japan either stockpiling wool or trans-shipping it to Germany and Italy.[13]

Frederick Booth's previous wartime experience made him a valuable resource. Nearing 60, he was first appointed to a subcommittee of the CWC to manage wool buyers signing up for the armed services.[14] So many did, along with shearers and wool classers, that manpower shortages affected the business of getting wool to Britain until in February 1942 those occupations were declared reserved and prohibited from enlisting. Booth later took charge of administering the NSW wool appraisals (dividing wool into different categories to determine prices within the predetermined average price).[15] His son James was also a wartime appraiser. The firm's other wool buyers had enlisted.[16]

With wool auctions suspended for the duration and Australian wool men enlisted, several Japanese wool buyers were appointed as appraisers, and, in a controversial CWC decision, some young Japanese men were accepted as apprentices. During 1941, however, on their government's orders, almost all the Japanese appraisers returned to Japan, with the last Japanese wool buyers departing in August 1941, with their final purchases, on the ship *Kashima Maru*.[17] Post-war, Booth saw that event "surely . . . intimating the coming of Pearl Harbor."[18] Australia had by then acceded to American pressure to stop selling wool to Japan, although government documents clearly show that Australian wool was being shipped to mills in Shanghai, China and Manchukuo—then occupied militarily by Japan and beholden to Japanese capital investment—until November 1941.[19]

* * *

Hard lessons about wool's long supply chain in 1914–1918 were relearned, and some previous mistakes avoided. Early in the war, with many Continental European wool contracts in abeyance, there was more wool in Britain than Bradford factories could process, even with production for civilian export markets, whose profits supported the war effort.[20] Australia's textile manufacturers could buy Australian wool at a discount subsidized by the federal government, for domestic civilian use.[21] Britain began to impose restrictions on textiles for civilians, issuing specifications for various types of "Utility Clothing."

After Britain imposed its commandeer, American manufacturers struggled, as in the previous war, to buy sufficient Australian wool for domestic requirements. They sought help from Ian Clunies Ross and the International Wool Secretariat (IWS), who argued that without sufficient wool the United States would turn to synthetics and blends. US threats to buy more South American wool was one effective bargaining chip. From its nadir in December 1939, the US allocation of Australian wool more than tripled by June 1940.[22]

Britain reassessed its strategy after the fall of Belgium, the Netherlands, and France to Germany in May–June 1940. From December 1940, the United States could buy unlimited Australian wool, with the price settling around a quarter higher than the average commandeer price.[23] In addition, the US and UK governments collaborated on a huge reserve cache: one million bales of wool from Australia, New Zealand, and South Africa; stored in the United States; owned by Britain; but available for purchase by the United States in an emergency. The whole reserve was eventually purchased by the United States once the UK was confident of its own supplies.[24] This irritated the Australian government and CWC, who were not consulted on the scheme.

Attitudes changed again in December 1941. The US Naval base at Pearl Harbor, Hawaii, was only one of Japan's targets that month, prompting the UK Board of Trade to cancel export licenses for "goods consigned to Japanese territory and countries contiguous to Japan, such as Manchuria, Korea, French Indochina, Thailand, and Portuguese Timor."[25] Australia was suddenly central to the Allies' war effort in the Pacific.

Despite the threat posed by the Japanese Navy, troop ships brought tens of thousands of US soldiers to Australia, returning across the Pacific laden with wool for the Reserve, some of it carried as deck cargo to protect ships from enemy bombs or fire.[26] Crucially for the Pacific theater's supply chain, Australian textile mills and factories produced wool (and cotton) uniforms and blankets for their own and US troops stationed locally. Lend-Lease arrangements supplied American weapons and munitions in return.[27] Unlike previous colonial mercantilism, war encouraged Australian wool manufacturing, which began exports to Allied nations including Canada, Brazil, Iraq, Mexico, and Turkey.[28]

During World War II, the United States bought more than four million bales of Australian wool, 55 percent of all Australian wool exports and nearly eight times as much as the UK approved for sale to European allies.[29] Fredk. H. Booth & Son alone sold almost 250,000 bales to the Massachusetts' Arlington Mills.[30] Most of it, from 1940, went into clothing the US military, which reached 11.4 million personnel at its 1945 peak. The QM Corps assumed that the wool of 26 sheep (about 100 pounds/45 kilograms) was needed to outfit a soldier for their first year of active service, compared to 20 in World War I. By contrast, the average American civilian had used around 2.2 pounds/1 kilogram of wool annually in the 1930s.[31]

Although expanded submarine warfare created greater shipping complexities for southern hemisphere wools, the American military remained committed to wool and "viewed the use of wool substitutes and extenders as a move to be taken only if other methods failed."[32] Foreshadowing the post-war Berry Amendment, the armed forces paid premium rates for US domestic wools, to encourage and protect a domestic source of supply.[33]

American woolen mills were at full tilt from 1941 onward, and textile production was classified as an essential activity from August 1942.[34] Julius Forstmann died in October 1939; his company, run by his son Curt, worked heavily on military contracts and even his yacht, the *Orion*, was acquired by the US Navy, becoming the patrol gunboat USS *Vixen*. New Jersey's Botany Mills regained profitability, while Arlington Mills ran entirely on military contracts. The year 1944 was the peak of

US woolen textile production, despite many mills struggling to find a sufficient workforce. Exports of woolen cloth to Allied nations including the Soviet Union grew to 60 times more than in 1939![35]

Despite importing vast amounts of raw wool, US supplies were still perceived as uncertain, and once war was declared the government put strict controls on how much wool would be allowed in civilian fabrics. From March 1942, the US War Production Board strictly reserved even woolen rags and wastes for use in military orders, citing "a shortage of wool for the combined needs of defense, private accounts, and export."[36] April brought instructions regarding "the manipulation of wool for civilian fabrics," requiring textile manufacturers to use "rayon, cotton, and other non-wool fibers . . . to provide adequately warm clothing." Blankets for civilians had to contain no more than 80 percent wool from April 1942, reducing to 65 percent later in the war.[37] Wool allocated for civilians dropped in 1942 to less than half the pre-war volume, but rose again the following year when supply concerns eased. Much of that rise appears to have been in wool-blend fabrics, although since Julius Forstmann's much-desired Wool Labeling Act had taken effect in 1941, fiber content had to be disclosed to consumers.

* * *

Although wool was sufficiently plentiful in Australia that blended fabrics were not required, rayon staple was still common in civilian clothing. As in most countries, clothing conformed to Utility or Austerity regulations, which limited the amount of fabric in any given garment. In a mid-1942 newsreel, John Dedman, Australia's Minister for War Organization of Industry, modeled the men's single-breasted woolen "Victory Suit," made with "no vest, no trouser turn up, no buttons on the sleeves," although Australia was producing twice as much woolen cloth as it had pre-war, barely three years earlier.[38]

In the UK, despite the IWS producing several films designed to keep "the desire for pure wool alive in the public," rationing favored rayon by allotting a much lower coupon value to rayon than wool.[39] Just as in Japan, Italy, and Germany several years earlier, military priority for wool accustomed US and UK civilians to fabrics that blended wool with other fibers.[40] Although the US trade journal *Textile World* featured all types of "Textiles in the War" in August 1942, the September issue's cover, and an entire section inside, proclaimed "Synthetics: Versatile for Victory," and continued pre-war "patriotic and modern" marketing, focusing on all the ways that synthetics (including rayon and nylon) were being called into service in military and civilian products. Wartime trends would have enduring effects.

In the Axis nations, as we've seen with the Japanese flying suit, rayon took on a very significant role. In German uniforms, for example, the percentage of rayon staple blended with wool increased regularly during the war. In 1939, Germany used a woolen yarn of 10 percent rayon staple and 90 percent new wool. In 1940, German uniforms combined both woolen and worsted yarns, blending more rayon with new wool and wool waste. By 1944, the woolen yarn was 35 percent rayon staple, 35 percent wool, and 30 percent waste and reworked wool, but the "worsted" yarn was 100 percent rayon staple.[41] For many reasons, chief among them warmth and flame resistance, this could not have passed unnoticed by the wearers.

The Japanese miscalculated how important textile production would be to their war effort. A significant portion of the country's textile machinery in several sectors was scrapped during the war and melted down for weapons. The woolen industry suffered the least from this shortsightedness, but Japanese civilians suffered serious shortages during the war.[42] German and Japanese textile factories were routinely the targets of bombing campaigns, affirming the strategic nature of textiles in wartime, despite their "soft" image.

* * *

General Douglas MacArthur directed the Pacific War from the Australian city of Brisbane in Queensland, suddenly full of American soldiers. Further west, Helen Close was growing up as the daughter of a woolgrower. With all the jackaroos gone to war and her elder brothers in boarding school, Helen was taught to drive a car at age nine to help her father run their sheep grazing property.[43] In NSW, Eberhard Noltenius, who had returned to Australia from Europe just days before war began, wrote Agnes Baldry, "I feel quite confident to face whatever there may be coming."[44] What came was internment for Eberhard and for his friend and distant relative Kurt Waldthausen, who, unlike his uncle Alfred Lohmann in 1914, had remained in Australia.

Eberhard was interned in several NSW locations before being dumped back onto the streets of Sydney in February 1940 with no means of support. He retreated to Wallendoon Station, where Agnes lived with her mother, sharing the house with her sister and brother-in-law, whose son Kenneth was in the UK training for the Royal Air Force. Amidst much local bad feeling about a German national in their midst, Eberhard was arrested in June 1940 and interned for the rest of the war. Some months later, the family at Wallendoon received the tragic news of Kenneth Baldry's death on a training flight in Wales. Sympathy letters to his parents include one from a family member saying he died "holding the Hun at bay."[45] Despite such sentiments, Agnes was Eberhard's primary support during the war, and they married soon after its end.[46]

By late 1944, with the end of war in Europe in sight, Britain held a stockpile of commandeered wools totaling more than 10 million bales: or two years' normal British requirements.[47] Australia and the UK ended their Wool Agreement a year early, in July 1945, amid fears that the overall wool market would decline once wartime demand abated, and until European mills were rebuilt. Australians were annoyed that wartime inflation was eating away at the value of the fixed price and that British growers had received higher annual increases in the commandeer price. Clearing the stockpile was handed over to what was known as the "Joint Organization" (JO), set up by the four Dominions and the UK.[48] All concerned were surprised when the stockpile began to clear much faster than anticipated, aided by the fact that Australian wool production had leveled out and even declined slightly as war continued, due to climate variation, labor shortages, and the less than exciting commandeer price.[49]

Replenishing the severely depleted stocks of wools in British mills was encouraged by nimble entrepreneurs again bridging wartime and peacetime production. Montague Burton by 1939 owned almost 600 retail menswear shops, and the factories to supply them. During World War II, Burton Menswear produced more than thirteen and a half million uniforms for Britain and its Allies' military personnel, a quarter of all uniforms produced in the UK.[50] The company was perfectly placed in 1945 to bid for peacetime contracts with the UK government for demobilization suits for each of the 90 percent of its five million service personnel that were male, getting the contract for a third of these.[51] In 1942, Burton had estimated that 75 percent of British men's suits were made-to-measure, but most demobilization suits were ready-to-wear. After years of clothing coupons and government-mandated Austerity suits, "demob suits" were made of quality wool, double breasted if desired, and included a waistcoat, felt hat, tie, and socks, details that had largely been scrapped during the war.[52] In 1945, novelist J. B. Priestly said these suits made a demobilizing serviceman a "prince among paupers."[53] These contracts greatly assisted Burton's transition to peacetime. Their menswear chain expanded to become the biggest "multiple tailor" in the world, combining manufacturing and retail.

Women's fashion also contributed to the rapid diminution of the stockpile. In 1946, David Jones (Australia's most prestigious department store for women's fashion) and the *Women's Weekly* (its largest circulation women's magazine), sent representatives to Paris to choose exclusive women's fashions containing Australian wool to feature in the magazine and in the store. A year later Christian Dior, the quintessential post-war French designer, brought out his "New Look." David Jones and its customers embraced with alacrity Dior's aesthetic of calf-length hemlines, plentiful fabric, and marked preference for fine wool. In 1948, David Jones brought Dior himself to Australia, accompanied by French models, to show his collection at special runway parades. Dior also visited Australian woolen mills to select fabrics for future designs. But the overnight obsolescence of the shorter, narrower, wartime silhouette was not universal. In the UK, for example, clothing and textiles were rationed until 1949.[54]

The UK's Bradford and Leeds mills came out of the war with fewer industrial, commercial, and political advantages than they had enjoyed for most of the previous century. This was partly because in dampening civilian demand, the UK government had ordered more than a third of Bradford's mills be decommissioned for the duration. Reopening after the war, these mills were handicapped by aging machinery which had received little wartime maintenance.[55] Britain was in debt, short of workers, and despite many of its woolen mills moving from steam to electric power in the immediate post-war years, had lost much of its competitive advantage in wool textile production.[56]

The United States, whose sheep numbers had declined during the war, like Australia, also saw its stockpile pulled quickly into manufacturers' waiting arms. In the immediate post-war years rising disposable incomes, millions of demobilizing men needing civilian clothes, and the need to replace rationed, worn-out consumer textiles, ensured a booming market for wool.[57] Synthetics, however, infiltrated that market very rapidly. The greater profitability of purpose-built mills for the new fibers in the largely non-union, pro-business southern states saw many well-known woolen manufacturers falter once military demand and the immediate post-war boom subsided.

Relief and rebuilding efforts in the nations that had suffered enemy occupation and those on the losing side also helped clear the stockpile. The Lend-Lease program that had provided vast quantities of woolen cloth to the Soviet Union ended abruptly in June 1945, casting that nation back on the open market to fill its needs. Mills in Belgium, France, and Italy had survived the war in better shape than anticipated and bought stock from the JO much faster than expected. The US government and an agency of the newly established United Nations purchased bulk wool from the JO for Eastern European nations including Poland, Greece, and Yugoslavia. The US's Marshall Plan financed woolen mill retooling, especially in countries that had been occupied by Germany. Auctions and free trading were reestablished by 1946–1947 with fewer tensions about the relation of stockpile wools to new season wools than in 1919.[58] Indeed from 1948–1949, wool prices rose sharply; by 1951 the stockpile was fully cleared and the price for wool was soaring to heights not seen before nor since.[59]

* * *

War was again responsible for this. In June 1950, with the backing of the newly minted Communist People's Republic of China, the Democratic People's Republic of Korea invaded the southern half of the

Korean peninsula, which had been under US occupation since Japan's defeat in August 1945. A United Nations coalition under US leadership was hastily put together to oppose the invasion. The Korean War featured fierce fighting of the conventional "hot" kind but also fomented the emerging Cold War between the United States and the Soviet Union and their respective allies. Korea has cold winters, the winter of 1950–1951 unusually so. In Australia and New Zealand the war caused a legendary boom when wool fleece was indeed golden, bringing wealth to many woolgrowers and a temporary fillip to wool exports. But it also hastened wool's diminution as a fabric of war—and of peace. Any commodity that boomed as quickly as wool created a bubble that would inevitably burst.

Compared to World War II with its 100 million military personnel, the Korean War was a minnow, whose six million combatants included small detachments from both Australia and New Zealand. But the US government and its QMs wanted wool and plenty of it, not only for winter uniforms in Korea, but for fear of war breaking out again in Eastern Europe amidst mounting anti-communist tensions. American wool manufacturers had canvassed the possibility in 1947 of the United States building up a peacetime wool stockpile, not having achieved that, they determined to secure adequate supplies immediately.[60] As prices more than doubled over a few months in 1950, American manufacturers blamed "the rather unfortunate amount of publicity concerning the probable requirements of this country."[61] Expectations of shortages drove many nations to panic-buy wool, and in June 1950 the International Wool Secretariat predicted even higher prices "as a result of 'no limit' buying at wool auctions."[62]

The early months of the Korean War saw new, and different, tensions between the UK and the United States over wool supplies. The United States, Australia, and New Zealand had been close allies throughout the Pacific campaigns of World War II, and the US government felt that it had earned preferred access to Australasian wools as another war in that region took shape. As the American wool manufacturers told it, in response to US complaints about wool prices, the UK recommended that the United States use less wool, and coarser wools, in its soldiers' uniforms. The United States retorted that before being asked to downgrade its military fabrics the British policy of shipping Empire wools to communist countries, "business as usual with China and Russia," should be "re-examined."[63]

In August 1950, ,US diplomats requested that Australia, New Zealand, and South Africa shut down their wool auctions, allocate wool to Allied countries as needed, establish a "fixed maximum price," and prevent "supplies . . . to unfriendly nations" (the USSR and its satellites).[64] New Zealand left Australia to lead the response to the proposal: the USSR was New Zealand's third largest wool customer after Britain and France, and US demand would likely evaporate when the war ended.[65]

The Australian government equivocated. The USSR and Poland were important customers, and a separate British proposal to acquire privileged peacetime access to Australian wool was being considered.[66] In the months before a formal response was given, wool rose to stratospheric prices, prompting the head of Australia's Treasury Department to warn against offending the United States lest it "encourage them to build up their flocks or use substitutes."[67] Australia refused to see the Korean conflict as a sufficient emergency to warrant shutting down auctions and counter-proposed that the United States could "buy wool for military requirements" prior to auction, but too late for implementation.[68] The auctions opened in November 1950 as usual and that month the US Congress authorized a "100 million pound military stockpile."[69] Charles Massy, woolgrower and historian, describes the upshot: "America . . . blew the market apart getting the wool they wanted to get through the war."[70] Fredk. H. Booth & Sons, for example, to keep the Arlington Mills supplied, bought West Australian wools for the first time, at the "absolute peak" of the wool bubble.[71]

Woolgrowers enjoyed a brief bonanza. Helen Close returned to her family's Rivoli Downs Station around the end of 1950, to help her father amidst the boom. In the late 1940s, a neighbor had needed to de-stock in a drought and sold Helen's father three thousand aging and unshorn ewes, many of them in lamb, for a paltry £35. Of the Korean wool boom, Helen recalls, "It must have been dramatic, because it made a dramatic difference." Suddenly, Helen's father had money to invest in his property and to have his first real holiday, and he employed Helen and her brother to collect the "pulled wool" from the many dead sheep in the paddocks. They made several hundred dollars and Helen and a friend went to New Zealand on their first overseas holiday.[72] Eberhard Noltenius and Agnes McKay, raising sheep at Wallendbeen, likely also enjoyed the boom.

The wool bubble was a complex blessing for wool exporting nations, fueling inflation and industrial trouble, especially in New Zealand. It was the last straw for many US wool manufacturers and buyers, and the military, not least because by the time of the Korean War, wool was *not* the only way of keeping a soldier warm. While the US military consumed a third of the wool used in the United States in 1951,[73]

> *The increasingly high cost of raw wool led to requests for synthetic and wool blends by the Army, Navy and Air Force. In April 1951, for example, the Marine Corps issued a directive specifying that all woolen and worsted fabrics procured in the future would contain 15 per cent of Dacron, previously known as Fiber V.*[74]

Dacron was DuPont's trade name (having bought the US patent) for Britain's fully synthetic Terylene polyester. Nylon, Orlon, and Dacron began to be blended with new wool and shoddy into fabrics for all American armed services.[75] And by 1952 sleeping bags were being filled with chicken feathers instead of wool, and down was being tested for cold weather insulation layering instead of wool jacket and trouser liners.[76] The US military used less of the wool stockpile than anticipated.

The Korean War led the US government and wool manufacturers to rethink supply chains. The 1933 Buy American Act, passed amidst the Great Depression, had required the government to buy goods from US suppliers whenever possible. These requirements were strengthened before the United States entered World War II, but American sources could not satisfy wartime demand. In 1952, at the behest of Congressman Berry, Congress amended the Act to state that all cotton and wool fiber required by the Department of Defense would come from domestic sources—unless "domestic wools cannot be procured at United States Market Prices."[77]

Wool prices did not stay stratospheric for long. Prices halved between March and June 1951 and fell another 20 percent by March 1952.[78] For wool manufacturers, the radical fluctuations of price and demand were disastrous: "they'd been forced to buy up *here*, the market collapsed, and it never recovered."[79] It took time for the woolen industry to understand that the decline was not just temporary. Economies of scale, simpler supply chains, and stable inputs made synthetics attractive. Manufacturers of ready-to-wear clothing increasingly adopted blends and straight synthetics and consumers followed. As prices for civilian woolens rose, so did consumer resistance to paying them, especially as alternatives, like the Lorette skirt, were available.[80]

Wool's wild price volatility had real consequences for wool's future. Bradford manufacturers noted with alarm that,

> *US consumption of wool during 1951 was the lowest for ten years. If account is taken of the considerable quantity used for military purposes, the drop in civilian consumption has been even more pronounced.*[81]

In 1952, the head of the huge conglomerate American Woolen Company addressed his industry, decrying the lack of productivity of "man and machine" in his mills; lamenting that wages and conditions were much higher than workers in the mostly southern synthetics factories experienced; and noting that although wool and worsteds were infinitely superior "they cost a lot more." Finally, he lectured: "We cannot depend upon war or the preparation for war to maintain our solvency and our existence."[82] The company soon canceled contracts with unionized workers.[83]

The Korean War ended in a 1953 armistice, by which time American wool manufacturers were distinctly and collectively downbeat. That year's secretary's report to the National Association described a "most difficult" year amidst "general prosperity." Government orders had largely dried up, civilian markets were shrinking, "profitable operations were truly the exception," and many companies had gone into liquidation.[84] By the end of the 1950s, Summer Street, the legendary Boston wool-buying district that had attracted Frederick Booth to learn its secrets five decades before, was a shadow of what it had been. Just a few wool brokers remained, and many of the mills they had bought wool for were closed.[85] Among them, the Arlington Woolen Mills (from around 1946 part of the William Whitman Company) entered voluntary liquidation in late 1951. Franklin Hobbs died in 1955; four years later his son Marland too was dead.[86] In 1955, the American Woolen Company merged with Textron, another large conglomerate, whose origins lay in Rhode Island's Atlantic Rayon Corporation. Their flagship mills were closed and sold off to an entirely different industry. In Passaic, Botany Mills closed in 1955, and Forstmann Woolens was bought by the J.P. Stevens Co. Stevens was originally a woolen manufacturer but by 1960 it was a mixed textile conglomerate with 50 facilities from Maine to South Carolina.

The remaining manufacturers kept reminding the US government that as wool was of "vital national interest in wartime," the nation must bear the costs.[87] In 1954, Congress passed a National Wool Act, offering substantial financial support for domestic woolgrowers "as a measure of national security."[88] This was "too little, too late." To take one state as an example, the number of sheep in California had almost halved between 1942 and 1950.[89] Wool manufacturers fought against tariffs on imported wools, imposed as part of complicated international free trade agreements.[90] But whatever support the American woolen industry received was insufficient for its health.

* * *

Meanwhile, synthetics manufacturers continued to win consumers' hearts and dollars. Mary found even two new dresses insufficient, and her brother also wanted a more varied wardrobe. In 1953, representatives of several chemical fiber makers were invited to address wool manufacturers on "The Place of Nylon, Orlon and Dacron." DuPont's spokesman claimed that the company's "aggressive promotion and advertising" campaign was an "important weapon for speeding [consumer]knowledge," and that it was through DuPont synthetics that "the textile industry is keeping in step with the trend of modern living—an easier life, more leisure, greater functionality, longer life" to ensure "a more profitable business for us all."[91] Union Carbide, Chemstrand Corporation, and the Virginia Carolina Chemical Corporation also pitched the positive attributes of their products. As a sop to the audience, the DuPont representative assured wool manufacturers that "your industry has become a good customer of ours," purchasing an increasing variety of synthetics for blended fabrics.[92]

Two years prior, another observer had pointed out that "all evidence points to a permanent shortage of wool for the world's growing population that only synthetics can fill," since there was no more land to devote to sheep. And as the Lorette skirt ad hinted, synthetics better complemented the central heating, automatic washing machines, and tumble dryers that became commonplace in the post-war United States. Production of the semi-synthetic rayon approximately doubled between 1950 and 1977. And fully synthetic fabrics, an almost infinitesimal part of the whole in 1950, by 1977 represented six times as much fiber as wool and two and a half times as much as rayon.[93]

* * *

If all of this sounds like wool became just a footnote to history after the Korean War, it did not. While the US wool market never fully recovered, global wool production grew steadily, only beginning to decline in 1970. So, what sustained wool for several decades after the early 1950s boom petered out?

A complete answer to this question is beyond our scope, but Frederick Booth's wool businesses can answer it in microcosm. As the Korean War began, Frederick was 70 and had handed over day-to-day company management to his son James. But in 1954, aged 47, James Booth died, collapsing after a busy day at a regional wool sale, and amidst debate about the company's future, especially vis à vis the United States. James's 19-year-old twin sons Jim and Donald were then in their first year of learning the family trade.[94] Frederick reengaged, acting as Chairman until at least 1967, but appointing Bruce Trebeck (who had worked for him since 1935), as managing director. Trebeck radically diversified the company, despite "constant arguments and friction" with Booth, "because F.H. . . . would not acknowledge that things were different to his old close knowledge of the American Trade."[95]

Trebeck wanted the company to be "International Wool Merchants," and from the late 1950s Booths found new clients in many countries including Poland, Belgium, Japan, Egypt, Mexico, and India. The Cold War indirectly underpinned many of these markets, and during a brief hot war between India and Pakistan over Punjab sovereignty, Booths was India's biggest supplier of raw wool.[96] Several company partnerships adjacent to Fredk. H. Booth and Son arose, including one with the Sir James Hill Group, a long-established Bradford top maker. The new partnership, Booth Hill, bought the Hill Group's raw wool for several decades from 1960. (Hill also produced DuPont's Orlon in Britain for blends.)[97] Zegna Baruffa, an Italian yarn-making company whose defining interest was the finest possible merino wool for high-fashion clothing, became a major client. A bale of ultra-fine wool once occupied a first-class seat in a Qantas plane bound for Italy.[98]

Following the Korean War's price gyrations, Australia had developed a wool futures market as a form of price insurance for growers and buyers.[99] But wool futures could also be risky. Early in 1979, an adjacent Booth company endured major losses in speculative futures trading. The wool price unexpectedly spiked after China briefly invaded Vietnam, sending Booth Hill into receivership for three months until new partners could be found.[100] Dieter Vollstedt, a West German international wool trader, invested in the firm, which became Booth, Hill, and New (BHN). Vollstedt's Neues Wollkontor company had grown from his establishing an export section of the Waldthausen wool company. It bought wool in Australia and elsewhere for processing and export to Eastern Europe.[101]

The new partnership further built Eastern European business, with governments or government agencies in Yugoslavia, Turkey, East Germany, Hungary, and Czechoslovakia among the main clients. Booth was the biggest single buyer of wool for Poland in the 1980s until Textilimpex, a Polish government agency, started buying wool directly. The Polish government once bought most of the merino wool at a Brisbane auction.[102]

What was all the wool for?

> *Uniforms. Not only army uniforms. It's railways, schools, banks. It's right across those communist-run governments. The easiest solution was to give everyone a wool uniform.*[103]

Government clients bought so much wool that Donald and Jim Booth, now running the company, watched for their ships, especially Russian and Yugoslav vessels, to arrive, knowing that wool prices would likely rise.[104] The Booth twins went regularly to Europe to meet clients. Business in Eastern Europe could be complex. In his 43-year career Jim Booth remembers only once meeting female wool buyers, in East Germany. "One," he said, "was a spy; the other one watched her because she was the Stasi. And the third one was very good at buying and selling wool."[105] Cheil Industries, a Korean wool manufacturer, also became an important client.[106]

This combination of diverse clients led to around a decade of economic good times for Booth, Hill, and New. Wool buyer and trader Scott Carmody remembers clients in myriad different nations when he started work in 1985.[107] BHN did not generally trade with Russia, other than two shipments helping a New Zealand company fill a huge order as the USSR was collapsing. Gaetan Pace, then the shipping manager, remembers that these orders presented challenges at a time when neither getting shipping containers back from Russia nor getting paid were guaranteed.[108]

* * *

By 1989–1990 the good times were coming to an end, not only for Booth, Hill, and New. Several factors intersected as the global wool trade unraveled. First, many Italian companies moved their scouring and top-making businesses to China, where wages were much cheaper. China had begun building up its wool manufacturing several years earlier, with Australasia its primary source of raw materials.[109] Second, an Australian Wool Price Reserve Scheme, started in 1970 to guarantee pastoralists minimum prices, had become divorced from underlying market trends by the end of the 1980s, even as numbers of sheep and bales of wool produced kept rising to earn what looked like easy money.[110] Third, these were years of widespread political and military turmoil disrupting the wool trade: Tiananmen Square; the fall of the Berlin Wall; the dissolution of the Soviet Union and Yugoslavia; the Gulf War. Western Europe had been buying less wool for some decades. Suddenly China,

Russia, and the satellites of the latter stopped buying almost completely. The result was a *huge* stockpile of wool in Australia, a smaller but significant stockpile in New Zealand and nervous governments, wool buyers, woolgrowers, and international clients. As the crisis peaked, Australian pastoralists were paid to slaughter millions of sheep.[111]

Late in 1990, as new head of the Australian Wool Exporters Council, Donald Booth joined a delegation including Australia's then Agriculture Minister, visiting China, Russia, Japan, Korea, and Europe. The delegation tried to restart trade (including offering Russia a line of credit to buy Australian wool) and assured their hosts that the Reserve Price would hold. It didn't. A free market for wool in Australasia was reestablished early in 1991, and prices fell significantly.[112] As at the end of the Korean War, many wool companies folded, including Booths. In Britain, the Sir James Hill group of companies was placed into administration.[113] From 1989, Dieter Vollstedt sold off his wool businesses in stages, including his share of BHN. By 1993, Bremer Woll-Kammerei (BWK), a German wool firm that was by then the world's largest, owned them all and a year later bought Booth's remaining wool business.[114] Not much more than a decade later, BWK itself collapsed.

* * *

As the wool market crisis unfolded, Malden Mills, a Massachusetts textile company, was working with the outdoor sportswear company Patagonia to develop a form of polyester that challenged wool in terms of warmth, comfort, and insulation, and was lighter, cheaper, and could be made from recycled PET plastic. Polarfleece was patented in 1981, widely used by the end of the 1980s, and ubiquitous by the end of the 1990s, morphing through several chemical formulas along the way.[115] Polyester fleece fabrics in many weights and textures became a dominant force in cold-weather apparel textiles.

Overall, wool lost market share continuously to other textiles across the twentieth century, including to cotton (another story, and not ours). Wars created huge demand for wool but greatly complicated the trade. Wool held its status as a prime strategic resource in World War II and the Korean War even as the wool "have-not" nations urged the synthetic genie out of the bottle. In 1900, wool represented 18.8 percent of the textiles produced globally; by 2000 this had dropped to 2.5 percent.[116] From about 1970, rayon use plateaued and full synthetics burgeoned, as manufacturers successfully convinced consumers that their products represented "Better Living." From the perspective of military quartermasters, the bubbles, busts, and supply chain dramas associated with wool in wartime could no longer be borne. Synthetics largely triumphed by offering cheaper and more reliable raw materials, amenable to chemical reinvention and economies of scale.

For families that had depended on wool for generations, the upshot varied. Yorkshire's Hainsworths continue to successfully navigate the contemporary woolen industry. The sixth generation of Booths worked briefly in wool before finding their paths elsewhere. Ditto the Waldthausens, although their last generation successfully computerized wool trading.[117] Members of the Mackay/Baldry/Jacobs family are still graziers and farmers at Wallendbeen, with wool now a much smaller part of their operations. Several members of Tup Bateman's extended family, including a granddaughter, still work in the wool industry and Tup periodically judges "wool handling" at shows across Australia. She and her late husband trained many of the next generation of shearers, an occupation desperate for new recruits. In the United States, Julius Forstmann's descendants found other occupations. Other wool families and companies moved into synthetics or found a path in wool through high-end branding or support from the Berry Amendment.

But that is not the end of the story. After the various wars, hot and cold, that so defined the twentieth century, since the early 1990s another war has arisen, with textiles at its heart in a different way.

Epilogue

Wool and the War on Waste

Control of wool as a strategic resource during the cold-climate wars of the twentieth century, and all that followed from that, eventually challenged wool's place in the textile world. Thirty-plus years from the end of the Cold War, synthetic textiles rule our world. They are integral to a fast-fashion universe dominated by brands such as Shein, Temu, and H&M. In a table showing which nation's citizens consume the most textiles and purchase them most cheaply, Australia tops the list, closely followed by the United States, both way ahead of "runners up" UK and China.[1]

Global textile production has nearly tripled since 1995 and is still rising, creating mountains of waste. Much of this is exported with the promise of reuse but in practice ends up clogging land and oceans in a process that has been dubbed "waste colonialism."[2] With castoff clothing and other textile waste desecrating places like Chile's Atacama Desert, and overflowing lands and waters in Ghana, Kenya, Nigeria, India, and Pakistan, literally no place on earth is untouched by humanity's overconsumption of textiles.[3] In 2025, the battle of greatest importance to the future of textiles is the metaphoric "War on Waste."[4]

Polyester accounts for 54 percent of current global textiles and a recent study reported that about 35 percent of microplastic particles in the oceans come from washing synthetic fabrics.[5] Microplastics are now found in our food and in our bodies. At a minimum they can cause inflammation, respiratory problems and intestinal microbiome disruption; researchers are investigating longer-term effects on fertility and immunity.[6] Recent research suggests that less than half of Australian consumers know that most of the textiles they wear and use are plastic, and that limiting synthetics is a vital part of cleaning up our environment and transitioning to a lower carbon economy.[7] It is unlikely that Australians are uniquely ignorant.

* * *

So where does that leave wool? It now represents just 1 percent of global textiles.[8] Australia grows 90 percent of the world's fine apparel wool, most of it manufactured into fabric in the People's Republic of China.[9] Wool prices have been depressed for many years, other than for ultra fine merino.[10] Wool has fallen well down the list of Australian exports, with many farmers now keeping sheep much more for their meat than their wool. In current clothing advertisements wool equals merino, and the market for apparel made from coarser varieties is much less obvious. Many of New Zealand's biggest wool producers are now Maori-owned enterprises producing "strong wool" for carpets and upholstery, although there are some large merino enterprises on the South Island. In the United States there are plenty of artisan Sheep and Wool Festivals, but wool has largely disappeared as an everyday textile.

Wool is now much more expensive than synthetic fibers and is mainly found in high-end fashion and/or in blends with synthetics. Italy's Zegna and other elite fashion brands continue to make pure wool garments. Merino wool, soft on the skin and with all the wearability advantages detailed in chapter 1, is prized as a base layer by outdoor/adventure sports outfitters such as New Zealand's Icebreaker, whose "Baacode" system allows consumers to trace woolen clothes back to the sheep station they came from. An innovative woolen yarn, called Optim™, in which fibers are stretched before spinning, is used for ultra water- and wind-resistant outer layers by brands such as Sweden's RÖJK. Other companies including Eileen Fisher, Patagonia and SmartWool aspire to sustainability and promote recycling. Wool's intrinsic circularity, especially when unblended with other fibers, is an important marketing angle.

Efforts to educate consumers and growers on wool's advantages including sustainability come from myriad national and international organizations, including the International Wool Textile Organization, the UK's Campaign for Wool, Australia's Woolmark and Australian Wool Innovation, the American Wool Council and American Sheep Industry Association, and South Africa's National Wool Growers Association.

Many military quartermasters are rethinking their relationship to wool, having largely abandoned it in the 1960s, apart from elite dress uniforms, blankets, overcoats and berets, or blended with synthetics in standard dress uniforms. The desert warfare of recent decades has highlighted two significant problems with field/combat uniforms made from synthetic fibers: they absorb body odors, making them unpleasant to wear, and more importantly, they can melt, which can greatly exacerbate burn injuries.[11] The American military, the largest consumer of American-grown wool, has since the early 2010s incorporated more wool into both field uniforms (for flame and odor resistance) and dress uniforms (for appearance, tailoring ease, and comfort). The Brickle Group, in Rhode Island, makes woolen blankets, berets, and pea jackets for the US military.[12] A key British brand is "Hainsworth Protective Fabrics," heavy-duty wool for "firefighters, police and the military," including ECO-DRY™ which blends wool with Tencel rayon.[13]

In a world that needs to limit carbon emissions, sheep emitting methane is a problem.[14] Many woolgrowers (including Charles Massy) now practice regenerative farming methods to limit their product's environmental impact and to mitigate the effects of climate change on their flocks.[15] In 2007, the New Zealand Merino Company adopted ethical sourcing standards for its woolgrowers, and their recent ZQRX initiative encourages regenerative agriculture, stewardship of the land, and ethical treatment of both sheep and the workers who care for them.[16] As the environment heats up, and wildfires feed on dry underbrush, some pastoralists and ranchers use herds of sheep and goats as "fire abatement crews" to graze undergrowth, leaving behind manure to enrich the soil. Bianca Soares in California considers this work her flocks do as "a small, but vital, piece of a much larger fire mitigation puzzle," in addition to their role as wool producers.[17] As nations worldwide transition to renewable energy, farms in Australia, Europe, and the United States have begun grazing sheep underneath huge solar arrays, the panels providing them with shade and shelter.[18] But textiles made with guaranteed sustainable grazing practices, sometimes allowing consumers to trace their garment back to a specific animal, are financially out of reach for most people.

A recent Woolmark advertising video powerfully evokes synthetics as made from fossil fuels. Within three months of release it had been seen by more than nine million people, mainly on social media.[19] But there are simply too many people in the world for humanity to rely solely on natural fibers. Synthetic fibers are cheaper, more uniform, and can be made to order. They are here to stay.

* * *

What then are the battles to be waged if this war on textile waste is to be won? The current overconsumption of cheap and poor-quality fabrics then donated to thrift stores is no solution. Nor is textile recycling a magic answer. Greenwashing, or purposely misleading consumers, is rife. To recycle the ubiquitous blended fabrics, such as cotton-polyester or wool-acrylic, requires separation into different components and is expensive, sometimes damaging, and largely futile. Currently, less than 1 percent of clothes globally are recycled back into apparel-quality textiles.[20] Textile recycling simply can't keep up with the amount of fiber encouraged by the drumbeat of "sale" and "trending now." Obscuring textile origins is also greenwashing, such as calling a fabric bamboo when it is simply rayon made from bamboo instead of wood, and therefore heir to most of rayon's environmental ills.[21]

If we really want to create change, consumer awareness of the true ecological, cultural, social, and economic costs of their textile choices is vital. A century ago, children learned where their clothing came from as part of their geography lessons.[22] Fifty years ago, girls at least learned something about textiles and clothing in Home Economics classes. Today, sewing and mending are no longer the norm, and few consumers understand how their textile and clothing choices are constrained by manufacturers' decisions.

Consuming as many textiles as we do today is simply not sustainable—no matter what they are made from. Notwithstanding encouraging recent reports of progress in chemical recycling of blended fabrics, and two high school students inventing a device to remove microplastics from wastewater, humans in the developed world consume thoughtlessly, and far too much.[23] There is only one serious remedy:

Consume less.
Buy better quality fabrics.
Wear clothes and use textile products for longer.
Wash your clothes less; air them between uses.
Mend, remake, recycle.
Commit to slow clothing.[24]

And ensure your clothes are truly recyclable, so when they do wear out they have a further purpose. Pure wool, for example, can be recycled into textiles (yes, our old friend "shoddy") until its fibers are too short even for that, at which point it can become fertilizer or mulch.

The future of the planet is in our hands. There will be many battles on the road ahead.

We all make choices in what we consume, who we vote for, which policies, products, and brands we support. Choose wisely.

Acknowledgments

A project involving two people living on opposite sides of the world, spanning several countries and filling 10 years accumulates a lengthy list of people to thank. First of all, the authors would like to acknowledge our research and writing partnership that has been intellectually challenging, enormously fun, and survived successes and disappointments with extraordinary humor and dedication to the final product. Our collegial friendship has become family, and through various stays in each other's countries has expanded in many directions.

Research support for the project has come from Griffith University; Australian Wool Innovation (which funded a short film: *Fabric of War: Why Wool?*); The Textile Society of America; Queensland-Smithsonian Fellowship (Trish FitzSimons, 2019); Fulbright Australia Senior Scholar Award (Madelyn Shaw, 2019), and a National Library of Australia Fellowship (Madelyn Shaw, 2022).

For research suggestions and assistance, technical and administrative support, reading drafts, giving interviews, access to collections, connecting us to publishers, taking photos, and in many cases for housing, feeding, and entertaining us, we sincerely thank:

In Australia: Ien Ang; John Atchison, Kathy "Tup" Bateman, Prudence Black, Frank Bongiorno, Helen and Cathy Booth, Jim and Margaret Booth, Nick Bradford, Scott Carmody, Jane Cavanough, Helen Close, Lorinda Cramer, Liz Cuninghame and Andrew FitzSimons, Jacqueline Dwyer, Deborah Edwards and Jim FitzSimons, Freya Edwards-FitzSimons, Merrie and David FitzSimons, Peter FitzSimons, Alex Fitzwater, Alison Flanagan, Hannah Forsyth, Rae Frances, Heather Goodall, Tom Griffiths, Ashley Hay, Janis Hanley, Nena Hicks, Cheryl Hill, Julie Hornsey, Luke Keogh, Richard Lander, Pat

Laughren, Charles Massy, Nicole McCuaig, Bec McElroy, Sandra McEwen, The Mackay Family Trust and the Jacobs/Baldry family, Trevor McKell, Jenny Meaney, Jane Milburn, Susan Morgan, Cathy Morrison, Stephen Muecke, Gaetan Pace, Bruce Pascoe, Pauline and Dennis Peel, David Peterson, Matt Pfeffer, Paul Read, John and Miranda Lucas, Bruce Scates, Llewellyn Stephens, Edite Vidins and Hal Wolter, Simon Ville, George Waldthausen, Alexander Wilkie, Mary Wilkie, Peter Williams, Sophie-Joy Wilson. *At:* The Australian War Memorial—Jane Peek, Dianne Rutherford; The Anthropology Museum, University of Queensland—Michael Aird, Mandana Mapar, Jane Willcock; Australian Wool Innovation—Laura Armstrong, Angus Ireland, Julie Davies; Brickendon, Tasmania—Richard and Louise Archer. Fulbright Australia—Karen Coleman, Thomas Dougherty, Tara Hawley, Pablo Jiménez, Alex Maclaurin; National Wool Museum, Geelong—Padraic Fisher; Griffith University—Damien Bickhoff, Trevor Case, Gerry Docherty, Susan Forde, Regina Ganter, Daina Garklavs, Keryn Gray, Donna Hamilton, Scott Harrison, Interlibrary Loan Librarians, Paul Jardine, Louise Johnson, Chris Little, Therese Nolan-Brown, Carey Ryan, Curtis Sullivan, Vanessa Tomlinson, Sandy Turner, Herman Van Eyken, Alex Waller, Brett Wiltshire, Adam Wolter, Ross Woodrow; National Archives Australia—David Fricker, Anne McLean, Louise Doyle; National Library of Australia—Kathryn Favelle, Susannah Helman, Matthew Jones, Simone Lark, Sharyn O'Brien, Kelly Torrens; Pioneer Park Museum, Dalby, Qld—Elaine Fox; Wally and Bev Lanagan; Powerhouse Museum, Sydney—Glynis Jones; Roger Leong; Queensland Museum—Paul Avern, Mark Clayton; State Library of Queensland—Joan Bruce, John Oxley Library staff, Jacinta Sutton; Tasmania Museum & Art Gallery—Tamzine Bennett, Jo Huxley; State Library of NSW—Stephanie Volkens, Mitchell Library Staff; UNSW Canberra at the Australian Defence Force Academy—John Connor, Shirley Scott; Warrock Station—Scott Farquharson; Smithsonian Scholarship Program, Department of Environment and Science, Qld—Sebastian Dimech, Grant Woolett. The Water Tower Historical Museum, Gunnedah, NSW—Marie Hobson; The Zara Clark Museum, National Trust, Qld—Erin Millar, Cindy Sesak.

In New Zealand: Maartje Abbenhuis, Kingsley Baird, Kirsty Cameron (The Woollover), Duane Harland, Kate Hunter, Mary Knox, Angela Lassig and Andrew Langridge, Jane Malthus, John MacGibbon, Gavin Tankersley; *at:* Atihau Whanganui Inc.—Mavis Mullins, Andrew Beijeman; Auckland War Memorial Museum Tāmaki Paenga Hira—Gail Romano; Otago Museum—Moira White. Te Papa Tongarewa Museum of New Zealand—Claire Regnault, Kirstie Ross, Mark Sykes, Awhina Tamarapa; Toitū Otago Settlers Museum—Sean Brosnahan, Claire Orbell.

In the United States: Pat Aufderheide, Deborah Baronas, Max and Sam Brickle (Northwest Woolen Mills), Ashley Callahan, Stephen Harrison, Vilsoni Hereniko and Jeanette Hereniko-Paulson, Patricia Nguyen, Ela Ramsey, Jen Swope, Margaret and Duncan Whitehead, Lauren Whitley; at the American Wool Council—Mitch Driggers, Christa Rochford; DAR Museum—Alden O'Brien; Bernice Pauahi Bishop Museum—De Soto Brown, Marques Marzan; George Mason University: Stephen Robertson; Hagley Museum & Library—Lucas Clawson, Kevin Martin, Eric Rau, Angela Schad, Ben Spohn; Hawaiian State Archive—Ju Sun; Hobart & William Smith Colleges—Anna Wager, Susan Gage; Library of Congress, Washington DC—Ronald Williams Junior; National Museum of American History—Frank Blazich, John and Sheryl De Jong, David Haberstich, Jennifer Jones; Newark Museum—Amy Hopwood, Andrea Ko; Oklahoma Humanities Review—Kimberly Robin; Oregon Historical Society—Scott Daniels, Helen Fedchak, Scott Rook; The Textile Museum and George Washington University—John and Tanya Wetenhall. Textile Society of America—Caroline Charuk, Lisa Kriner; US Army Quartermaster Museum—Luther Hanson, Weldon Svoboda. Willamette Heritage Center—Michelle Cordova, Kaylyn Mabey, Kylie Pine; Winterthur Museum & Library—Linda Eaton; University of Hawaii at Manoa—Jodie Mattos, Stuart Dawrs.

In the United Kingdom: Peter Ackroyd, Nigel Gosse, Tom and Roger Hainsworth, John and Liz Knox, Ruth Strong; at the Association of Dress Historians—Jennifer Daley; The Company of the Merchants of the Staple—Robert Hall, Anthony Robinson.

In Europe: (Sweden) Désirée Koslin and Johan Mörner, Gornilla Törnvall; at the Livrustkammaren (Royal Armory), Stockholm—Annika Nylander, Andreas Olsson, Augusta Persson; Armémuseum (Army Museum), Stockholm—Rebecka Karlsdottir, Martin Markelius. (Belgium) Stijn Coninx, International Wool Textile Organization, Dalena White; Germany—Dieter Vollstedt.

In Asia: (Japan) Koichi Okamoto; (India)Radhika Singh.

For getting this book into print: Charles Harmon, Elaine McGarraugh, and the team at Rowman & Littlefield/Bloomsbury, Mitchell Krieger for the introduction, and Sue Jarvis for the index.

For keeping us sane, making us laugh, and putting up with our obsession: Erika Addis, Anna Bourke, Julie Broadfoot and Colin Bennett, Ann Burrola, Kathy Clarendon, Therese Collie, Amanda and David Coultas-Roberts, Ellen Ferrin, Andrew and Isabelle FitzSimons-Reilly, Jennifer Gibson, and Harry Rand, Georgina Greenhill, Karen Herbaugh, Annie and Susie Jacobs and David Robinson, Carolyn Kibbe and Jayne Stokes, Stuart Malone and Catherine White, Priscilla Maxwell, Christine Morgan and Patrick Sidwell, Sandra Novocewski, Annabelle Quince, Chris Sayer, Sue Schneider, Joyce Van Der Ham.

Finally, and always, our deepest appreciation of Gary Reilly, Jonathan Howard, and Angela K. Shaw, for their love, enthusiasm, support, and endless patience.

Abbreviations

AWC—American Woolen Company, United States
AWM—Australian War Memorial, Canberra, Australia
AWMM— Tāmaki Paenga Hira Auckland War Memorial Museum, New Zealand
BNAWM—Bulletin, National Association of Woolen Manufacturers, United States
CWC—Central Wool Committee, Australia
DHM—Deutsches Historisches Museum, Germany
GPO—Government Printing Office, United States
HMSO—His/Her Majesty's Stationery Office, United Kingdom
IWM—Imperial War Museum, United Kingdom
IWS—International Wool Secretariat
LOC—Library of Congress, United States
LOC/PP—Library of Congress, Prints & Photographs Division
NAA—National Archives, Australia
NARA—National Archives, United States
NAWM—National Association of Woolen Manufacturers, United States
NCWSBA—National Council of Wool Selling Brokers of Australia
NLA—National Library, Australia
NMAH/SI—National Museum of American History, Smithsonian Institution, United States
NSW—New South Wales, an Australian state
POW—Prisoner/s of War
PTJ—Posselt's Textile Journal
QLD—Queensland, an Australian state
QM—Queensland Museum, Australia

QM—Quartermasters, United States
RG—Record Group
RTM—Rayon Textile Monthly, United States
SLNSW—State Library of NSW
SLQ—State Library of Queensland
SNIA—Società di Navigazione Italo-Americana
TWJ—Textile World Journal, United States
TPT/MNZ—Te Papa Tongarewa Museum of New Zealand
TSA—Textile Society of America
UK—United Kingdom
UNSW—University of New South Wales, Australia
USDA—US Dept. of Agriculture
USDOC/BFDC—US Dept. of Commerce, Bureau of Domestic and Foreign Commerce
USQM—US Army Quartermaster
USTC—US Tariff Commission
VDL—Van Diemen's Land Company
VGF—Vereinigte Glanzstoff-Fabriken, Germany
WA—Western Australia, an Australian state
WRTW—Wool Record and Textile World, United States

Notes

Preface

1. Gerda Blau, "Wool in the World Economy," *Journal of the Royal Statistical Society* 109 (1946), 1. https://doi.org/10.1111/j.2397-2335.1946.tb04664.x.

Chapter 1

1. Donald M. Blinken, *Wool Tariffs and American Policy* (Washington, DC: Public Affairs Press, 1948), 57.
2. https://issuu.com/nationaltrustsaustralia/docs/trust_news_feb_2015final/24; See also, Te Papa Tongarewa Museum of New Zealand (TPT), https://collections.tepapa.govt.nz/object/364206.
3. Jim McDonald has no known grave and is commemorated on the Menin Gate Memorial. https://vwma.org.au/explore/people/107204.
4. Frank L. Walton, *The Thread of Victory* (New York: Fairchild, 1945), 69.
5. Trevor McKell, "Thomas Blacket Stephens 1819–1877: History of Stephens Shire," unpublished; Llewellyn Stephens, "The Stephens Family" in *Annals of Annerley: Proceedings of the Annerley Conference*, July 17, 1994, Royal Historical Society of Queensland, 1997.
6. https://www.gutenberg.org/files/2895/2895-h/2895-h.htm#ch13.
7. For a concise view of the importance of uniforms see: Stephen J. Kennedy and Alice F. Park, "The Army Green Uniform," Technical Report 68-41-CM (March 1968), Introduction. https://www.quartermasterfoundation.org/the-army-green-uniform/.
8. Richard Walker, *Savile Row: An Illustrated History* (New York: Rizzoli, 1989), 21, 27–31.
9. National Museum of American History, Smithsonian Institution (NMAH/SI): http://americanhistory.si.edu/collections/search/object/nmah_449194.
10. Claudia A. Kidwell and Margaret Christman, *Suiting Everyone: The Democratization of Clothing in America* (Washington, DC: Smithsonian, 1974), 75.
11. Pennant TPT, https://collections.tepapa.govt.nz/object/1296244.
12. Gas mask: Queensland Museum, https://collections.qm.qld.gov.au/objects/SH3827/gas-mask-hypo-helmet.

13. Thomas J. Mayock, *The Government and Wool: 1917–20,* Miscellaneous Publications 329493 (Washington, DC: USDA Economic Research Service, 1943), iii.

14. Diary entry, March 23, 1865, William Bluffton Miller, in Jeffrey L. Patrick and Robert J. Willey, eds. *Fighting for Liberty and Right: The Civil War Diary of William Bluffton Miller* (Knoxville: University of Tennessee Press, 2005), 325–26.

15. R. Van Emden, ed. *Sapper Martin: The Secret Great War Diary of Jack Martin* (London: 2009). 95. Quoted in Catherine Price-Rowe, *First World War Uniforms* (Barnsley, UK: Pen and Sword, 2018), 99.

16. Diary entry, March 15, 1865, William Wiley, in Terence J. Winschel, ed. *The Civil War Diary of a Common Soldier: William Wiley of the 77th Illinois Infantry* (Baton Rouge: Louisiana State University, 2001), 143.

17. "The Graybacks So Tenderly Clinging." Words: Anonymous, Music by Henry Clay Work. *Old War Songs* (Syracuse, NY), 29. https://www.libraryweb.org/~digitized/musicscores/ This_song_souvenir_of_old_war_songs_Rochester.pdf.

18. William Davis Years, "Knitted Articles in War Service Equipment," *Textile World Journal (TWJ)* 53, no. 38 (March 23, 1918), 37.

19. Smithsonian American Art Museum (SAAM), https://americanart.si.edu/artwork/christmas-boxes-camp-christmas-1861-harpers-weekly-january-4-1862-36961.

20. French *mutilés,* Library of Congress, Prints & Photographs Division (LOC/PP) http://hdl.loc.gov/loc.pnp/anrc.02144; NZ amputees, TPT, https://collections.tepapa.govt.nz/object/900527; Shipboard lessons, Australian War Memorial (AWM), https://www.awm.gov.au/collection/C987601.

21. NMAH/SI; The International Quilt Study Center, Lincoln, Nebraska; Colonial Williamsburg Foundation, Virginia.

22. Burnett pullover: AWM, https://www.awm.gov.au/collection/REL33118.

23. https://www.youtube.com/watch?v=jreDWCWWEpE; https://www.manfromsnowyrivermuseum.com/, Corryong, Victoria, Australia.

24. Textile Museum (Washington, DC) Exhibition loan records, 1997, *Knitting & Looping: A History*; Interview with Alice and Paul Takemoto, Japanese-American Museum of San Jose. https://www.jamsj.org/manabu/paul-alice-takemoto.

25. Union Infantry Overcoat, M-851 model, 1861? QMR-85.10.03. U.S. Army Quartermaster Museum (USAQM), Ft. Gregg-Adams, VA.

26. Boy's Suit: 1985.252.M2487, Atlanta History Center, Atlanta, Georgia, USA.

27. Radhika Singh, "The Short Career of the Indian Labour Corps in France, 1917–1919." *International Labor and Working-Class History*. 87 (2015a), 27–62.

28. AWM relics: https://www.awm.gov.au/articles/blog/sir-john-monashs-german-shoulder-strap-collection; Collar fragment: RELAWM07839.012.

29. Columella, *On Agriculture*. https://www.loebclassics.com/view/columella-agriculture/1941/pb_LCL361.21.xml., 21.

30. K. G. Ponting, *The Wool Trade: Past and Present* (Manchester, UK: Columbine, 1961), 24.

31. See for example, E. Ciani et al., On the origin of European sheep as revealed by the diversity of the Balkan breeds and by optimizing population-genetic analysis tools. *Genetics Selection Evolution* 52, no. 25 (2020). https://doi.org/10.1186/s12711-020-00545-7.

32. Charles Massy, *The Australian Merino* (Viking O'Neil, 1990),143.

33. Massy, *Australian Merino*, 197–236.

34. Richard C. Kugler, "The Collaborations of Paul Cuffe and Isaac Cory," October 3, 2009. 4. https://paulcuffe.org/wp-content/uploads/2018/02/Kugler_Richard-.pdf.

35. Carroll W. Pursell, Jr. "E. I. duPont and the Merino Mania in Delaware," *Agricultural History* 36, no. 2. (April 1962). https://www.jstor.org/stable/3740945.

36. Chester Whitney Wright, *Wool-Growing and the Tariff* (Boston: Houghton Mifflin, 1910); The United States Tariff Commission, *The Wool-Growing Industry* (Washington: GPO, 1921); Edward N. Wentworth, *America's Sheep Trails: History, Personalities* (Ames: Iowa University Press, 1948).

37. Joan Hughes, (ed.), *Australian Words and Their Origins* (Melbourne: Oxford University Press, 1989), 155.

38. Dorothy M. Zimmern, "The Wool Trade in Wartime," *The Economic Journal* 28, no. 109 (March 1918), 8.

39. USDA Wool Standards Boxes, 1926 and 1946, USAQM.

40. Ponting, *The Wool Trade*, xiv.

CHAPTER 2

1. *Just Wool,* British Pathe Newsreel, 1933. https://www.britishpathe.com/asset/189043/.

2. John James, *History of the Worsted Manufacture in England* (London: Longman, 1857).

3. Parliament Rolls, September 1353, quoted in Susan Rose, *The Wealth of England: the Medieval Wool Trade and Its Political Importance 1100–1600* (Oxford, UK: Oxbow, 2018), 74.

4. Eileen Power, *Medieval People,* 10th edition (New York: Harper & Row, 1963), 125.

5. Nestor Rodriguez, *Capitalism and Migration: The Rise of Hegemony in the World System* (Austin, TX: Springer, 2023), Section 2, 35–37.

6. Sally Coulthard, *A Short History of the World According to Sheep* (NY: Head of Zeus, 2020), 187; Rose, *Wealth of England,* 60.

7. James, *Worsted Manufacture*, 82, 157 (note 13).

8. Rodriguez, *Capitalism and Migration,* 56.

9. Power, *Medieval People*, Chapter VIII, Thomas Paycocke.

10. James, *Worsted Manufacture*, 115–16.

11. Coulthard, *According to Sheep*, 207–209.

12. Julian Hoppit, "The Political Economy of Wool 1660–1824," in *Britain's Political Economies: Parliament and Economic Life 1660–1800* (Cambridge, UK: Cambridge University Press, 2017), 241, https://doi.org/10.1017/9781139057875.010; P. J. Bowden, "The Wool Supply and the Woollen Industry," *The Economic History Review* 9, no. 1 (1956): 45–46, https://www.jstor.org/stable/2591530.

13. Hoppit, "Political Economy of Wool," 223.

14. Hoppit, 217.

15. Hoppit, 223.

16. Adam Smith, *On the Nature and Causes of the Wealth of Nations* (1776). https://www.gutenberg.org/files/3300/3300-h/3300-h.htm.

17. Hoppit, "Political Economy of Wool," 218.

18. Viking Ships Museum. https://www.vikingeskibsmuseet.dk/en/professions/boatyard/experimental-archaeological-research/maritime-crafts/maritime-technology/wool-sailcloth?amp=336&sword_list%5B0%5D=cloth&cHash=3d63343460bd5fd5c9b860984f38ab60.

19. John W. Klein, *War Records Project Monographs, No. 7 - Wool During World War II* (Washington: USDA, Bureau of Agricultural Economics, 1948), 41.

20. Tom Hainsworth, interview *Fabric of War: Why Wool?*, Video, 2018. See also: https://www.awhainsworth.co.uk/about/our-heritage/.

21. Ruth Strong, *The Hainsworth Story: Seven Generations of Textile Manufacturing* (Lindley, UK: Jeremy Mills, 2006), 41–43.

22. Arthur H. Cole, *The American Wool Manufacture* (Cambridge: Harvard University Press, 1926); Frank Ormerod, *Wool.* Staple Trades and Industries series, Gordon D. Knox, ed. (New York: Henry Holt, 1919); Alfred L. Lomax, *Pioneer Woolen Mills in Oregon: History of Wool and the Woolen Textile Industry in Oregon, 1811–1875* (Portland, OR: Banford & Morts, 1941).

23. Unknown author, *The Marland Family of Andover*, p. 1. Typescript digitized by Memorial Hall Library, Andover, MA. https://mhl.org//sites/default/files/files/Abbott/Marland%20Family.pdf.

24. *Fourth Exhibition of the Massachusetts Charitable Mechanic Association at Quincy Hall in the City of Boston September 16 1844* (Boston: Crocker and Brewster, 1844), 52–53.

25. *History of American Textiles* (Boston: American Wool & Cotton Reporter, 1922), 52.

26. Originally viewed at the Osborne Library, American Textile History Museum, transferred to Cornell University in 2018. ATHM finding aid: Cocheco Woolen Mfg. Co. MSS 66. Financial Records. Series 11, Ledgers and Series 12, Journals. Book 10, Mill Journal. 4 (August 22, 1863); 21 (November 28, 1863); 31 (February 29, 1864); 62 (April 30, 1865). Book 8, Mill Ledger, 3–4. Stevens Companies, Woolen Mills. MSS 60, Section I, Series 57. Stevens Woolen Mill, North Andover, MA. George Stevens Correspondence, Clark & Perkins,

1862–1865 (August 9, 1862, July 22, 1863, August 12, 1863, June 3, 1864, August 2, 1864); Folder 155.49, T. S. Mitchell correspondence 1861–1862; Folder 155.56 Mudgett & Co. correspondence 1860–1861.

27. Cole, *American Wool Manufacture*, 343 note 1.

28. See, for example: "The Simmons-Underwood Tariff," *Bulletin, National Association of Wool Manufacturers* (*BNAWM*) 43. (September 1913), 209–59.

29. "The American Wool Trade," *Maitland Weekly Mercury* (November 7, 1896), 10. Trove.

30. Frederick Booth to Marie Booth in Sydney, Australia, from St. Louis, MO. July 31, 1905; Frederick Booth to James Booth in Sydney, Australia, from Philadelphia, PA, September 2, 1905, Booth Family Archive.

31. "An Honor for Mr. Hobbs," *BNAWM* 43 (September 1913), 318.

32. Donald McLeod, *History of the destitution in Sutherlandshire. Being a series of letters published in the Edinburgh Weekly Chronicle . . . with an appendix containing some additional information* (Edinburgh: 1841).

33. Hoppit, "Political Economy of Wool," 241.

34. P. A. Pemberton, *Pure Merinos and Others: The Shipping Lists of the Australian Agricultural Company* (Canberra: Australian National University Archives of Business and Labour, 1986), updated for web publication 2011. https://imagedepot.anu.edu.au/sis/archives/publications/pure_merinos_and_others_-pa_-pemberton.pdf.

35. Simon Ville, "The Relocation of the International Wool Market for Australian Wool" (2005), https://ro.uow.edu.au/commpapers/93.

Chapter 3

1. Lyndall Ryan, "No Right to the Land": The Role of the Wool Industry in the Destruction of Aboriginal Societies in Tasmania (1817–1832) and Victoria (1835–1851) Compared," in Mohamed Adhikari, ed. *Genocide on Settler Frontiers: When Hunter-Gatherers and Commercial Stock Farmers Clash* (New York: Berghahn Books, 2015), 76.

2. Emmanuel Mauro and Stephane Delorme, *Rapanui: A Hidden History of Easter Island* (France: Drole de Trame Television, 2014).

3. Alberto Harambour-Ross, "Sheep Sovereignties: The Colonization of the Falkland Islands/Malvinas, Patagonia, and Tierra del Fuego, 1830s–1910s," *Latin American History* (Oxford Research Encyclopedias, September 2016). https://doi.org/10.1093/acrefore/9780199366439.013.351.

4. Dale Kerwin, "Aboriginal dreaming paths and trading ways," *Queensland Historical Atlas* (August 26, 2010). https://qhatlas.com.au/content/aboriginal-dreaming-paths-and-trading-ways.

5. CO 202/6, Secretary of State for the Colonies Dispatches, National Archives Kew, in S. Fergusson, "The History of Textile Manufacture in Australia, 1788–2020" (Melbourne, Australia: PhD Thesis, RMIT University, 2021), 26.

6. Margaret Steven, "John Macarthur," *Australian Dictionary of Biography* 2 (1967). https://adb.anu.edu.au/biography/macarthur-john-2390.

7. Laycock, quoted in Charles Massy, *The Australian Merino* (Melbourne: Viking O'Neil, 1990), 28.

8. "Statement of the Improvement and Progress of the Breed of fine-woolled Sheep in NSW; presented by Captain Macarthur at the Right Honourable Lord Hobart's office, 26 July, 1803," in *The Philosophical Magazine*, Series 1, 16, no. 64 (1803), LXV11.

9. John Thomas Bigge, "Third Report to Earl Bathurst, Jan 1823." http://gutenberg.net.au/ebooks13/1300241h.html.

10. Damaris Bairstow, *A Million Pounds, a Million Acres: The Pioneer Settlement of the Australian Agricultural Company* (Sydney: Self-published, 2003), 5–7.

11. John Atchison, "The Lure of Distant Profits: The Australian Agricultural Company in Early New South Wales" (Canberra: PhD Thesis, Australian National University, 1973), 3–7.

12. Geoff Lennox, "The Van Diemen's Land Company and the Tasmanian Aborigines: a reappraisal," *Papers and Proceedings, Tasmanian Historical Research Association* 37, no. 4 (1990), 25. https://search.informit.org/doi/10.3316/ielapa.910707697.

13. Goldsbrough Mort & Co, *Wool and the Nation: A Sketch of the Wool Industry in Australia*, 3rd ed. (Geelong: National Wool Museum, 1960), 13.

14. Joan Hughes, *Australian Words and Their Origins* (Oxford, UK: Oxford University Press, 1989), 537.

15. John C. Weaver, "Beyond the Fatal Shore: Pastoral Squatting and the Occupation of Australia 1826–1852," *The American Historical Review* 101, no. 4 (October 1996), 984–86.

16. Weaver, "Beyond the Fatal Shore," 988–89.

17. Ryan, "No Right to the Land," 197.

18. Henry Reynolds and Jamie Dalziel, "Aborigines and Pastoral Leases: Imperial and Colonial Policy 1826–1855," *UNSW Law Journal* (1996), 323.

19. Sir Richard Bourke to Lord Glenelg, October 1835, in Reynolds and Dalziel, "Aborigines and Pastoral Leases," 323.

20. David Marr, *Killing for Country: A Family Story* (Melbourne: Schwartz Books, 2023), 171.

21. Reynolds and Dalziel, "Aborigines and Pastoral Leases," 323–33. Weaver, "Beyond the Fatal Shore," 1002–04.

22. Eric Rolls, *A Million Wild Acres: 200 years of Men and an Australian Forest* (Melbourne: Thomas Nelson, 1981), 165.

23. Ryan, "No Right to the Land," 188.

24. G. A. Robinson to La Trobe, October 7, 1842, in Jan Critchett, *A Distant Field of Murder* (Melbourne: Melbourne University Press, 1992), footnote 23.

25. Ryan, "No Right to the Land," 197; Marr, *Killing for Country*, 178.

26. Gunditjmara People and Gib Wettenhall, *The People of Budj Bim: Engineers of aquaculture, builders of stone house settlements and warriors defending country* (Heywood, Vic: Press Publishing, 2010), 30.

27. Ray Kerkhove, *How They Fought: Indigenous Tactics and Weaponry of Australia's Frontier Wars* (Brisbane: Boolarong Press, 2023), 130–32.

28. Howard Pederson and Banjo Woorunmurra, *Jandamarra and the Bunuba resistance* (Broome: Magabala Books, 1995), 43.

29. Lennox, "The Van Diemen's Land Company," 165–208.

30. Rachel Perkins, Blackfella Films, *Australian Wars* (SBS TV, Sydney, Australia, 2022).

31. Marr, *Killing for Country*, 172–82; Jonathan Richards, *The Secret War: A True History of Queensland's Native Police* (Brisbane: University of Queensland Press, 2008), 176–200.

32. Mary Durack, *Kings in Grass Castles* (London: Corgi, 1959), 159.

33. Marr, *Killing for Country*, 87, 114–15.

34. John Connor, *The Australian Frontier Wars, 1788–1838* (Sydney: UNSW Press, 2002), 107–11.

35. Stan Ewing, Handwritten document recounting his father, J. P. Ewing's memories (Canberra: Institute of Aboriginal Affairs, 1945), 1. Viewed in Water Tower Museum, Gunnedah, NSW.

36. "Wonderful Woman, The Late Mrs Mary Cain, First Half Caste born on the Castlereagh," Obituary, *Western Age Dubbo*, August 22, 1929. Trove.

37. Mary Jane Cain, Letter of 19th June 1893 to the Colonial Secretary, CSIL 5/6137 in Margaret Somerville et al., *'Sun Dancin:' People and Place in Coonabarabran* (Canberra: Aboriginal Studies Press, 1994), 74–75.

38. Massy, *Australian Merino*, 197–236.

39. Adam Robertson, *Warrock Station: A Life Built Worth Settling For* (Portland: Portland Council, undated), 11–14.

40. Richard Grace, *Opium and Empire: the lives and careers of William Jardine and James Matheson* (Montreal: McGill-Queens University Press, 2014), 286.

41. Grace, *Opium and Empire*, 299–300.

42. R. A. Littlejohn, *An Australian Pioneer: Alexander Mackay 1815–1890* (Wallendbeen: self-published, Ian Baldry, 1992), 17–27.

43. Littlejohn, *Mackay*, 91–92.

44. Littlejohn, 104–105.

45. Phillip McMichael, *Settlers and the Agrarian Question: Foundations of Capitalism in Colonial Australia* (Cambridge, UK: Cambridge University Press, 1984), 220–29.

46. Littlejohn, *Mackay*, 106, 110–11; Grace, *Opium and Empire*, 300–301.

47. Database, Centre for the Study of the Legacies of British Slavery, University College London. https://www.ucl.ac.uk/lbs/.

48. David Alston et al., *Slaves and Highlanders: Silenced Histories of Scotland and the Caribbean* (Edinburgh: University of Edinburgh Press, 2021), 245.

49. Mark Dunn, *Benjamin Boyd's Role in 19th Century Blackbirding in the Pacific for Labour in New South Wales* (NSW National Parks and Wildlife, 2021), 3–4. https://www.environment.nsw.gov.au/-/media/OEH/Corporate-Site/Documents/Parks-reserves-and-protected-areas/Parks-management-other/ben-boyd-blackbirding-evaluation-report.pdf.

50. Dunn, *Ben Boyd*, 4–5.

51. Mary Jane Cain obituary, August 22, 1929.

52. "Mary Jane Cain handwritten memoir," September 30, 1920 (State Library of New South Wales).

53. Art Gallery of NSW. https://www.artgallery.nsw.gov.au/collection/works/648/ and National Gallery of Victoria (NGV), https://www.ngv.vic.gov.au/explore/collection/work/2920/.

54. NGV. https://www.ngv.vic.gov.au/explore/collection/work/3051/.

55. Ryan Butta, *The Ballad of Abdul Wade* (Melbourne: Affirm Press 2022), 49–50.

56. Ryan, "No Right to the Land," 185.

57. Bill Carter and John MacGibbon, *Wool: A History of New Zealand's Wool Industry* (Wellington: Ngaio Press, 2003), 9–20.

58. John MacGibbon, interview with Trish FitzSimons, Masterton, New Zealand, April 30, 2017.

59. Simon Ville, *The Rural Entrepreneurs: A History of the Stock and Station Agent Industry in Australia and New Zealand* (Cambridge: Cambridge University Press, 2000), 1, 10.

60. Mark Sykes, interview with Trish FitzSimons, Wellington, New Zealand, April 28, 2017.

61. Carter and MacGibbon, *Wool*, footnote 27, 346 quoting *A Pioneer Missionary among the Maori 1850–1878: being letters and Journals of Thomas Samuel Grace.*

62. Paintings by Gotfried Lindauer, 1885 and 1915; Charles F Goldie, 1906, 1910, 1939. Auckland Art Gallery.

63. Carter and MacGibbon, *Wool*, 10.

64. Edward N. Wentworth, *American's Sheep Trails: History—Personalities* (Ames, IA: State College Press, 1948).

65. Ned Blackhawk, *Violence Over the Land: Indians and Empire in the Early American West* (Cambridge, MA: Harvard University Press, 2008).

66. G. J. Tucker, "Historical sketches of the Wallowa National Forest" (1962). https://www.fs.usda.gov/detail/wallowa-whitman/landmanagement/resourcemanagement/?cid=stelprdb5275839; David P. Del Mar, "The World Rushed In: Northeastern Oregon," Section 2, "Losing the Land (2005). https://oregonhistoryproject.org/narratives/the-world-rushed-in-northeastern-oregon/contact-and-settlement-2/losing-the-land/#.Ww21O-4vypo.

67. See E. Kalbfleisch and J. C. Berlo, "Indigenous Textiles of North America," in *A Companion to Textile Culture*, J. Harris (ed.). https://doi.org/10.1002/9781118768730.ch22.

68. T. L. West, "Centennial mini-histories of the Forest Service," FS-518. (Washington: USDA Forest Service, 1992); Iker Saitua. *Basque Immigrants and Nevada's Sheep Industry: Geopolitics and the Making of an Agricultural Workforce,* 1880–1954 (Reno: University of Nevada Press, 2019).

69. G. D. Best, "Wallowa County Agriculture Reports (1934–1958)," cited in Jennifer Williams and Erin Melville, "The History of Grazing in Wallowa County, (September 2005). https://www.co.wallowa.or.us/media/3901.

70. Peter Mills et al., "The Paradox of the 'Paniolo': An Archeological Perspective of Hawaiian Ranching," *Historical Archaeology* 47, no. 3 (2013): 115–19. www.jstor.org/stable/43492148.

71. Edward Stepien, *"Ni'ihau: A Brief History Pt 1"* (Manoa: Center for Pacific Island Studies, University of Hawaii, 1988).

72. Elama Kanahele, Kimo Armitage, Keao NeSmith, *Aloha Ni'ihau: Oral Histories* (Waipahu: Island Heritage Publishing, 2007), 85–87.

73. Harambour-Ross, "Sheep Sovereignties," 7.

74. Harambour-Ross, 4.

75. Harambour-Ross, 11.

76. Steven Fischer, *Island at the End of the World: The Turbulent History of Easter Island* (London: Reaktion Books, 2005); Mauro & Delorme, Rapanui.

77. David Merrett and Simon Ville, "Accounting for the Nonconvergence in Global Wool Marketing before 1939," *Business History Review* 89 (Summer 2015), 232. doi.10.1017/S0007680515000641.

78. Merrett & Ville, "Nonconvergence," 244.

79. Simon Ville, "The Relocation of the International Market for Australian Wool," *Australian Economic History Review* 45, no. 1 (March 2005), Table, 80.

80. Ville, "Relocation," 82.

Chapter 4

1. Testimony of John P. Wood, January 7, 1918, *Investigation of the War Department: Hearings before the Committee on Military Affairs, US Senate, 65th Congress, 2nd session* (Washington, DC: GPO, 1918), 1463.

2. *Annual Wool Review 1917* (Boston: Rockwell and Churchill, 1918), 48; Stanley Hart, *Wool: The Raw Materials of the Woolen and Worsted Industries* (Philadelphia: Textile School, 1917), Tables B, C, D, G, and M-R, 191–202; Empire Marketing Board, *Wool survey: a summary of production and trade in the empire and foreign countries* (London HMSO, July, 1932).

3. "The Woollen Trade," *The Times* (London, England), January 22, 1915, 7.

4. Frank Ormerod, *Wool* (New York: Henry Holt, 1919), 67.

5. J. H. Clapham, *Economic Development of France and Germany, 1815–1914* (Cambridge, UK: Cambridge University Press, 1928), 249, 292–95.

6. Jane Tynan, "When they ran out of khaki: improvised uniforms and Kitchener Blue." http://ww1centenary.oucs.ox.ac.uk/author/jtynan/.

7. Roger Hainsworth, interview with T. FitzSimons, October 2016; Mark Keighley, *Wool City: A history of the Bradford textile industry in the 20th Century* (Bradford: Whitaker, 2007), 19.

8. Frank G. Carpenter. "Twenty Sheep Needed For Every Soldier." *The Boston Globe,* January 27, 1918, SM9. Newspapers.com.

9. "Wool Products Dwindling: War Demands Have Caused a World Shortage." *Scientific American,* Supplement 2216 (June 22, 1918), 392–93.

10. Leonard P. Ayres. *The War With Germany: A Statistical Summary.* Chapter IV, Table 3, "Clothing Delivered to the Army April 6, 1917, to May 31, 1918" (Washington: GPO. 2nd Edition, August 1, 1919). https://net.lib.byu.edu/estu/wwi/memoir/docs/statistics/stats1-4.htm.

11. Ayres, *The War with Germany,* Chapter IV, Diagram 22.

12. Letter, Julius Forstmann to Senator Joseph S. Frelinghuysen, December 28, 1917. *Investigation of the War Department* (1918), 1207.

13. Clapham, *Economic Development,* 294.

14. "Wool for Germany," *Brisbane Courier*, October 7, 1914, 7. Trove.

15. "Extracts from Dalgety's Review," *Annual Wool Review 1915*, 56.

16. "International Law Topics: Documents on Neutrality and War with Notes," Volume 15 (1915). International Law Studies. U.S. Naval War College. https://digital-commons.usnwc.edu/ils/vol15/iss1/9; *Papers Relating to the Foreign Relations of the United States, 1915, Supplement, The World War*, Part II, Neutral Rights, Documents 123–1088 (Washington: GPO, 1928). https://history.state.gov/historicaldocuments/frus1915Supp.

17. Charles Massy, interview with T. FitzSimons, August 20, 2016.

18. "The Ambassador in Great Britain to the Secretary of State, January 29, 1915," *Papers Relating to the Foreign Relations of the United States, 1915, Supplement, The World War.* Document 922. https://history.state.gov/historicaldocuments/frus1915Supp/d922; Edwin J. Clapp, *Economic Aspects of the War: Neutral Rights, Belligerent Claims, and American Commerce in the Years 1914–1915.* (New Haven, CT: Yale University Press, 1915), Chapter XII. The Import Situation. http://www.gwpda.org/wwi-www/Clapp/Clapp5.htm.

19. Frederick Booth to A. W. Elliott, June 10, 1915. Booth Family Archive.

20. Mariya Grinberg, "Wartime Commercial Policy and Trade between Enemies," *International Security* 46, no. 1 (2021) 33–34. doi: https://doi.org/10.1162/isec_a_00412.

21. "Agreement of May 29, 1918, between the 'Associated Governments' and Sweden, the United States Memorandum of Adherence, and Annexed Letters," *Papers Relating to the Foreign Relations of the United States, 1918, Supplement 1, The*

World War, Vol. II. Document 350. https://history.state.gov/historicaldocuments/frus1918Supp01v02/d350.

22. "Personals," *Textile World Journal* (*TWJ*) 51, no. 33 (July 15, 1916) 77; "Personal Page," *TWJ* 51, no. 40 (September 2, 1916), 17.

23. Christopher Fyfe, *Gentlemen's Agreements: Australian Wartime Wool Appraisements* (Dalkeith, WA: Lana Press, 1996), xxiii.

24. Thomas J. Mayock, *The Government and Wool, 1917–20,* Agricultural History Series No. 6 (Washington, DC: USDA, 1943), 30.

25. "First Conference of Representatives of the Wool Industry with the Hon. Minister of Agriculture," November 14, 1916. H38-B, II, 4. https://paperspast.natlib.govt.nz/parliamentary/appendix-to-the-journals-of-the-house-of-representatives.

26. *Papers Relating to the Foreign Relations of the United States, 1916, Supplement, The World War.* Part II: Neutral Rights. https://history.state.gov/historicaldocuments/frus1916Supp/comp3 and *Papers Relating to the Foreign Relations of the United States, The Lansing Papers, 1914–1920, Vol. I—The World War: Period of American Neutrality.* https://history.state.gov/historicaldocuments/frus1914-20v01/comp1.

27. Attorney General's Department, November 16, 1915. File of Papers, Wool: Export to Italy. A456/3 W/29/13/5 76583. National Archives of Australia (NAA).

28. "Cotton Manufactures: Indirect Routes to Germany Shut Off," *TWJ* 51, no. 35 (July 29, 1916), 47.

29. Dorothy Zimmern. "The Wool Trade in Wartime." *The Economic Journal* 28, no. 109 (March 1918), 14.

30. "Seeking Substitutes for German Exporters of English Textiles" *TWJ* 51, no. 40 (September 2, 1916) 57.

31. Tom Hainsworth, interview with T. FitzSimons, October 6, 2016.

32. Franklin W. Hobbs, "Textiles—The Backbone of New England. An Address Before the Boston Art Club." *Bulletin of the National Association of Woolen Manufacturers* (BNAWM) 67 (1917), 83.

33. "American Dyestuffs," *BNAWM* 48 (1918), 356–64; https://www.firstworldwar.com/source/deutschland1.htm; http://www.colorantshistory.org/SubmarineDeutschland.html.

34. Zimmern, "Wool Trade," 14.

35. Australian Government internal cable, June 2, 1916, in White, *Wool in Wartime,* 5.

36. *Trade of the United States with the World: 1916 and 1917,* Miscellaneous Series, No. 63, Department of Commerce (Washington: GPO, 1918); "The Wool Trade: Government Intervention," *Sydney Morning Herald* (August 12, 1916), 11. Trove.

37. Fyfe, *Gentlemen's Agreements,* 3–14.

38. "Australian PM to Governor General, Secret, January 11, 1917" A11803, 1917//89/334 1804494. NAA, Canberra.

39. John Knox, interview with T. FitzSimons, October 6, 2017.

40. Keighley, *Wool City*, 23.

41. "New England Mills Prosper From War" *The Boston Globe* (December 31, 1914), 1. Newspapers.com; Clapp. *Economic Aspects*, Chapter 11.

42. "Britain Stands Pat," *TWJ* 51, no. 48 (October 28, 1916), 16.

43. "Export Trade Futures," *TWJ* 51, no. 32 (July 8, 1916), 16.

44. "Sheep Campaign Develops." *TWJ* 51, no. 41 (September 9, 1916), 17, 19; Poster, "Join a Sheep Club" 1917–1918. Library of Congress Prints and Photographs Collection: http://hdl.loc.gov/loc.pnp/cph.3g07465; "1917—Shepherdesses Drive Flock on Michigan Avenue." NARA 31481135; American Unofficial Collection of World War I Photographs, 1917–1918. RG 165: Records of the War Department General and Special Staffs, 1860–1952. https://catalog.archives.gov/id/31481135.

45. "Wilson to Sell 48 Prize Sheep," *Washington Post*, August 1, 1920, 2. ProQuest Historical Newspapers.

46. Statement of Winthrop L. Marvin, *Investigation of the War Department*, 1385.

47. "Cooperating with the Government," *BNAWM* 48 (1918), 287.

48. "Completion of Wool Work," Hearings Before Subcommittee of House Committee on Appropriations, 70th Congress, 1st Session (Washington, DC: GPO, 1928), 873–80; "Case No. 2621, August 28, 1920. Claim of Wool Growers Central Storage Co." *Decisions of the Appeal Section, War Department, Claims Board* 7 (Washington, DC: GPO, 1921), 483–505.

49. "Active and Idle Machinery," *BNAWM* 48 (1918), 375–77.

50. "Cooperating with the Government." *BNAWM* 48 (1918), 286.

51. "Deutsche Textilfabriken in den Vereinigten Staten," *Leipziger Monatsschrift für Textil-Industrie* (October 4, 1899), 1. https://digital.slub-dresden.de/kollektionen.

52. Julius Forstmann, Letter and Statement, *Investigation of the War Department*, 1206–11, 1299–1321.

53. "Hearing Transcripts," *TWJ* 53 (March 23, 1918), 31–33; (April 6, 1918), 65–66, (April 13, 1918), 24–25.

54. "Control Enemy Plants: Alien Property Custodian Appoints Directors for New Jersey Mills," *TWJ* 53, no. 40 (April 6, 1918), 65.

55. Donna F. LaVallee, "Picturing the Transformation of a Nation's Textile Traditions: Meiji Era Woodblock Prints," in *Appropriation, Acculturation, Transformation, Textile Society of America 9th Biennial Symposium* (2004), 237.

56. Hisashi Oyama and Gotaro Ogawa, *Expenditures of the Russo-Japanese War* (Oxford, UK: Oxford University Press, 1923), Table, 196.

57. "Typewritten List of Wool Purchases/ers, April 20–22, 1915," Brisbane Wool Selling, Brokers Association Archive, Collection 99208443402061, Box 76, OMA 7/1 and OMA 7/2, State Library of Queensland.

58. "Japanese Aggressiveness," *TWJ* 53, no. 42 (April 20, 1918), 28.

59. Letter, Prime Minister to the Governor General, September 19, 1916, A456, W/29/4/2, Export Wool to Japan. Attorney General's Department. NAA, Canberra.

60. Wool Situation in Japan. p. 63–71. EF Crowe, Enclosure 4 in No 1, memorandum (B). Notes on the Japanese Woollen and Worsted Industries—followup to report of February 1, 1916. 63–64. SC 52, Wool for Japan. A3932. NAA, Canberra.

61. Gus C. Roeder, "Raw Material Enough for Years in Germany," *The Boston Globe,* January 6, 1916, 10. Newspapers.com.

62. "US Third Army, Report, November 20, 1918," *United States Army in the World War, 1917–1919. Reports by the Commander-in-Chief, Staff Sections, and Services,* Volume 11. Reprint (Washington, DC: Center of Military History, United States Army. 1991), 16.

63. "The Mobilization of War Raw Materials in Germany," *Scientific American* 53, Supplement 2062 (July 10, 1915).

64. "Französische Granaten auf St. Quentin" (1917), Bundesarchiv, Spiel- und Dokumentarfilme, EFG1914—Filme zum 1 Weltkrieg; "Gathering raw materials in Craiova. August 1917," Official German WWI Photo, German Military Activities and Personnel, 1917–1918, RG 165. https://catalog.archives.gov/id/17390988; "This Won't Please the Germans, 1919," American National Red Cross photograph collection, Library of Congress. http://hdl.loc.gov/loc.pnp/anrc.03686.

65. "Red Cross Salvage," American National Red Cross Photograph Collection, Library of Congress. http://hdl.loc.gov/loc.pnp/anrc.11709.

66. C-in-C Rept. File: Fld. 317: Report—Quartermaster Corps. Tours, France, March 12, 1919, *United States Army in the World War*, 91.

67. C-in-C Rept. File: Fld. 317: Report—Quartermaster Corps. Tours, France, March 12, 1919, *United States Army in the World War*, 96–97, 297.

68. Louis Filler, *Laundry and Related Activities of the Quartermaster General,* Q.M.C. Historical Studies, No. 13 (Washington, DC: Office of the Quartermaster General, 1946), 11.

69. Isaac Marcosson, *The Business of War* (New York: John Lane Co., 1918), 180–86.

70. Ernest Brooks, "Salvage of the battlefield near Bapaume," National Library of Scotland. https://digital.nls.uk/74545996.

71. "Foreign Wools," *BNAWM* 48 (1918), 109.

72. Fyfe, *Gentlemen's Agreements,* 72.

73. F. P. Huddle, "Disposal of surplus war materials," *Editorial research reports 1943,* II (Washington: CQ Press, 1943). http://library.cqpress.com/cqresearcher/cqresrre1943113000; Fyfe, *Gentlemen's Agreements,* 76.

74. "The Economic Position of Europe: Finance and Industry," *The Textile Journal of Australia* 5. (May 15, 1930), 156. Reprint from Canadian Bank of Commerce Monthly Commercial Letter.

CHAPTER 5

1. Appendix, Report to A. Bonar Law by Messrs. Freshfield on the workings of the Textile Alliance, November 24, 1916, A 11803, 1917/89/40 (Wool Export

to the United States. Governor General's Office), National Archives of Australia (NAA), Canberra.

2. The second suit is: 23.1537A-C. Gift of Ferdinand J. and Henry F. Herpers, 1923.

3. "Kiwanians Hear About Paper," *The Paper Industry* 8, no.2 (May 1926), 299.

4. *Draft book, 1860–1867*, Charles Noska, Manayunk, PA. Acc.# 2017x85.44, Winterthur Museum & Library.

5. Madelyn Shaw, "Slave Cloth and Clothing Slaves: Craftsmanship, Commerce, and Industry," *Journal of Early Southern Decorative Arts* (2012). https://www.mesda-journal.org/2012/slave-cloth-clothing-slaves-craftsmanship-commerce-industry/.

6. Cartoon, Special Collections, University of Chicago Library, Illustrated in Mark Wilson, *The Business of Civil War* (Baltimore: Johns Hopkins University Press, 2006).

7. "G. H. Crosman sworn, Philadelphia: March 6, 1862," Congressional Select Committee on Government Contracts, 37th Congress, Congressional Serial Set, Vol. 1143, 880.

8. See Chapter 5, "Mobilizing Industry," in Madelyn Shaw & Lynne Z. Bassett, *Homefront & Battlefield: Quilts & Context in the Civil War* (Lowell, MA: American Textile History Museum, 2012).

9. "QM Dept. Memoranda Book Relating to Agents and Supplies 1864, Mr. Thomas Sharpe June 8th to self" RG 109, Confederate Quartermaster Records, Ch. V, Vol. 227, 46. National Archives (NARA).

10. "The Blanket Question," *New York Times,* November 2, 1861.

11. Sheet Music, *The Shoddy Ball,* F. E. Garrett, 1863. Library of Congress (LOC). https://lccn.loc.gov/2023783060.

12. John L. Hayes, *The Fleece and the Loom: An Address Before the National Association of Woollen Manufacturers, Sept 6, 1865* (Boston: John Wilson, 1866), 5, 23–24.

13. David T. Jenkins, "Transatlantic Trade in Woollen Cloth 1850–1914: The Role Of Shoddy," *Textile Society of America Symposium Proceedings* (1990), 27, https://digitalcommons.unl.edu/tsaconf/607.

14. Dorothy M. Zimmern, "The Wool Trade in Wartime," *The Economic Journal* 28, no. 109 (March 1918), 28.

15. "New uniforms from those collected on the battlefield," *Posselt's Textile Journal* 21, no. 6 (December 1917) vii.

16. Roger Hainsworth, interview with Trish FitzSimons, Pudsey, UK, October 2016.

17. "Wool Trading in General is Quiet," *Boston Globe*, August 20, 1915. Newspapers.com.

18. "Operations Base Section Plant. NY April 14, 1919." Photographs of American Military Activities, ca. 1918–ca. 1981. RG 111. https://catalog.archives

.gov/id/86700549; Historical Film No. 1191 (ca. 1918) "Quarter Master Salvage Operations in the U. S. A." https://catalog.archives.gov/id/24696. Both: NARA.

19. "Testimony of Winthrop A. Marvin, Resumed," January 18, 1918, U.S. Congress, Senate, Committee on Military Affairs. *Investigation of the War Department.* 65th Congress, 2nd Session (Washington, DC, GPO, 1918), 1467.

20. "Statement of Samuel McGowan," January 9, 1918, *Investigation of the War Department,* 1560–65.

21. "Statement of Col. Elmer Lindsley," January 4, 1918, *Investigation of the War Department,* 1330–35.

22. "The Supplying of Army Fabrics," *Bulletin of the National Association of Wool Manufacturers* (*BNAWM*) 47, no. 2 (April 1918) 185.

23. J. Merritt Matthews, *The Textile Fibers,* 4th edition (NY: John Wiley, 1924) 395–99; "Peruvian Cotton Production," *Posselt's Textile Journal* 21, no. 1 (July 1917) xxi.

24. Fleisher samples: Textiles Dept, NMAH/SI. Accession #63045, Gift of S. B. and B. W. Fleisher, Inc., 1918.

25. Madelyn Shaw, "H.R. Mallinson & Co." in *American Silk: Entrepreneurs and Artifacts* (Lubbock: Texas Tech University Press, 2006) 208–209.

26. Photograph, Connecticut State Council of Defense War Exhibit. October 18, 1918. Acc. # 165-WW-135A-054. American Unofficial Collection of World War I Photographs, 1917–1918. RG 165. NARA. https://catalog.archives.gov/id/26432867.

27. STYCOS Wool Substitute. Cat. # T2367, Acc. # 57996. Gift of the Superior Thread & Yarn Co., 1915. Textiles Dept., NMAH/SI.

28. Howard W. Adams, "The German Vegetable Fiber Industry," *Commerce Reports,* No. 262 (Washington, DC: Department of Commerce, November 6, 1920) 597–98.

29. "Sammelt Brennesseln, die Deutsche Baumwolle!" Fritz Wolffhügel, München. http://hdl.loc.gov/loc.pnp/cph.3g11900; "Sammelt Brennessel! Wenn ihr Kleidung und Faden wollt!," Geis. http://hdl.loc.gov/loc.pnp/cph.3g11557. Prints & Photographs Division, LOC.

30. "Nettle Fibers Used in Cloth Making," *Posselt's Textile Journal* XX, no. 2 (February 1917) xii; Chauncey Depew Snow and J. J. Kral, *German Trade and the War: Commercial and Industrial Conditions in War Time and the Future Outlook,* Department of Commerce Miscellaneous Series, no. 65 (Washington, DC: GPO, 1918) 51.

31. Matthews, *Textile Fibers,* 807–809.

32. "Intelligence Summary, 2d Section. General Staff No. 4, Third Army. November 20, 1918," *United States Army in the World War, 1917–1919. American Occupation of Germany,* Vol. II. (Washington, DC: U.S. Army Center of Military History, 1991), 193–201.

33. Matthews, *Textile Fibers,* 771.

34. "Statistics for the Manufacture of Textiles, Thirteenth Census of the United States" (Washington, DC: Department of Commerce, 1910), 25–34.

35. Division of Political & Military History (Acc 059777), and Consular Collection, Textiles Dept., Division of Home & Community Life (Acc. # 67246), NMAH/SI.

36. Carl Bailey Hurst, "Cloth from Paper," *Bradstreet's Weekly: A Business Digest* 35 (May 18, 1907), 318–19.

37. Hurst, "Cloth from Paper," 319.

38. "Paper Replaces Cotton," *Textile World Journal (TWJ)* 51, no. 48 (October 28, 1916), 22.

39. Cited in Snow and Kral. *German Trade and the War,* 52.

40. "Clothing of Enemy Troops." *The Land* (Sydney), April 20, 1917, Trove; Photographs, PH-ALB-419-H509 or PH-ALB-419, collection of the Auckland War Memorial Museum. Tāmaki Paenga Hira (AWMM). https://www.aucklandmuseum.com/collections-research/collections/record/am_library-photography-18470?k=Hun%20AND%20wool&ordinal=0.

41. Snow and Kral, *German trade and the war,* 50–53.

42. "Yarns and Woven Goods of Paper in Germany," *The Economic World* 101 (March 2, 1918), 319.

43. Imperial War Museum, London (IWM). For example: EPH 7877, Catalogue, ersatz samples, German; UNI 11991, Woven paper nightdress. See also: Deutsche Historisches Museum: Inventarnr. KTe 74/17, Leibchen für Mädchen, 1916/18; and Inventarnr. KTe 67/108, Herrenhose 1916–1918.

44. Capt. H. B. C. Pollard, "The New Land of Paper," *Newcastle Morning Herald and Miners' Advocate* (NSW, Australia) July 20, 1918.

45. IWM, sample records: German Entrenching Tool, M1887; German Water bottle, EQU 3800.2; Cloth shoulder strap, INS 18604. NMAH/SI examples: Accession # 070063.

46. AWMM, Accession numbers, 1929.162.3; W1349.1–3; 1935.351; W1352; W1351; W3061; W3307; 1995x2.96–99; 2004.125; 2013.40.1; NN121; NN133. We are grateful to curator Gail Romano for drawing our attention to this group.

47. Australian War Memorial, Canberra: Prosthetic leg with puttee, RELAWM07698; Jumping-off tape, RELAWM04459.

48. Pollard, "The New Land of Paper," 4.

49. Hamilton C. Claiborne, "English Production of Paper Textiles," *Commerce Reports* 3, no. 154 (July 3, 1917), (Washington: Dept. of Commerce, 1917), 20.; G. H. Brock, "Europe's War-time Uses of Paper Textiles," and "European Processes of Paper-Textile Manufacture," *Commerce Reports*, 4, nos. 230–306 (October–December 1918), (Washington, DC: Department of Commerce, 1919), 872–77; 922–26.

50. "To Make Paper Garments" *British Market* 56, (July 1919), 21; "Photograph of the Textilite Engineering Co., Ltd., London, August 1918," Accession 20253, Textiles Dept., NMAH/SI.

51. Lincoln Eyre, "Conditions in Germany," *St. Louis Post-Dispatch* (Missouri), December 26, 1918.

52. I. Newton Kugelmass, "A Paper Suit for One Dollar," *Popular Science* 98, no. 2 (February 1921), 33.

53. Howard Priestman, "Artificial Silk," *BNAWM* 43, no. 3 (September 1913), 274–97.

54. Jonas Scherner and Mark Spoerer, "Infant company protection in the German semi-synthetic fiber industry," *Business History* (2021), 2. DOI: 10.1080/00076791.2021.1900118.

55. "Status of German Fiber Substitutes," *TWJ* 61, no. 20 (May 20, 1922), 25–26; P. A. Koch, "New and Interesting European Staple Fibers," *Rayon Textile Monthly* 18, no. 11 (November 1937), 53.

CHAPTER 6

1. Narrator, *Just Wool,* British Pathé Newsreel, March 9, 1933. https://www.britishpathe.com/asset/189043/.

2. Steven Bellowin, et al., "Compression, Confidentiality and Comprehension: A look at Telegraphic codes" (Columbia University, March 2009) 1. https://www.cs.columbia.edu/~smb/papers/codebooks.pdf.

3. *Colonial wool telegraph book between Messrs. Fredk. Huth and Co London & [blank],* 1884 with additions 1887 and 1890. State Library of Queensland (SLQ).

4. Bill Carter and John MacGibbon, *Wool: A History of New Zealand's Wool Industry* (Wellington, NZ: Ngaio Press, 2003), 52.

5. Thomas J. Mayock, *The Government and Wool 1917–1920* (Washington, DC: USDA, August 1943), 7.

6. "The Personal Page," *Textile World Journal (TWJ)* 54, no. 26 (December 28, 1918), 32.

7. Global Nonviolent Action Database: https://nvdatabase.swarthmore.edu/content/lawrence-mill-workers-strike-against-wage-cuts-1919.

8. Jacob F. Brown, "The Situation in Raw Wool," *TWJ* 60, no. 24 (December 10, 1921), 31–33.

9. United States Tariff Commission, *The Wool Growing Industry* (Washington, DC: GPO, 1921), 90.

10. Tilden, Leonard E. "New England Textile Strike." *Monthly Labor Review* 16, no. 5 (1923), 13–36. http://www.jstor.org/stable/41828627.

11. John Knox, interview with Trish FitzSimons, October 6, 2016; Mark Keighley, *Wool City: A History of the Bradford Textile Industry in the 20th Century* (Ilkley, UK: Whitaker, 2007), 53.

12. Hughes cable to Goldfinch, December 1919 in Kosmas Tsokhas, *Markets, Money, and Empire: The Political Economy of the Australian Wool Industry* (Melbourne: University Press, 1990), 38.

13. AA, CP 361/1 Bundle 1, File 1, Hughes papers May 1920 in Tsokhas, *Markets,* 43.

14. Tsokhas, 39.

15. Tsokhas, 45.

16. Les White, *Wool in Wartime: A Study in Colonialism* (Sydney: Alternative Pub. Co-op., 1981), 24.

17. White, *Wool in Wartime,* 21.

18. U.S. Tariff Commission, *Recent Tendencies in the Wool Trade With Special Reference to Their Tariff Aspects: 1920–1922* (Washington, DC: GPO, 1922).

19. White, *Wool in Wartime,* 25.

20. "Sydney Sheep Show," *Smith's Weekly*, July 7, 1923. Trove.

21. "Australia Comes a Cropper from the Sheep's Back," *Truth Sydney,* May 17, 1925, 8. Trove.

22. "The Wool Crisis; Brisbane Sales Postponed," *The Telegraph*, Sydney, May 6, 1925. Trove.

23. R. W. Thompson, *Down Under: An Australian Odyssey* (London: Duckworth, 1932), 78.

24. Cyril Briggs, "Passaic Today," *Organized Labor* 28, no. 4 (January 22, 1927). https://cdnc.ucr.edu/?a=d&d=OLSF19270122.2.61.

25. "Workers' Toil Buys Yacht," *The Daily Worker*, September 26, 1929, Final City Edition, 2. Library of Congress, Chronicling America.

26. "Statement of Mr. Henry H. Van Bilderbeck," *Tariff Act of 1929: Hearings before a Subcommittee of the Committee on Finance, United States Senate, Seventy-First Congress, First Session on H.R. 2667, Schedule 4,* 11 (1929), 231–33.

27. John Knox, interview, October 6, 2016; Keighley, *Wool City*, 53.

28. Peter Burness, "James Alexander Kenneth Mackay" *Australian Dictionary of Biography,* 10, 1986. https://adb.anu.edu.au/biography/mackay-james-alexander-7379.

29. Helen Close, interview with Trish FitzSimons, September 21, 2022.

30. Close, interview.

31. Helen Close, unpublished personal memoir, 2013.

32. James Edward Cain; Virtual War Memorial, https://vwma.org.au/explore/people/176225.

33. *Wool Statistics and Related Data, 1920–1964.* Statistical Bulletin No. 363 (USDA Economic Research Service, July 1965); U.S. Tariff Commission, "United States Wools: Production by Regions and by Grades, 1936–40" (March 10, 1942). Typescript, NLA.

34. Letter, Henry Barwell to Billy Hughes, October 13, 1921, CSO 1097/21, B512603, NAA.

35. Georg Waldthausen (Unpublished Speech notes, Lohmann Company Dinner 1955), trans. by Regina Ganter. Waldthausen family personal archive.

36. "Wollstra," *Sydney Morning Herald,* March 14, 1935, 10. Trove.

37. D. F. Nicholson, *Australia's Trade Relations: An Outline History of Australia's Overseas Trading Arrangements* (Melbourne: F. W. Cheshire, 1955), 129.

38. John Perkins, "The German Australian Chamber of Commerce in the Interwar Era," in *Zeitschrift fur Unternehmensgeschicht/Journal of Business History,* (1995), 45.

39. German Ministry of Economics to Foreign Ministry, October 1, 1934, in Perkins, "German Australian Chamber," 46.

40. "An Economist," *Trade without Money! An Examination of the German Barter System, with Particular Reference to Australian Wool* (Sydney, 1935): 9.

41. *Sydney Truth,* December 17, 1934, in Perkins, "German Australian Chamber," 46.

42. "Wollstra," *Sydney Morning Herald* (March 14, 1935), 10–11. Trove.

43. Perkins, "German Australian Chamber," 35–48.

44. Letters: Eberhard Noltenius to Agnes Mackay, September 5, 1932; Noltenius to Mackay, January 26, 1933; Noltenius to Mackay, from Brisbane, May 16, 1933. ALL: Box 19, Folder 74, MS 10290. Mackay Family Papers, NLA.

45. Noltenius to Mackay, November 6, 1933, B19, F74, MS10290.

46. Nicholson, *Australia's Trade Relations,* 129–32.

47. John R. Stewart, "Manchuria as Japan's Economic Life-Line," *Far Eastern Survey* 4, no. 23 (November 20, 1935), 183. https://www.jstor.org/stable/3022242.

48. *Just Wool,* British Pathé Newsreel, 1 minute, 29 seconds.

49. J. G. Latham, *Report of the Australian Far Eastern Mission* (Canberra:1934), Part 16, 1935, 21. A 981, NAA.

50. Ian Clunies Ross, *A Survey of the Sheep and Wool Industry in North and Eastern Asia with special reference to Manchukuo, Korea, & Japan.* 1936. Pamphlet #65, In CSIR Pamphlets 3, nos. 51–75 (Melbourne, CSIR, 1932–1938).

51. Clunies Ross, *Survey,* 39–42.

52. Noltenius to Mackay, August 14, 1936, B19, F77, MS 10290.

53. *Australian Japanese Trade: statement issued at the direction of the General Council of the Grazier's Association of NSW* (Sydney: Harbour Press, 1936), Archive Item 382.099405/2, Mitchell Library, SLNSW.

54. D. C. S. Sissons, "Private diplomacy in the 1936 trade dispute with Japan," *Australian Journal of Politics and History* 27, no. 2 (1981), 145.

55. Noltenius to Mackay, January 11, 1937, B19, F37, MS 10290.

56. Nicholson, *Australian Trade Relations,* 1935, 122–24; Tsokhas, *Markets,* 118.

57. J. F. Guthrie, Typescript, Speech to the International Textile Organization, 1937. MSS 2317, J.F. Guthrie Papers, NLA.

58. His Imperial Japanese Majesty's Consulate General, Letter to the Asst. Comptroller General (Tariff), Department of Trade and Customs, Australia, March

9, 1938, A1667, 194/B/5,33533777, NLA; "Pact with Japan—Wool Imports," *Sydney Morning Herald*, July 4, 1938, 11. Trove.

59. Carter and MacGibbon, *Wool,* 59–60; Simon Ville and David Merrett, "Too Big to Fail: explaining the timing and nature of intervention in the Australian wool market, 1916–1991," *Australian Journal of Politics and History* 62 no. 3 (2016), 7.

60. "Use More Wool: Worldwide Campaign Suggested," *Manilla Express,* May 17, 1929, 6. Trove.

61. "Central Wool Fund," *New Zealand Herald,* December 4, 1930, in Carter and MacGibbon, *Wool,* 59.

62. Keighley, *Wool City*, 78–79.

63. Carter and MacGibbon, *Wool,* 71–79.

64. "Outlook for Wool Fabrics in U.S.A.," *The Wool Record & Textile World (WRTW)* 55 (March 16, 1939): 24, 28, 46.

65. "Raw Wool for Germany, German Buying in South Africa," *WRTR* 55 (January 26, 1939), 3.

66. Australian Trade Commissioner, *Confidential Report on the Market for Wool in U.S.A.* (Canada: 1938), 25. NLA.

67. "Outlook for Wool Fabrics" *WRTW* 55 (March 16, 1939), 24.

68. "Outlook for Wool Fabrics" 47.

69. Pedlar, "Access to Raw Materials," *WRTW* 51 (January 21, 1937), 13.

70. "FH Booth's New Building Opened," *The Sun*, September 9, 1938, 14. Trove.

71. "Topics of the Week—French Army Contracts," *WRTW* 55 (April 20, 1939), 3.

72. The Bradford Market—Pieces," *WRTW* 55 (August 31, 1939), 1.

73. "Press Release: Bureau of Fashion Trends" (April 7, 1939), Eleanor Roosevelt Papers: Visit of British Royalty 1939. Preparations for Visit. https://fdrlibrary.wordpress.com/2011/03/24/found-in-the-archives/.

74. *Western Star and Roma Advertiser* (Queensland), August 19, 1939, 4; "Thermos Wool," *Dominion* 32, no. 264 (August 5, 1939), 5, Supplement. Trove.

75. Nicholson, *Australian Trade Relations,* 131.

76. Noltenius to Mackay, May 3, 1937, B19, F77, MS 10290.

77. Noltenius to Mackay, September 22, 1937, B19, F77, MS 10290.

78. Noltenius to Mackay, Brisbane, January 16, 1938, B20, F78, MS 10290.

79. John Morecombe, "Joseph Binstead: the Manly Man Who Survived the 1937 Stinson Crash," *Manly Daily*, June 25, 2021.

80. Noltenius to Mackay, October 6, 1938, B20, F78, MS 10290.

81. "Cotton and Wool Claimed as 'Immovable,'" *Daily News* (London) October 8, 1938, 1. British Newspaper Archive.

82. Noltenius to Mackay, in envelope, November 3, 1937, B19, F77, MS 10290.

83. Noltenius to Mackay, March 14, 1939, B20, F78, MS 10290.

84. Noltenius in Berchtesgaden, Germany to Mackay, u.d. prob. July 1939, B20, F78, MS 10290.

85. Noltenius to Mackay, August 29, 1939, B20, F78, MS10290.

Chapter 7

1. *Shepparton Advertiser*, October 16, 1939, 20. Trove.

2. "Rental supply The Yokosuka Military Department/Year and Month of production—The year of 17 [Japanese imperial calendar, Showa], the month of 12 (December 1942)/Size 4/Name (blank)," Translated by Koichi Okamoto, Professor, International Liberal Studies, Waseda University, Tokyo, Japan. Via Email Correspondence, May 16, 2019.

3. "Growth of the Japanese Wool Manufacture," *Bulletin, National Association of Wool Manufacturers (BNAWM)*, 54 (April 1924), 306.

4. Wally Lanagan, filmed interview with Trish FitzSimons, May 27, 2019.

5. Grace Hutchins, *Labor and Silk* (New York: International Publishers, 1929), 62–81, 68.

6. Howard Priestman, "Artificial Silk," *BNAWM* 43 (September 1913), 274–97.

7. Hutchins, *Labor and Silk*, 65.

8. James Chittick, *Silk Manufacturing and its Problems* (New York: James Chittick, 1913), 69–70.

9. Grace Hutchins, *Women Who Work* (New York: International Pamphlets, 1932), 9.

10. Paul David Blanc. *Fake Silk: The Lethal History of Viscose Rayon,* (New Haven, CT: Yale University Press, 2016), 78-84, and notes.

11. F. Charnley et. al., *Developments in the Cotton, Rayon and Silk Industries in Germany 1939–1945.* B.I.O.S Overall Report No. 13 (London: British Intelligence Objectives Sub-Committee, 1949), 11, 81.

12. Jocelyn Gottschalk, "Competing Images: Silk and Rayon in Popular U.S. Publications of the Nineteen Thirties," *Textile Society of America Symposium Proceedings, 2002*. 390. https://digitalcommons.unl.edu/tsaconf/390.

13. Ephraim Freedman, "The History of Rayon in the Retail Field," *Rayon Textile Monthly* (*RTM*) 18, no. 7 (July 1937), 35–36, and no. 8 (August 1937), 33–34.

14. Earnest Elmo Calkins, "False Bargains Betray Us," *The Atlantic Monthly* (December 1932), 667–75.

15. John A Spooner, "Rayon Specifications," *Commercial Standards Monthly* (August 1931), 53; "Note of the Month—Consumer Wear Testing," *RTM* 18, no. 11 (November 1937), 37.

16. British Celanese Ltd. Advertisement, *Wool Record & Textile World (WRTW)* 51 (April 29, 1937), 38–39.

17. Letter from Edith Cox, February 15, 1939. Folder: PMs Dept: Substitutes for Wool. A461/9 N325/1/8 93145. NAA, Canberra.

18. C. H. Ward-Jackson, *History of Courtaulds: An Account of the Origin and Rise of the Industrial Enterprise of Courtaulds Limited and of its associate The American Viscose Corporation* (London: Courtaulds, 1941), 112–13.

19. Ward-Jackson, *History of Courtaulds*, 114–18.

20. Dr. F. Bonnet, "The Manufacture and Uses of Cut Rayon Staple," *RTM* 18, no. 6 (June 1937), 32–36.

21. Louis Domeratzky, *The International Cartel Movement, Trade Information Bulletin No. 556* (Washington, DC: Bureau of Foreign and Domestic Commerce, Department of Commerce, 1928), 54.

22. John E. Bassill, "The Rayon Industry," Scoville Hamlin, ed. *The Menace of Overproduction: its Causes, Extent, and Cure* (New York: Wiley, 1930), 44–45.

23. Domeratzky, *International Cartel Movement*, 53–55.

24. Celanese advertisement, *The Textile Manufacturer* 60, no. 709 (January 1934), 44.

25. *Industrial Fibers: A Summary of Figures of Production, Trade and Consumption Relating to Cotton, Wool, Silk, Flax, Jute, Hemp and Rayon* (London: Intelligence Branch, Imperial Economic Committee, 1936), 96, 116.

26. J. F. Guthrie, *Sniafil's Challenge to Wool* (Undated). National Library of Australia.

27. "No Warmth in It," *Mudgee Guardian and North-Western Representative,* May 26, 1930, 15, Trove.

28. Benito Mussolini, quoted in Jeffrey T. Schnapp, "The Fabric of Modern Times," *Critical Inquiry* 24 (Autumn 1997), 195.

29. F. F. Robinson, "Wood Fibers—Their Relation to Wool," *Dennys, Lascelles Annual Report* (Geelong, Australia: August 1926), 17.

30. V. Cerretano, "Multinational business and host countries in times of crisis: Courtaulds, Glanzstoff, and Italy in the inter-war period," *Economic History Review* 71, no. 2 (2018), 540–66.

31. Schnapp, "Fabric of Modern Times," 215.

32. Schnapp, 212.

33. "New Italian Wool Substitute From Milk," *Belfast Telegraph,* January 8, 1936, 8. British Newspaper Archive.

34. Marinetti, *Poema non umano dei tecnicismi* in Schnapp, "Fabric of Modern Times," 205–208.

35. Jonas Scherner and Mark Spoerer, "Infant company protection in the German semi-synthetic fiber industry," *Business History* (2021), 2. DOI: 10.1080/00076791.2021.1900118.

36. "Richtiges und Falsches über die Zellwolle," *Der Führer,* January 21, 1938, 6. Translation by Dr. Regina Ganter.

37. Helmut G. Bodenbender, *Zellwolle Kunstspinnfasern: ihre Herstellung, Verarbeitung und Wirtschaft* (Berlin: 1937).

38. "Extract from Zellwolle und Deutsche Kunstseiden-Zeitung, March 1939. Dr. Richard Hünlich," Imperial Economic Committee, Wool/Release No. 2/1939. Dated 20/4/1939. NAA, Canberra.

39. Newspaper clippings and Notes by J. F. Guthrie, compiled for an unfinished memoir, James F. Guthrie Papers, MSS 2317, Folder 2. NLA.

40. Dept. of Post War Reconstruction, Australia, *Wool & Synthetics* (Canberra: February 1945), 6.

41. Shinichi Suzuki, "The Rayon Industry in Japan," *Economic Geography* 11, no. 1 (January 1935), 105–107.

42. Grace Hutchins, *Japan's Drive for Conquest* (New York: International Pamphlets, 1935), 26.

43. W. F. A. Turgeon, *Report of the Royal Commission on the Textile Industry* (Ottawa: King's Printer, January 1938), 27.

44. "Textile/Wool Arrangement," Record Group A1667; and 194/B/3/A7-01, Trade and Customs Dept., Japan Treaty Negotiations, Textile/Wool Arrangement. Trade Agreement, Treaty Series No. 66 (1938) NAA, Canberra.

45. H. W. Rose, *Rayon and Synthetic Fiber Production of Japan* (New York: Textile Research Institute, 1946), Chapter 6.

46. Paul Douglas, quoted in Bassill, "The Rayon Industry," 47.

47. Madelyn Shaw, "American Fashion: The Tirocchi Sisters in Context," in *From Paris to Providence: Fashion, Art and the Tirocchi Dressmakers Shop, 1915–1937*. Susan Hay, ed. (Providence: RISD Museum, 2000). http://tirocchi.stg.brown.edu/essays/shaw_01.html.

48. Advertisement, DuPont Rayon Staple. *RTM* 18, no. 6 (June 1937), 22–23.

49. Dana H. Gillingham, "Rayon's Progress in New England," *RTM* 18, no. 1 (January 1937), 43–44.

50. "Advantages of Rayon Shown by N.R.W.A." *RTM* 18, no. 2 (February 1937), 30.

51. F. K. Howell, "Latest Foreign Developments in the Continuous Drying of Staple Rayon," *RTM* 18, no. 1 (January 1937), 75–76.

52. General Electric Advertisement, "Mary has two dresses," *RTM* 18, no. 6 (June 1937), 8–9.

53. Memorandum, May 14, 1938, "Rayon Participation," New York World's Fair 1939. Box 439, Folder 9. New York World's Fair Incorporated Records, New York Public Library. We are grateful to Lauren Whitley for sharing this document and her World's Fair knowledge with us.

54. Brochure, *Du Pont Presents the Wonder World of Chemistry*, New York World's Fair (1940), 3. Uploaded Courtesy of Cathy Scibelli. https://www.1939nyworldsfair.com/worlds_fair/wf_tour/zone-5/dupont_chemistry/dupont_chemistry.aspx; Peter J. Kuznick, "Losing the world of tomorrow: The battle over the presentation of science at the 1939 New York World's Fair," *American Quarterly* 46, no. 3 (1994), 341–73.

55. Lammot Du Pont, "Chemical Research," *The Wonder World of Chemistry—1939*, 3. Uploaded Courtesy of Laurel Phelan. https://www.1939nyworldsfair.com/DuPont/Dupont_Chemistry.aspx.

56. John V. Haggard, *Procurement of Clothing and Textiles, 1945-53*, QMC Historical Studies Series II, No. 3 (Washington, DC: Office of the QM General, 1957) 83–84.

Chapter 8

1. "Fanfare for a New Fabric," *Life* 32, no. 20 (May 19, 1952), 142.

2. Dr. Joseph Quig, DuPont News Release (December 2, 1948), in Orlon folders, Hagley Library and Archive, Delaware (HLA).

3. R. M. Hoffmann and J. B. Quig, "A Summary of Defects of 'Orlon' Acrylic Fiber" (July 1–August 8, 1952), Orlon folders, HLA.

4. Mary Bellis, "The History of Polyester," *ThoughtCo* (February 16, 2021), thoughtco.com/history-of-polyester-4072579.

5. Les White, *Wool in Wartime: A Study in Colonialism* (Alternative Publishing Cooperative, 1981), 64.

6. Sir Owen Dixon, comments, N. W. Yeo, *The Wartime Administration of the Central Wool Committee* (Sydney, Economics Society of NSW, 1949), 33.

7. Yeo, *Wartime Administration*, 7.

8. White, *Wool in Wartime*, 83.

9. White, 64–76.

10. White, 85; Mark Keighley, *Wool City: A history of the Bradford textile industry in the 20th century* (Ilkley, UK: G. Whitaker & Co, 2007), 85.

11. Letter from J. M. Felgate, October 1939, quoted in White, *Wool in Wartime*, 84.

12. Frederick Booth comments, Yeo, *Wartime Administration*, 34–35.

13. Kosmas Tsokhas, *Markets, Money and Empire: The Political Economy of the Australian Wool Industry* (Melbourne: Melbourne University Press, 1990), 168–77; Nicholson, *Trade Relations,* 126; Yeo, *Wartime Administration*, 13–14; Christopher Fyfe, *Gentleman's Agreements: Australian Wartime Wool Appraisements* (Perth: Lana Press 1996), 308–309.

14. Fyfe, *Gentlemen's Agreements,* 168.

15. Fyfe, 176.

16. N. B. Trebeck, "Wool Trade Story," Typescript work history, nd, Booth Family Archive, 1.

17. Fyfe, *Gentlemen's Agreements*, 168–69.

18. Frederick Booth comments, Yeo, *Wartime Administration*, 1949, 31.

19. Fyfe, 308-9; "Wool to Shanghai, November 20, 1941," A1539/1, 1941/W/1333b, 6972833; File of cables/telegrams, "Clearances of wool to Shanghai," A1539/1, 1941/W/13266, 6937975. Both: NAA.

20. White, *Wool in Wartime*, 99.

21. Yeo, *Wartime Administration*, 13.

22. Fyfe, *Gentlemen's Agreements*, 278–79; "Discussion of wool questions," March 16, 1940, Clunies Ross et al. in White, *Wool in Wartime*, 98.

23. White, *Wool in Wartime*, 99–101.

24. Yeo, *Wartime Administration*, 11–12.

25. "The Bradford Market—Far East and Export Trade," *The Wool Record & Textile World* (WRTW) (December 11, 1941), 1.

26. Fyfe, *Gentlemen's Agreements*, 300, 305; Bill Carter and John MacGibbon, *Wool: A History of New Zealand's Wool Industry* (Wellington: Ngaio Press, 2003), 100.

27. "Curtin Explains how US Aids Australian Lend-lease Plan," *Daily Mirror*, September 4, 1942, 9. Trove.

28. Yeo, *Wartime Administration*, 20.

29. White, *Wool in Wartime*, 76; Yeo, *Wartime Administration*, 11.

30. N. B. Trebeck, "An Outline of Commercial Involvement," typescript work history, u.d. but likely 1978, Booth Family Archive, 1.

31. John Klein, *Wool During World War II, War Records Project Monograph No 7* (Washington: USDA, May 1948), 7; U.S. Tariff Commission, *US Stockpile wools, War Changes in Industry Series, no. 3* (Washington, DC: GPO, May 1944), 1.

32. Klein, 8–9.

33. Klein, 30.

34. War Manpower Commission, "List of Essential Activities" (August 14, 1942), Columbia Empire Industries, Thomas Kay Mill Archive (TKMA), Salem, Oregon.

35. Klein, *Wool During World War II*, 38.

36. National Defense War Production Board Part 1086 Regulations, OD [Olive Drab] Wool Clips, General Preference Order M-87 (March 10, 1942). TKMA.

37. "Letter from the War Production Board, Washington DC to Manufacturers of Wool Products," April 2 1942, and "National Defense War Production Board Order M-73 Curtailing the Use of Wool," TKMA; Klein, *Wool During World War II*, 49.

38. *The Victory Suit*, newsreel, Commonwealth Dept. of Information, 1942. https://anzacportal.dva.gov.au/resources/victory-suit; Lorinda Cramer and Melissa Bellanta, "'Clothes Shall Mark the Man': Wearing Suits in Wartime Australia, 1939–1945," *Cultural and Social History* 19, no. 1 (2022), 62–65, DOI: 10.1080/14780038.2022.2031424.

39. Carter and MacGibbon, *Wool*, 79.

40. Klein, *Wool During World War II*, 38.

41. Stephen J. Kennedy, "Fiber Blends in Military Textiles," *Journal of the Textile Institute Proceedings*, 43, no. 8 (1952), 681–98. DOI:10.1080/19447015208664085; Leroy H. Smith, et. al., *New Fibers and Their Applications in Germany During the War Period* (Field Information Agency-Technical) (FIAT). Final Report No. 44, September 14, 1945); P. Alexander and C. S. Whewell, *Some Aspects of Textile*

Research in Germany. British Intelligence Objectives Sub-Committee (BIOS) Final Report No. 1472, Item No. 22 (London: HMSO, 1946).

42. John R. Stewart, *Japan's Textile Industry* (New York: International Secretariat, Institute of Pacific Relations, 1949), 36–41.

43. Helen Close, interview with Trish FitzSimons, September 21, 2022.

44. Eberhard Noltenius to Agnes Mackay, August 29,1939, B20, F78, MS10290, NLA.

45. Gerard Baldry to Aldred Baldry, December 27, 1940, B26, F98, MS10390, NLA.

46. Noltenius to Mackay, from Tatura intern camp, various dates, B2, F9, MS10290, NLA.

47. White, *Wool in Wartime,* 90–91; Carter and MacGibbon, *Wool*, 100.

48. Fyfe, *Gentlemen's Agreements*, 356; Carter and MacGibbon, 101–105.

49. The National Council of Wool Selling Brokers of Australia (NCWSBA), *Wool Review (1942–43)*, Table, State Library of NSW.

50. Danielle Sprecher, "Demob Suits: One Uniform for Another? Burtons and the Leeds Multiple Tailors Production of Mens' Demob Tailoring after the Second World War," *Costume* 154, no. 1 (2020), 110, footnote 4, 127.

51. Sprecher, 115, 108.

52. Sprecher, 112–13, 116.

53. Sprecher, 128.

54. Tiffany Dunk, "How the Weekly Brought Dior to Australia," *The Australian Women's Weekly,* June 5, 2024. https://www.womensweekly.com.au/fashion/how-the-weekly-brought-dior-to-australia/.

55. Keighley, *Wool City,* 85, 88.

56. Keighley, 108.

57. Klein, *Wool During World War 11,* 75–76.

58. Carter and MacGibbon, *Wool,* 104–105.

59. Keighley, *Wool City,* 95.

60. A. J. Little, "Aspects of the World Wool Market 1939–1952," *Australian Economic Papers* (June 1967), 175.

61. "Secretary's Report," *Bulletin of the National Association of Wool Manufacturers* (*BNAWM*) 80 (1950), I-38.

62. Carter and MacGibbon, *Wool*, 118.

63. "Secretary's Report," *BNAWM* 80 (1950), I-38–40.

64. Carter and MacGibbon, *Wool*, 118; Little, "Aspects of World Wool," 176.

65. John MacGibbon, interview with Trish FitzSimons, April 29, 2017.

66. "Secretary's Report," *BNAWM* 80 (1950), 1–38.

67. Roland Wilson in Charles Massy, *Breaking the Sheep's Back* (Brisbane: University of Qld Press, 2011), 19.

68. "Enter the Politicians," *WRTW* 79, no. 2173 (January 4, 1951), 3; Little, "Aspects of World Wool," 176.

69. Carter and MacGibbon, *Wool*, 118.
70. Charles Massy, interview with Trish FitzSimons, August 20, 2016.
71. Trebeck, "Outline of Commercial Involvement," 2.
72. Close, Interview.
73. "Secretary's Report," *BNAWM* 81 (1951), I-54.
74. "Secretary's Report," *BNAWM* 80 (1950), I-66.
75. Little, "Aspects of World Wool," 173.
76. "Secretary's Report," *BNAWM* 82 (1952), I-45.
77. Valerie Bailey Grasso, *The Berry Amendment: Requiring Defense Procurement to Come from Domestic Sources* (Washington, DC: Congressional Research Service, 2014), 12. https://sgp.fas.org/crs/natsec/RL31236.pdf; "Secretary's Report," *BNAWM* 83 (1953), I-53.
78. Little, "Aspects of World Wool," 173.
79. Massy, Interview.
80. Little, "Aspects of World Wool," 171, 174.
81. *WRTW* 81 (January 17, 1952), 3.
82. "Francis White, American Woolen Co., Jan 17, 1952," *BNAWM* 81 (1951), 3–26.
83. WRTW (Jan 24, 1952), 47 (303).
84. "Secretary's Report," *BNAWM* 83 (1953), 1–37.
85. Massy, Interview.
86. "Franklin W. Hobbs, Nationally Known Textile Official, 86," *The Boston Globe,* June 17, 1955, 10. https://bostonglobe.newspapers.com/newspage/433635253/; Marland C. Hobbs, *The Boston Globe,* January 19, 1959. 2;3; Trebeck "Outline of Commercial Involvement," 2.
87. "Statement Submitted to the Commission on Foreign Economic Policy," *BNAWM* 83 (1953), 59.
88. United States Public Law 690, "National Wool Act" (August 28, 1954), Sec 702.
89. Edwin C. Voorhies and Robert Rudd, *Sheep and Wool Situation in California* (Berkeley: The College of Agriculture, University of California, 1950).
90. Edwin Wilkinson (V.P., NAWM), U.S. Congress, "Hearings before the Committee on Ways and Means: Trade Agreements Extension," Part 2 (January 17–February 7, 1955), 1723–24.
91. Donald Holmes, "The Place of Nylon, Orlon and Dacron," *BNAWM* 83 (1953), 106, 110.
92. Holmes, 102.
93. White, *Wool in Wartime,* Table 6, 156.
94. Jim Booth, interview with Trish FitzSimons, September 22, 2014.
95. Trebeck, "Outline of Commercial Involvement," 4.
96. Trebeck, "Outline," 4; Booth, Interview.
97. Keighley, *Wool City*, 141, 185.

98. Booth, Interview; Georgina Safe, "Fashion: it's a superfine romance," *Sydney Morning Herald,* March 8, 2012. https://www.smh.com.au/lifestyle/fashion/its-a-superfine-romance-20120307-1ukcv.html.

99. Stephen Calder et al., *Future Stock: A Full Introduction to the World of Futures Trading* (Sydney: Horwitz Grahame, 1986), 14–15.

100. Patrick Lindsay, "Speculating on Wool: A Broker's tale from Go to Woe," *The Australian, Business,* ud. late 1979, Booth Family Archive.

101. "The BWK in the globalized wool industry 1993–2000," (Oct 2015). Blog: *Sheep, wool and fashion: Information and work materials on sheep, wool and fashion.* https://schafwolle-und-mehr.blogspot.com/2015/10. Site's English translation.

102. Booth, Interview; Scott Carmody, interview with Trish FitzSimons, April 11, 2024.

103. Scott Carmody, 2nd interview with Trish FitzSimons, May 9, 2024.

104. Gaetan Pace, interview with Trish FitzSimons. January 25, 2024.

105. Booth, Interview.

106. "Cheil Industries," English language translation (accessed July 31, 2024). https://en.namu.wiki/w/%EC%A0%9C%EC%9D%BC%EB%AA%A8%EC%A7%81.

107. Carmody, 2nd Interview.

108. Pace, Interview.

109. Booth, Interview; Carter & MacGibbon, *Wool,* 293, 302, 320.

110. Massy, *Breaking the Sheep's Back,* 108.

111. Massy, 312.

112. Massy, 325–26; Carter and MacGibbon, *Wool,* 324–25.

113. "Buyers Needed for Crisis Group," *Yorkshire Post,* October 2, 1990.

114. "BWK in the globalized wool industry."

115. Hilary Greenbaum and Dana Rubenstein, "The Evolution of Fleece, from Scratchy to Snuggle," *New York Times*, November 25, 2011. https://www.nytimes.com/2011/11/27/magazine/fleece-scratchy-to-snuggie.html.

116. Graph, from the International Rayon and Synthetic Fibres Committee, in Carter and MacGibbon, *Wool,* 311.

117. https://www.talman.com.au/.

Epilogue

1. Nina Gbor and Olivia Chollet, *Textile Waste in Australia: Reducing Consumption and Investing in Circularity* (Canberra: Australia Institute, May 2024), graph, 6.

2. This term was coined in 1989 by the United Nations Environmental Working Group Basel Convention.

3. For example: Zoya Wazir, "How Fast Fashion Dumps into the Global South, *U.S. News & World Report*, November 11, 2021, 6:00 a.m. https://www.usnews.com/news/best-countries/articles/2021-11-11/how-dead-white-mans-clothing-is

-clogging-the-global-south; *Textile Mountain: The Hidden Burden of Our Fashion Waste*. https://www.textilemountainfilm.com/.

4. Craig Reucassel, *War on Waste*, Series 3 (Sydney, Australia: ABC Television, 2023), Ep 3 focuses on textiles.

5. The Textiles Exchange, *Materials Market Report,* 10th Edition (Lamesa, TX: December 2023), graphs 9–10. https://textileexchange.org/; F. De Falco et al. "The contribution of washing processes of synthetic clothes to microplastic pollution," *Scientific Reports* 9, no. 6633 (2019). https://doi.org/10.1038/s41598-019-43023-x.

6. Yongin Lee, et. al., "Health Effects of Microplastic Exposure: Current Issues and Perspectives in South Korea," *Yonsei Medical Journal* 64, no. 5 (May 2023), 301–308. https://www.ncbi.nlm.nih.gov/pmc/articles/PMC10151227/.

7. *Textile Waste in Australia,* graph, 11.

8. Materials Market Report, 11.

9. *Wool: a sustainable solution*, Australian Wool Innovation (AWI), Woolmark (Sydney: 2021), 13.

10. Andrew Woods, "Merino Price in US and Aussie dollar terms," *Mecardo*, July 23, 2024, 1. https://mecardo.com.au/merino-price-in-us-and-aussie-dollar-terms/.

11. "Wool & the Military," *American Wool,* November 10, 2020. https://www.americanwool.org/wool-and-the-military/ (November 10, 2020); "Army Develops Wool-Blend Uniform," November 28, 2016. https://www.military.com/kitup/2016/11/wool-blend-uniform.html; Mitch Driggers, "Wool in the Military," *Sheep Industry News,* January 2017. https://www.sheepusa.org/blog/newsmedia-sheepindustrynews-pastissues-2017-january2017-woolinthemilitary.

12. The Brickle Group. https://thebricklegroup.com/.

13. "241 years of Weaving Wool at AW Hainsworth," *Beyond the Bale* (AWI, 98) 56.

14. Kirsi Niinimaki et.al. "The Environmental Price of Fast Fashion," *Nature Reviews: Earth and Environment,* April 1, 2020, 194.

15. W. H. E. J. Van Wettere, S. Culley, A. M. F. Swinbourne, et al. Heat stress from current and predicted increases in temperature impairs lambing rates and birth weights in the Australian sheep flock. *Nat Food* 5 (2024), 206–10. https://doi.org/10.1038/s43016-024-00935-w.

16. Lucianne Tonti, "Why regenerative garments are the ultimate status symbol," *The Guardian,* Wednesday May 8, 2024. https://www.theguardian.com/fashion/article/2024/may/08/why-regenerative-garments-are-the-ultimate-status-symbol.

17. Christina Couch, "With 7,000 Sheep and Goats, This Mother-Daughter Team is Playing a Part in California's Fight Against Wildfires." *Vogue,* September 29, 2021. https://www.vogue.com/article/star-creek-land-stewards-california-wildfire-mitigation.

18. Caitlin Fitzsimmons, "It's beneficial for the sheep: The surprising 'win-win' for solar panels on farms," *Sydney Morning Herald*, August 18, 2024.

19. "Wear Wool, Not Fossil Fuel," AWI, Woolmark, August 17, 2022. https://www.youtube.com/watch?v=DTpyVxYRQGA.

20. Nikolina Sajn, *European Parliament Textile Impact Report,* Briefing to the European Parliament, January 2019, 5.

21. Hyesim Seo and B. Ellie Jin, "Greenwashing: Behind the Scenes of Sustainable Fashion," Fashion and Textile Business Excellence Cooperative, N.C. State University (September 20, 2023). https://ftbec.textiles.ncsu.edu/greenwashing-behind-the-scenes-of-sustainable-fashion/.

22. For example: Frank Carpenter, *The Clothes We Wear: A Journey Club Reader* (1926: American Book Co.) and J. F. Chamberlain, *How We are Clothed: A Geographical Reader* (New York: MacMillan, 1918).

23. Erha Andini et al., "Chemical recycling of mixed textile waste," *Science Advances* 10, no. 27 (2024). DOI:10.1126/sciadv.ado6827; Alex Scott, "Chemical Recycling of Textiles Advances, Shakily," *Chemical and Engineering News* (March 15, 2024). https://cen.acs.org/environment/green-chemistry/Chemical-recycling-textiles-advances-shakily/102/web/2024/03; Justin Huang and Victoria Ou, "Acoustic Filtration: Harnessing Ultrasonic Technology for the Streamlined Removal of Microplastic Particles From Water Flow." https://www.societyforscience.org/isef/awards/gordon-e-moore-awards/.

24. Jane Milburn, *Slow Clothing: Finding Meaning in What We Wear* (Brisbane: Textile Beat, 2017). https://textilebeat.com/slow-clothing/.

Bibliography

Select Bibliography

Research for this project has continued for a decade. The authors have previously produced several short films as well as multiple articles. This is a select bibliography of sources germane to the overall topic. Additional source details can be found in chapter endnotes.

Archives and Digital Repositories

1914–1918-online. International Encyclopedia of the First World War. https://encyclopedia.1914-1918-online.net/home.html.

Anzac Portal. Dept. of Veterans Affairs, Australian Government. https://anzacportal.dva.gov.au/resources/victory-suit.

Auckland War Memorial Museum Research Library.

Australian National University, Archives of Business and Labour.

Bernice Pauahi Bishop Museum.

Booth Family Archive (privately held).

British Newspaper Archive: https://www.britishnewspaperarchive.co.uk/.

British Pathé Newsreels: https://www.britishpathe.com.

Deutsches Zeitungsportal: https://www.deutsche-digitale-bibliothek.de/.

Hagley Library and Archive, Wilmington, Delaware.

Hathi Trust Digital Library: https://www.hathitrust.org/.

Hawaiian State Archives.

International Law Studies. U.S. Naval War College. https://digital-commons.usnwc.edu/

Internet Archive: https://archive.org/.

Library of Congress: in person and online at: Chronicling America: https://www.loc.gov/collections/chronicling-america/; Prints & Photographs Division: https://www.loc.gov/pictures/.

National Archives of Australia: in person and online at https://www.naa.gov.au.

National Archives (United States): in person and online at: https://www.archives.gov/.

National Library of Australia: in person and online through Trove: https://trove.nla.gov.au/.

National Library of New Zealand, Papers Past: https://paperspast.natlib.govt.nz/.

National Museum of American History Library: https://siris-libraries.si.edu/.
Newspapers.com: https://www.newspapers.com/.
Proquest Historical Newspapers: https://about.proquest.com/en/products-services/pq-hist-news/.
Queensland Museum.
State Library of New South Wales.
State Library of Queensland.
Thomas Kay Mill Archive. Salem, Oregon.
U.S. Army Center of Military History: https://history.army.mil/.
[U.S.] Army Quartermaster Foundation: https://www.quartermasterfoundation.org/articles/.
U.S. Congressional Archive: https://www.congress.gov/.
U.S. Dept. of Commerce, Commerce Research Library: https://library.doc.gov/home.
U.S. Dept. of State, Office of the Historian: https://history.state.gov/.
University of Hawai'i at Manoa, University Archives & Manuscripts.
Waldthausen Family Archive (privately held).
World War I Document Archive: Brigham Young University Library.

Textile Trade Journals

American Silk & Rayon Journal, Rayon Textile Monthly, Rayon and Synthetic Textiles (United States).
Annual Wool Review (United States).
Bulletin of the National Association of Wool Manufacturers (United States: quarterly issues bound as annual volume with Secretary's Report).
Dalgety's Review (Australia).
Dennys, Lascelles Limited, Annual Review (Australia).
Posselt's Textile Journal (United States).
Textilberichte. It reviewed and summarized important articles from other textile industry-related journals.
Textile World Record, Textile World Journal, Textile World (United States).
The Melliand (United States) English language version of the German *Melliand Textileberichte.*
The Textile Journal of Australia.
The Wool Record and Textile World (United Kingdom).
Wool Review (Australia).

Books and Articles (apart from trade journals and newspapers)

Alexander, P. and C. S. Whewell (British Intelligence Objectives Sub-Committee), *Some Aspects of Textile Research in Germany*. B.I.O.S. Final Report No. 1472. Item No. 22. London: HMSO, 1946.
American Wool & Cotton Reporter. *History of American Textiles,* Boston: 1922.

Australian Trade Commissioner. *Confidential Report on the Market for Wool in U.S.A.* Canada: 1938.

Australian Dictionary of Biography (various authors, subjects, volumes, years) Canberra: Australian National University, https://adb.anu.edu.au/.

Ayres, Leonard P. *The War With Germany: A Statistical Summary.* Washington: GPO. 2nd Edition, August 1, 1919.

Blanc, Paul David. *Fake Silk: The Lethal History of Viscose Rayon.* New Haven: Yale University Press, 2016.

Blinken, Donald M. *Wool Tariffs and American Policy.* Washington: Public Affairs Press, 1948.

Bowden P. J. "The Wool Supply and the Woollen Industry," *The Economic History Review* 9, no. 1 (1956).

Bureau of Statistics, U.S. Treasury Department. *Wool and Manufactures of Wool: Special Report.* Washington, DC: GPO, 1888.

Carter, Bill and John MacGibbon. *Wool: A History of New Zealand's Wool Industry.* Wellington, NZ: Ngaio Press, 2003.

Cherington, Paul T., *The Wool Industry: Commercial Problems of the American Woolen and Worsted Manufacture.* Chicago: A.W. Shaw, 1916.

Clapham, J. H. *Economic Development of France and Germany, 1815–1914.* Cambridge, UK: Cambridge University Press, 1928.

Clapp, Edwin J. *Economic Aspects of the War: Neutral Rights, Belligerent Claims, and American Commerce in the Years 1914–1915.* New Haven, CT: Yale University Press, 1915.

Clunies-Ross, Ian. *A Survey of the Sheep and Wool Industry in North and Eastern Asia with special reference to Manchukuo, Korea, & Japan.* Pamphlet #65, 1936. Melbourne: CSIR, 1932–1938.

Cole, Arthur H. *The American Wool Manufacture.* Cambridge, MA: Harvard University Press, 1926.

Coulthard, Sally. *A Short History of the World According to Sheep.* London: Head of Zeus, 2020.

Daws, Gavin, *Shoal of Time: A History of the Hawaiian Islands,* Honolulu: University of Hawaii Press, 1968.

Empire Marketing Board, *Wool survey: a summary of production and trade in the empire and foreign countries.* London: HMSO, July 1932.

Fyfe, Christopher. *Gentlemen's Agreements: Australian Wartime Wool Appraisements.* Dalkeith WA: Lana Press, 1996.

Furneaux, Holly and Sue Prichard. "Contested Objects: Curating Soldier Art," *Museum & Society*, 13 (4), 447–61.

Grace, Richard, *Opium and Empire: the Lives and Careers of William Jardine and James Matheson*, Montreal: McGill-Queens University Press, 2014.

Grinberg; Mariya. "Wartime Commercial Policy and Trade between Enemies." *International Security* 46, no. 1 (2021).

Harambour-Ross, Alberto, "Sheep Sovereignties: The Colonization of the Falkland Islands, Malvinas, Patagonia, and Tierra del Fuego, 1830s–1910s," *Latin American*

History (*Oxford Research Encyclopedias,* September 2016). https://doi.org/10.1093/acrefore/9780199366439.013.351.

Hart, Stanley. *Wool: The Raw Materials of the Woolen and Worsted Industries.* Philadelphia: Textile School, 1917.

Hoppit, Julian. "The Political Economy of Wool 1660–1824," in *Britain's Political Economies: Parliament and Economic Life 1660–1800.* Cambridge, UK: Cambridge University Press, 2017.

Huddle, F. P. "Disposal of surplus war materials." *Editorial research reports 1943,* II. Washington, DC: CQ Press, 1943.

James, John. *History of the Worsted Manufacture in England.* London: Longman, 1857.

Jenkins, David T. "Transatlantic Trade in Woollen Cloth 1850–1914: The Role of Shoddy." In *Textiles in Trade: Proceedings of the Textile Society of America Biennial Symposium.* 1990.

Keighley, Mark. *Wool City: A History of the Bradford Textile Industry in the 20th Century.* Bradford, UK: Whitaker, 2007.

Kennedy, Stephen J. "Fiber Blends in Military Textiles," *Journal of the Textile Institute Proceedings* 43, no. 8 (1952).

Klein, John W. *War Records Project Monographs, No. 7 - Wool During World War II.* Washington, DC: USDA, Bureau of Agricultural Economics, 1948.

Little, A. J., "Aspects of the World Wool Market 1939–1952." *Australian Economic Papers,* June 1967.

Marcosson, Isaac. *The Business of War.* New York: John Lane Co., 1918.

Marr, David. *Killing for Country: A Family Story,* Melbourne: Schwartz Books, 2023.

Massy, Charles. *The Australian Merino,* Melbourne: Viking O'Neil, 1990.

———. *Breaking the Sheep's Back.* Brisbane: University of Qld Press, 2011.

Matthews, J. Merritt. *The Textile Fibers.* 4th edition. New York: John Wiley, 1924.

Mayock, Thomas. *The Government and Wool: 1917–20.* Agricultural History Series, Bureau of Agricultural Economics. Washington, DC: USDA, 1943.

Nicholson, D. F. *Australia's Trade Relations: An Outline History of Australia's Overseas Trading Arrangements.* Melbourne: F.W. Cheshire, 1955.

Ormerod, Frank. *Wool.* Staple Trades and Industries series, Gordon D. Knox, ed. New York: Henry Holt, 1919.

Perkins, John. "The German Australian Chamber of Commerce in the Interwar Era," in *Zeitschrift fur Unternehmensgeschicht/Journal of Business History.* 1995.

Perkins, Rachel, Blackfella Films, *Australian Wars* (SBS TV series, Sydney, Australia, 2022).

Ponting, K. G. *The Wool Trade: Past and Present.* Manchester, UK: Columbine Press, 1961.

Price-Rowe, Catherine. *First World War Uniforms.* Pen and Sword Archaeology, 2018.

Pursell, Carroll W. Jr. "E. I. duPont and the Merino Mania in Delaware." *Agricultural History* 36, no. 2 (April 1962). https://www.jstor.org/stable/3740945.

Reynolds, Henry and Jamie Dalziel, "Aborigines and Pastoral Leases: Imperial and Colonial Policy 1826–1855," *UNSW Law Journal* (1996), 323.

Rodriguez, Nestor. *Capitalism and Migration: The Rise of Hegemony in the World System.* Austin, TX: Springer, 2023.

Rose, Susan. *The Wealth of England: the Medieval Wool Trade and its Political Importance 1100–1600.* Barnsley, UK: Oxbow, 2018.

Ryan, Lyndall. "No Right to the Land": The Role of the Wool Industry in the Destruction of Aboriginal Societies in Tasmania (1817–1832) and Victoria (1835–1851) Compared," in Mohamed Adhikari, ed. *Genocide on Settler Frontiers: When Hunter-Gatherers and Commercial Stock Farmers Clash,* New York: Berghahn Books, 2015, 76.

Säckel, Sarah. "'Dirty Clothes,' their 'Greenwashing' and a Call for Change in Andrew Morgan's Film *The True Cost* (2015)." *Context: Dress, Fashion, Textiles. Journal of the Costume and Textile Association of New Zealand.* Issue 32, Winter 2016.

Scherner, Jonas and Mark Spoerer. "Infant company protection in the German semi-synthetic fiber industry," *Business History* (2021).

Shaw, Madelyn. "Slave Cloth and Clothing Slaves: Craftsmanship, Commerce, and Industry," *Journal of Early Southern Decorative Arts* (2012). https://www.mesdajournal.org/2012/slave-cloth-clothing-slaves-craftsmanship-commerce-industry/.

Shaw, Madelyn and Lynne Z. Bassett. *Homefront & Battlefield: Quilts & Context in the Civil War.* Lowell, MA: American Textile History Museum, 2012.

Singh, Radhika. "The Short Career of the Indian Labour Corps in France, 1917–1919." *International Labor and Working-Class History* 87 (2015a).

Sissons, D. C. S., "Private diplomacy in the 1936 trade dispute with Japan," *Australian Journal of Politics and History* 27, no. 2 (1981).

Smith, Leroy H. et. al. (Technical Industrial Intelligence Committee). *New Fibers and Their Applications in Germany During the War Period.* Field Information Agency, Final Report No. 44 (September 14, 1945).

Sprecher, Danielle. "Demob Suits: One Uniform for Another? Burtons and the Leeds Multiple Tailors Production of Mens' Demob Tailoring after the Second World War." *Costume* 154, no. 1 (2020).

St. Clair, Kassia, *The Golden Thread: How Fabric Changed History,* London: John Murray, 2018.

Strong, Ruth. *The Hainsworth Story: Seven Generations of Textile Manufacturing.* Yorkshire, UK: Jeremy Mills, 2006.

Tsokhas, Kosmas. *Markets, Money, and Empire: The Political Economy of the Australian Wool Industry.* Melbourne: University Press, 1990.

Ville, Simon. "The Relocation of the International Wool Market for Australian Wool" (2005). https://ro.uow.edu.au/commpapers/93.

Ville, Simon and David Merrett. "Too Big to Fail: explaining the timing and nature of intervention in the Australian wool market, 1916–1991." *Australian Journal of Politics and History* 62, no. 3 (2016).

Voorhies, Edwin C. and Robert Rudd. *Sheep and Wool Situation in California.* Berkeley: The College of Agriculture, University of California, 1950.

Walton, Frank L. *Tomahawks to Textiles: The Fabulous Story of Worth Street.* New York: Appleton-Century-Crofts, 1953.

Walton, Frank L. *The Thread of Victory*. New York: Fairchild Publishing Co., 1945.

Wentworth, Edward N. *America's Sheep Trails: History, Personalities*. Ames: Iowa State College Press, 1948.

White, Les. *Wool in Wartime: A Study in Colonialism*. Sydney: Alternative Pub. Co-op., 1981.

Wright, Chester Whitney. *Wool-Growing and the Tariff*. Boston: Houghton Mifflin, 1910.

U.S. Tariff Commission. *The Wool-Growing Industry*, Washington, DC: GPO, 1921.

———. "US Stockpile Wools." *War Changes in Industry Series, No. 3*, Washington, DC: GPO, May 1944.

———. *Wool Statistics and Related Data, 1920-1964*. Statistical Bulletin No. 363. USDA Economic Research Service, July 1965.

Yeo, N. W. *The Wartime Administration of the Central Wool Committee*. Sydney: Economics Society of NSW, 1949.

Zimmern, Dorothy M. "The Wool Trade in Wartime." *The Economic Journal* 28, no. 109 (March 1918).

Index

About the Authors

Trish FitzSimons is adjunct professor at the Griffith Film School, Griffith University, Brisbane, Australia. She is a documentary filmmaker and exhibition curator with a passion for social and cultural history. Interview has been a defining component of her practice for the past 40 years. Her intellectual and creative interests are eclectic and had not included textile history prior to this shared research project with Madelyn. A cache of family letters and documents was her way into this fascinating field. She is one of three authors of *Australian Documentary: History, Practices, Genres* (2011). Her exhibitions include *Channels of History: The Women, Land and History of Qld's Channel Country* (State Library of Queensland and national tour 2002–2005) and *Navigating Norman Creek* (Museum of Brisbane 2015). Her broadcast documentaries include *Snakes and Ladders: A Film About Women, Education and History* (ABC TV Australia, Ch 4 UK) and *Another Way?* (SBS TV—Australia).

Madelyn Shaw is a curator and author specializing in the exploration of American culture and history, and its international connections, through textiles and dress. She has held curatorial and administrative positions at the National Museum of American History, Smithsonian Institution; the Museum of Art, Rhode Island School of Design; New Bedford Whaling Museum; The Textile Museum, Washington DC; and the Museum at the Fashion Institute of Technology, New York City. She has curated more than 50 exhibitions and published widely on topics related to the development of the American textile and fashion industries, the China Trade, Slave Cloth, and Aviation clothing and popular culture. Books include *Dress in Colonial British North America* (2013, with Kathleen Staples), *Homefront & Battlefield: Quilts & Context in the American Civil War* (2012, with Lynne Bassett); and the case study "H. R. Mallinson & Company of New York, New Jersey and Pennsylvania" in *American Silk: Artifacts and Entrepreneurs, 1830–1930* (2007).